STRUGGLE FOR A CONTINENT

Glen Barclay

STRUGGLE FOR A CONTINENT

The Diplomatic History of
South America
1917-1945

NEW YORK UNIVERSITY PRESS
NEW YORK 1972

First published by New York University Press
in the United States of America 1972

Copyright © 1972 New York University

Library of Congress Catalogue Card Number: 79-166505

SBN 8147-0969-9

Printed in Great Britain

TO ELIZABETH

TO ELIZABETH

Acknowledgements

I wish to record my appreciation of the absolutely invaluable assistance rendered by Dr Claudio Veliz, Professor of International Relations, University of Santiago, Chile; Professor Cleantho de Paiva Leite, Executive Director of the Instituto Brasileiro de Relacoes Internacionais; and the staffs of the Hispanic and Luso-Brazilian Councils, Canning House, and of the Royal Institute of International Affairs, Chatham House, London.

Contents

Prelude

THE POSITION IT DESERVES
(1917-1919)

The Republics of Latin America had been practising their diplomatic skills industriously ever since they had gained independence. But it was not until the First World War that they had the opportunity to exercize these talents significantly outside the limits of their own hemisphere. This was not to say that they had been quite isolated from world events before 1914. They had not, indeed, made much impact upon the world outside; but the world outside had made considerable impact upon them, most conspicuously by way of a series of forays against Latin independence made by Britain, France, Spain, and latterly the United States. As the Great War across the Atlantic became more extensive in its scope, the world outside began to threaten their sovereignty and welfare again. This time, however, the relationship was not an essentially one-sided affair. The Latins had found the will and the opportunity to impose their own wishes upon Europe and North America. Canning's rhetoric had come true after ninety years. A new world was making its presence felt in the international community. But the form that Latin intervention would take was something that not even the most prescient of statesmen could possibly foretell.

There was certainly no indication at first that a new era of Latin American independence was at hand. Events seemed to follow the traditional pattern of the Latins being assailed by Europe, and called to order by the United States. The crisis was, of course, precipitated by the declaration of the German Imperial

11

Government on 31 January 1917 that unrestricted submarine warfare would be enforced around the coasts of the Western Allies. This in itself had serious implications for Latin American commerce. But what was far more significant in every way was the reaction of the United States. The economic recovery of that country had come to depend on its developing to the utmost its sea-borne trade with the Western Allies. In their attemps to safeguard these economic links President Wilson and his advisers had manoeuvred themselves into a position in which their only consistent response to the German challenge would have been to sever diplomatic relations. Even this most drastic of international actions short of war was not necessarily going to secure the other vital United States interest, the right to participate in the reordering of the world once peace had been restored in Europe. The only reasonable presumption was, therefore, that the United States would regard the re-introduction of the submarine blockade as an occasion for entering the war against Germany as a full belligerent. The only real question for the other American Republics was whether they had any option but to do the same.

Wilson certainly lost no time in presenting this question to the Latins as directly as he could. The United States severed diplomatic relations with Germany on 1 February; four days later, Wilson expressed the hope, quite unmistakable in its implications, that 'other neutral powers will find it possible to assume the same position';[1] and on the same day, the United States Minister in Ecuador, the weakest of the South American Republics and therefore the one most likely to be influenced by pressure of this kind, asked the government of that hapless country to state clearly whether or not it was disposed to accede to Wilson's wishes.[2] Countries even weaker and more vulnerable than Ecuador did not need such a reminder of where their true interests lay. The 'banana belt' of Caribbean vassals was already hastening to fall in line with Washington. Cuba, whose economy was almost totally controlled by United States capital, whose export trade was, for all practical purposes, dependent upon the United States market,

[1] Benson to Muller, *Foreign Relations of the United States*, 5 February 1917
[2] Hartman to Tobar, *Informe que el Ministerio de Relaciones Exteriores presenta a la Nacion en 1917*, p. 235

and which was in any case bound to the United States by a treaty of mutual defence imposed in 1903, severed diplomatic relations with Germany immediately. It was followed in this course three weeks later by Panama, a creation of Theodore Roosevelt's and virtually a protectorate of the United States under the terms of the treaty of 1904. The Panamanian Government responded even more promptly to the American declaration of war against Germany on 6 April, actually entering the war itself on the same day. Cuba predictably followed suit within twenty-four hours. On 27 April, the Guatemalan dictatorship, to the best of its abilities the most repressive, illiberal, and militaristic upon earth, proclaimed its unity with the United States in 'lofty principles . . . for the good of humanity'.[1] Haiti, a protectorate of the United States since 1915 and burdened with a government whose capacity for humanly worthwhile achievement was lower than that of Guatemala's, severed relations with Germany on 11 May and declared war a year later, giving as its reason its disgust with German methods, which indeed differed considerably from those in vogue in the Caribbean. Meanwhile, the dictatorship of Honduras, dependent on United States connivance for its tenure of office, broke off relations with Germany on 17 May. So on the following day did Nicaragua, completely dependent financially on American capital, and with a ruling conservative oligarchy kept in power only by the presence of United States Marines on Nicaraguan territory. The most interesting diplomatic situation was created by the revolutionary junta of Costa Rica, which severed diplomatic relations with Germany on 21 September, thereby withdrawing recognition from the only Government in the world which recognized its own legitimacy.

This impressive unanimity in the Caribbean hardly added up to a triumph for United States diplomacy, however. With such allies one hardly needed enemies. Nothing could have given more moral prestige to the German cause than the fact that some of the most disreputable regimes in the world had entered the war on the side of the Western Allies, for the least inspiring reasons. In any case, the banana belt could make little material contribution to the war effort against Germany to compensate for its moral liabilities. All

[1] *Boletin Oficial de la Secretaria de Estado,* April 1917, pp. 207-211

it could provide was naval bases which the United States would undoubtedly have seized anyway had it become necessary to do so. What was necessarily more significant in every way was the reactions of the great republics of the southern continent, relatively rich in resources, reputable in their forms of government, and unsusceptible to external coercion. Here, it was very clear that things were not going according to Washington's plan. Wilson had initially tried to intimidate the big Latin powers of Argentina, Brazil, and Chile by warning them that German activities might threaten the stability of their 'ABC' alignment, which had been conceived as an association of mutual friendship under the terms of a treaty signed in Buenos Aires on 25 May 1915. But this argument had no appeal to the Argentine President, Hipolito Yrigoyen,[1] who had refused to ratify the ABC Treaty anyway, and had already determined to let it die from neglect. Even little Ecuador attempted to evade the immediate issue; its Government responded to Wilson's demand for clarification by calling for a Pan-American Conference to formulate a united Latin response to the new international situation. Of course this was not going to work, as no Latin government would ever acknowledge an initiative launched by the least powerful of Latin states. The Republics seemed far more likely to follow the lead of their largest member, Brazil, which warned Germany on 9 February that it did not recognize the legitimacy of unrestricted submarine warfare. This action had already been given some justification by the sinking of a Brazilian merchant ship, the *Rio Branco*, by a German U-Boat on 2 May 1916. This indiscretion had made Brazil the only American Republic apart from the United States which had genuine material grounds for a quarrel with Germany; and these grounds were made even more substantial by the most inopportune sinking of a second Brazilian ship, the *Parana,* on 5 April 1917.

Yet, even as Brazil moved towards war, the prospects of a united Pan-American front against Germany were becoming increasingly remote. A new and unpredictable element was entering the scene. The Argentine Government had at first seemed to approve the decisions being taken in Washington and Rio. It had resoundingly proclaimed the justice of the American decision

[1] 1852–1933. President of Argentina 1916–22 and 1928–30

for war on 10 April 'as being founded on the violation of principles of neutrality consecrated by the rules of international law which are regarded as achievements of civilisation'.[1] On 12 April the great and influential *porteno* daily, *La Presna*, the most respected organ of sophisticated Argentine opinion, commented that : 'If Argentine vessels had been sunk . . . this country could have done no less than the United States.' In fact, an Argentine vessel had already been sunk. A U-Boat had torpedoed the *Monte Protegido* the day before the sinking of the *Parana*, but the government of Hipolito Yrigoyen had not responded by declaring war or even by breaking off diplomatic relations. It had merely demanded compensation and apologies. Nor was this all. Yrigoyen had accompanied his warning to Berlin with his own variation of the neglected Ecuadorean initiative. On 8 May 1917, Argentine diplomats presented to the other Latin Governments a proposal from Yrigoyen for a Pan-American Conference, 'to find among the American nations a decision in respect to the war which every day extends more widely in the world . . . this Government considers that the American nations should create a common association to establish . . . the situation and position of the American nations in the general concert of nations.'[2]

This could only be regarded as a fully conscious challenge to United States leadership in the hemisphere. Wilson had already defined a situation and position for the American Republics : one of opposition to the Central Powers under the guidance of Washington. Nor were the other Latin governments in any doubt as to what had happened. The Uruguayan Ambassador in Buenos Aires told Yrigoyen's Foreign Minister, Honorio Pueyrredon, that : 'It is neither admissible nor tolerable that when the United States adopts an attitude towards the present war in Europe . . . it should expect that other republics, whether they agree or not, should align themselves with it.'[3] Yrigoyen's challenge was unquestionably ill-timed. It might have been successful in February

[1] Isidoro Ruiz-Moreno, *Historia de las Relaciones Exteriores Argentina*, Editorial Perrot, Buenos Aires, 1961, p. 315
[2] Argentina, Ministerio de Relaciones Exteriores y Culto, *Memorias*, 8 May 1917
[3] Roberto Etcheparaborda, 'Presidencia Yrigoyen', *Historia Argentina*, Plaza y Jares, B.A., 1968, p. 3374

when it was floated by Ecuador; but any prospects of a common position had already been lost. The United States was at war; Brazil had renounced its position of neutrality; and Chile was unwilling to commit itself to an association which would necessarily be dominated by Argentina, since it would have to exclude the United States and Brazil. The other prong of Yrigoyen's diplomatic thrust, however, had been admirably aimed. Berlin hastened to mollify offended gaucho pride. The Germans expressed 'sincere regrets for the loss of the Argentine bark'; offered to pay reparation for the damage caused; and promised that their fleet would 'avail itself of the first opportunity to salute the Argentine flag', as a proof that the attack on the *Monte Protegido* was in no way to be construed as showing a lack of respect for that particular symbol of national sovereignty.[1]

This was, of course, completely satisfactory. Germany's willingness to make amends to Argentina in this way was made the more gratifying by its refusal to do the same for Peru in the case of the *Lorton*, sunk on 4 February in similar circumstances. Yet there were two factors which rather diminished Yrigoyen's triumph. One was his decision to place an embargo on exports of grain across the Atlantic from Argentina, which could only be regarded as a concession to the German blockade. The other and more serious was that U-Boat attacks on Argentine commerce did not cease with the German apology. Two more Argentine ships, the *Oriana* and the *Toro*, were sunk in quick succession on 6 and 22 June respectively. Pueyrredon accordingly demanded on 4 July that the German Government promise to respect the right of Argentine ships to the freedom of the seas. The language of the Argentine demand moved the German Ambassador in Buenos Aires, Count Karl von Luxburg, to describe it as tantamount to an ultimatum. The United States hopefully seized the opportunity to strengthen resolve in Buenos Aires by proposing that a squadron of American warships call there on a goodwill visit after leaving Rio. This might, indeed, have served to deter the Germans. In fact, it only worsened Argentine–United States relations. The Americans most unfortunately linked their offer of

---

[1] Luxburg to Pueyrredon, *Memorias,* 2 May 1917

a goodwill visit with a request that the American ships be allowed to enter Argentine waters 'unconditionally', on the grounds that their safety might be endangered if their movements in neutral waters were subject to any restrictions. Determined to avoid any appearance of gratitude for United States support, Yrigoyen announced that Argentina did not give 'unconditional' invitations to anyone, and that the American ships would be required to offer due 'respect and courtesy' if they wanted to visit Argentine ports. Ambassador Stimson insisted that the safety of the fleet required him to reject this demand. Yrigoyen then stated flatly that the United States fleet would not be allowed to enter Argentine waters unless the request for 'unconditional' entry were withdrawn. Washington immediately responded to the gaucho spur. A reply came within twenty-four hours withdrawing the offending expression; explaining that the whole affair was merely the result of an unfortunate misunderstanding by Ambassador Stimson; and respectfully seeking permission for the American squadron to visit Buenos Aires.

Meanwhile, Berlin also had fallen into line. Pueyrredon repeated his demands on 4 August, adding the remarkable argument that : 'It is inconceivable that . . . [Argentina's] natural products should at any time be qualified as contraband of war . . . [as] . . . they are the fruits of the efforts of the nation in its vital work, not to satisfy war requirements, but to meet the normal needs of humanity.'[1] This novel doctrine might, indeed, have marked 'a distinct step forward in the domain of international law', as Professor Martin suggests.[2] Essentially, it was merely restating in peculiarly nationalistic terms the distinction between 'free goods' and 'contraband of war' traditionally made by international lawyers when considering the legitimacy of a blockade. But it was, of course, irrelevant in the present context of a submarine blockade, as such a blockade could only be effective, and therefore legitimate according to international law, if submarines were freed from the obligation to halt and search merchant ships running the blockade. The Germans nonetheless tried to meet Pueyrredon's impossible

[1] Molina to Zimmermann, *Memorias,* 4 August 1917
[2] P. A. Martin, *Latin America and the War,* John Hopkins, Baltimore, 1925, p. 210

requirements. They agreed on 28 August to indemnify Argentina for the loss of the *Toro* on the same basis as that accepted in the case of the *Monte Protegido*; claimed that 'the freedom of the seas, in which Argentina has an immediate interest, is one of the principal [German] objects of the war'; and accepted with pleasure the rules of international law.[1] Buenos Aires had won again, hands down.

Once again, however, Yrigoyen and Pueyrredon had their victory soured for them by circumstances. In a second attempt to force Argentina's hand after the farce of the 'unconditional' goodwill visit, the United States released for publication a series of intercepted telegrams from Luxburg to Zimmermann, in which this most indiscreet of German Ambassadors rather unhelpfully recommended that Argentine ships entering the war zone should be either compelled to go back, sunk without trace, or allowed to go through. He also referred to the dignified and pedantic Pueyrredon as, successively, 'a notorious ass and Anglophile', 'a theatrical person who has shown an insane cunning in preventing me from having an interview with the President', and 'probably bribed'.[2] Germany was always sadly out of luck with its diplomatic representatives in Latin countries. However, it is difficult to imagine how even a diplomat as unperceptive as Luxburg could have imagined that any foreign government would have been likely to hire the services of Pueyrredon, who was manifestly giving satisfaction to none of them; or to have fancied that he would have been any the wiser for an interview with Yrigoyen, ponderous, morose, and wrapped in an aura of Basque mystery which invariably left his interlocutors wondering what secrets it concealed.

The chief secret of the President was unquestionably his own incipient madness. Certainly, his diplomacy could hardly have been less complex. Yrigoyen had come to office on a policy of strictly domestic reform without any preconceptions about foreign affairs. The principles he now used as guides in that field were the traditional ones of Argentine diplomacy in their simplest possible

---

[1] Luxburg to Pueyrredon, *Memorias,* 28 August 1917
[2] Luxburg to Zimmermann, *Official Bulletin,* (Washington) 21 December 1917

form. They had never been very complicated. President Bartolome Mitre had first given them formal expression at an Inter-American Conference in Lima in 1865 when he rejected the concept of multilateral security arrangements as being incompatible with the doctrine of national sovereignty. This point of view was never wholly inflexible, however. Mitre himself showed this the following year when he aligned Argentina with Brazil and Uruguay in the War of the Triple Alliance against Paraguay. But the peculiarly uninhibited way in which Argentine jurists and politicians were wont to insist upon the absolutely prior claim of the sovereign state over any international limitations whatsoever naturally disturbed many foreigners. Professor Martin records that: 'Competent and discriminating foreign observers, such as Bryce and Clemenceau, have remarked on this cult of the *patria* [in Argentina] at times becoming almost a mania. The Argentines were therefore quite capable of judging the war and its issues on the basis of criteria in which their own national interest and own national point of view were prominent factors.'[1] This was hardly the point. No representative national government would be justified in assessing external events in any other manner, even if it had the inclination to do so. What was really significant was that other Latin countries normally sought their individual self-interest through active co-operation with their neighbours and with the United States. The Argentines sought theirs through the rejection of any foreign entanglements whatever.

Foreigners were not likely to find this way of thinking appealing. It was nonetheless understandable in the case of a people whose population had increased nearly five times in fifty years, and who could justifiably expect to enjoy in the future one of the highest standards of living in the world. The policy was triumphantly carried into practice by Hipolito Yrigoyen during the last quarter of 1917. His position was made tactically easier by Pueyrredon's opportune illness. The Argentine Constitution divided control over foreign affairs between the Executive Power and Congress, reserving to the President the right to make diplomatic initiatives, but requiring Congress to ratify any agreements with foreign powers. Congress at the time was clamouring for a breach with

Martin, *op. cit.*, p. 177

Germany, but with Pueyrredon temporarily out of the way there was no one to explain Executive policy to Congress or to convey Congressional opinion back to the Casa Rosada. Yrigoyen had it all to himself. His first move was to give Luxburg his passports and declare him *persona non grata* in Argentina. This produced the desired response from Berlin of repudiating unreservedly the views of its former Ambassador. Yrigoyen then dealt with the 'war party' at home; he told the Comite Nacional de Juventud that: 'Argentina cannot be dragged into war by the United States, and the nation must take the position it deserves in the American Continent.'[1] He then furiously rebuked the British Ambassador, Sir Reginald Tower, who was quoted in *La Nacion* as having said that public demonstrations in Buenos Aires and the views expressed in Congress indicated general support for the Allies and dissatisfaction with the vacillating nature of official Argentine policy. Yrigoyen threatened to treat Tower in the same way as he had Luxburg if he insisted on issuing misleading statements in his capacity of diplomat. Tower duly withdrew the remarks attributed to him. Then, in a last bid to rally continental support for Argentine neutrality, Yrigoyen called again for the governments of South America to convoke 'a Latin American Conference to agree upon a common action . . . to avoid their nations becoming compromised individually'.[2]

Yrigoyen's unpromising attempt to renew the concept of a 'League of Neutrals' was inspired by the decision of Brazil to go to war with the Central Powers. His appeal was launched even as Francophile, Germanophobe Ruy Barbosa called for a united transatlantic front against Germany in the Brazilian Senate: ' . . . Europe is with America, America is with Europe . . . in unity with the United States, in unity with England, in unity with France, with Portugal, with Italy.'[3] There were obviously two voices trying to speak for Latin America. On the evidence, the far less melodious one of Hipolito Yrigoyen proved the more persuasive. Chile, faced with the reality of the breakdown of the

[1] *La Presna*, 27 September 1917.
[2] *La Presna*, 29 October 1917
[3] Ruy Barbosa, *A Grande Guerra*, Editora Guanabara, Rio de Janeiro, 1932, p. 222

ABC alignment, elected to preserve the rigorous neutrality it had initially proclaimed;[1] so did Colombia, Venezuela, and Paraguay; only Peru, Bolivia, and Ecuador severed relations with Germany; and Brazil alone followed the Caribbean vassals into the war.

Neutrality did not, however, mean indifference, as Argentine diplomats never tired of explaining during the Second World War. Argentina had presented its challenge to United States domination of the hemisphere by remaining neutral. After this, the problem was to ensure that the moral prestige thus obtained was not bought at any material cost. The most obvious danger was that the Allied and Associated Powers might accord some favours to Brazil as a co-belligerent which they might withhold from neutral Argentina. Indications of what might happen were given when Brazil was invited to the Inter-Allied Conference held in Paris between 30 November and 3 December 1917. Yrigoyen accordingly hastened to make a bid for Allied goodwill by organizing an impressive ceremonial welcome for the new Belgian Ambassador, Auguste Melot. He assured Melot that the cause of Belgium 'was the cause of independence and the right of nations', and that he himself believed 'in the power and sovereignty of these principles, indestructible throughout the history of the world'.[2] In the same week, post-war Argentine economic prosperity was assured by a Convention under which France and Great Britain undertook to purchase two and a half million tons of Argentine agricultural products. The needs of its co-belligerents forced the United States also to come to terms. Washington had threatened to place an embargo on shipments of coal to Argentina when Yrigoyen stopped grain exports the year before. Now the Americans hastened to give assurances that ships arriving at Argentine ports to take on the foodstuffs contracted for would bring 'coal for the requirements of the Argentine people'.[3] Yrigoyen followed up this success with a series of extraordinary interviews with visiting American diplomats and journalists in which he sought to give the impression that he and

---

[1] Luis Galdames, *Historia de Chile,* University of North Carolina Press, 1941, p. 410

[2] *La Presna,* 11 January 1918

[3] Stimson to Pueyrredon, *F.R.U.S.,* 14 January 1918

Wilson had always been basically in accord in their thinking on international affairs. He finally placed Argentina firmly on the side of the angels when he hailed the cessation of hostilities in November 1918 with the claim that he had always sought a peace based on the rule of liberty, justice, and law.

The triumph of Argentine diplomacy was undoubtedly complete,[1] at least in the sense that Argentina had won every hand in a game where the prizes were the very fundamental ones of prestige and wealth. Buenos Aires had challenged Washington and Berlin and had won. It had also become rich. Argentina had ranked eleventh among both trading and exporting countries in 1913. By the end of the war it had improved its position to tenth and seventh respectively. The Argentine *peso* had become the strongest currency in the world. It was true that this achievement had been gained at the cost of offending every country with which Argentina had had to deal over the past two years; but on the other hand it was by no means clear that Argentina's position could possibly have been improved had its policies been conciliatory and obliging instead of being ruthlessly self-centred and intransigent.

Brazil had certainly been as conciliatory and obliging as possible. That country's motives for entering the war had been interpreted in a number of bizarre ways.[2] They were, in fact, as simple as Argentina's motives for staying out. Brazilian diplomats had traditionally sought to maintain the most cordial relations possible with the United States.[3] Their object in doing so was to avoid anything like a struggle for primacy between the two largest American powers, which Brazil could not hope to win, and to assure Brazil as far as possible of United States support against foreign aggression either from Europe or from across the Rio de la Plata. President Braz could thus quite reasonably state, when calling for a declaration of war against Germany, that : 'Brazil, in taking her place once more at the side of the United States, has

---

[1] Etcheparaborda, *op. cit.,* p. 3382
[2] Albert Haas, 'The Foreign Policy of the ABC Powers', *Deutsche Politik,* 2 July 1921
[3] Nilo Pecanha to Alcibiades Pecanha, *Brazilian Green Book,* p. 70

remained faithful to her political and diplomatic traditions of continental solidarity . . . '[1]

This was an eminently rational policy. It remained to be seen whether it was a particularly profitable one. Brazil's external trade had indeed benefited impressively from Allied war contracts, but its relative economic position had scarcely improved. Brazil in 1913 had ranked fifteenth among trading nations and thirteenth among exporters. Its position as a trading nation was unchanged in 1919, although it had moved from thirteenth to twelfth place among the exporters. However, Brazil could still hope to reap any material advantages accruing from being junior partner of the United States among the American Republics. It was naturally the object of Argentine diplomacy to ensure that Brazil did not gain any preferential benefit in this manner, and the Argentines had an unbeatable trump card to hand. This was quite simply the fear that they inspired in their neighbours by reason of their size, their resources, their superb economic development, and, above all, their strident doctrine of national self-interest. It did not matter that Argentina had never in fact attempted to assert its authority by force over other Latin countries. For practical purposes it did not have to do so as long as it possessed the capacity to intimidate them. The 'cult of the *patria*' was a safe and inexpensive substitute for a policy of aggression. Its effect was that Uruguay and Paraguay for certain, and probably Bolivia as well, could be counted on to give some measure of consent to the initiatives of Buenos Aires; that Chile would be afraid to oppose them too openly; and that Brazil itself would probably be forced to co-operate in order to avoid becoming isolated in the continent. The United States, of course, had the capacity to restore the balance. But Buenos Aires was distant from Washington by three times the width of the Atlantic, and anyway, the last thing that the United States wanted was to become involved in an overt struggle for power in the hemisphere. United States policy was becoming increasingly oriented towards the goal of Pan-American solidarity; but solidarity was impossible as long as Argentina was prepared to defy the wishes of Washington and was able to drag about three-quarters of the continent along with it. The answer to the equation was simple. Pan-Americanism meant that the United States would

[1] Jose Mario Bello, *A History of Modern Brazil, 1889–1964*, Stanford, 1966, p. 222

have to learn to neglect its friends and conciliate its enemies in the hemisphere.

It was perhaps the first time that a really great power had to learn this particular lesson. The Americans were certainly never allowed to forget it for the next twenty-five years. For a quarter of a century, the American Hemisphere and to a great extent the world outside formed the arena for a power struggle between Washington and Buenos Aires. The North Americans were assisted neither by their own vastly greater material resources nor by the fact that they usually took up moral positions which were considerably easier to defend than those of their gaucho opponents. The Argentines won almost every round. They defied a world in arms, and grew rich. What ultimately halted the gaucho march of triumph was mainly the weather. But its eventual failure did not diminish the incredible success of Argentine diplomacy in demonstrating the ways in which a relatively small nation can defy the greatest of superpowers with impunity and profit. They had taught a lesson and provided a technique for Paris and Bucharest, for Havana and Lima. They were the first Gaullists.

Chapter I

A TEMPLE OF HONOUR, RIGHT, AND JUSTICE (1920-1930)

Brazil naturally represented the main obstacle to Argentine pretensions. Although it could hardly compete with Argentina in any economic or financial sense it was still the largest Latin country; its army was more numerous and its navy probably more formidable than those of Argentina; and it possessed, as a co-belligerent of the victorious western allies, a claim to international importance which Argentina could not match. This importance was already becoming enhanced by Brazil's close involvement in the creation of the tremendous new international factor of the League of Nations.

This concept of President Wilson's was by any standards the most portentous initiative yet made in the history of international politics. Its significance was even greater for the Latin Americans than for any other members of the world community. In the first place, it was reasonable to regard Bolivar himself (the liberator of the Spanish America colonies) as 'the first modern pioneer of the organisation of peace',[1] and therefore as the spiritual progenitor of the League. In the second, the League could provide a bridge linking the Latins with their cultural homelands in Europe, and enabling them at last to take their parts in the drama of world politics. Above all, it was obvious that the great Latin republics represented ideal potential members of the League. Both the material strength and moral prestige of the European Great Powers had been seriously eroded by the events of the First World

[1] Martin, *op. cit.*, p. 177

War. Germany, Austria, and Russia had been practically eliminated as world powers, at least for the time being. Britain, France, and Italy had been seriously weakened physically by their efforts in the war. All had to some extent been discredited by revelations of diplomatic and military incompetence and unworthy motives and methods.

If the stature of the Great Powers had been diminished, the new states created from the wrecks of the Russian and Austrian Empires could not be said to have acquired any. The fact was that Argentina, Brazil, and Chile appeared at the time to be positively outstanding in comparison with the Europeans in terms of both constitutional stability and fidelity to democratic principles. Argentina had enjoyed constitutional government since the presidency of Bartolome Mitre in 1862; Chile had been a stable republic since 1831, and a parliamentary one since 1891; and Brazil had developed with impressive calm from a regency to an independent empire in 1822, and to a constitutional republic in 1891, interrupted only by three years of arbitrary rule under Floriano Peixoto. Moreover, the three nations had been independent for nearly 100 years; they had managed to live at peace with one another for nearly the whole of that period; and they possessed material resources which rendered them vital elements in the world economy.

Nor were the Latins insignificant even in military terms, although it was naturally hoped that the time had passed for settling international differences by force of arms. All the ABC peoples had performed impressively in the past against European invaders who threatened their independence; Argentina and Brazil had made great and sustained military efforts in the dreadful War of the Triple Alliance, the second most deadly ever fought in the American Hemisphere;[1] and Chile's raid against Peru and Bolivia in the War of the Pacific ranked as one of the most efficient and financially successful wars in the history of armed aggression. Moreover, all three possessed naval power distinctly

[1] Statistics for this incredible war are highly unreliable, but it is conservatively assumed to have resulted in about 500,000 deaths in all. By contrast, the American Civil War claimed one million casualties in all, including 617,000 dead

formidable by the standards of 1919. Chile's excellently trained sailors manned a fleet consisting of 2 venerable battleships, 2 armoured cruisers, 4 light cruisers, 14 destroyers and torpedo boats, and 6 submarines; Brazil could deploy 2 really formidable capital ships, 2 armoured cruisers, 6 light cruisers, 11 destroyers and torpedo boats, and 3 submarines; and Argentina's navy numbered 2 battleships of gun power equivalent to the Brazilians, 4 armoured cruisers, and 15 destroyers and torpedo boats. All this, of course, did not amount to anything like Great Power striking capacity, even in combination. Italy, the least considerable of the Great Powers, could, for example, put to sea no less than 22 battleships, 12 armoured cruisers, 13 cruisers, 130 destroyers and torpedo boats, and 43 submarines. But the ABC fleets were still stronger even individually than those of any of the lesser European states except Spain, or of any non-European country except the United States and Japan.[1]

What really mattered was that the great Latin Republics represented at the time literally the only group of historically mature, constitutionally stable, traditionally peaceful, and physically secure sovereign states to be found anywhere in the world. They were, therefore, as has been said, ideal potential members of the League of Nations. Moreover, they lost no time in showing that they were fully aware of the roles they were qualified to play.

Naturally Brazil had the inside running. The Peace Conference of 18 January 1919 had decided to go ahead with implementing Wilson's concept of a world organization to maintain and preserve international peace. Latin America had been represented only by the belligerents of the banana belt, Ecuador and Brazil. The former Brazilian President, Epitacio Pessoa, was chosen to be a member of the committee charged with drafting the original Covenant of the League. Wilson himself recommended on 28 April that Brazil should be included with Spain, Belgium, and Greece to make up the four countries entitled to elect members of the Council of the League.

It was time for the Latin neutrals to take action to safeguard their own positions. The Chilean Government hastily announced

[1] *Jane's Fighting Ships* 1920

on 19 March 1919 that it also accepted the ideas of the League of Nations. Yrigoyen's task was more difficult. He had to reconcile participation in an effective world organization which it might be inexpedient to stay out of, with traditional Argentine doctrines of unlimited state sovereignty. Nobody was going to believe that Argentina accepted the ideas of the League of Nations. Still, Yrigoyen instructed the Argentine Ambassador to France to assure the delegates at the Peace Conference that Argentina would adhere to the League without any reservations once the Covenant of the world body had been ratified by Congress.[1] This in fact was only saying that Argentina would do whatever its Government decided to do; but this was not the impression created in Paris. Impressive, dignified, and wildly ambitious, Marcelo T. de Alvear simply told the Secretary-designate of the League, Sir Eric Drummond, that Argentina wished to adhere to the League. The surprised Drummond replied that this was not possible as the League was not yet formally constituted. He accordingly asked Alvear if he wished him to understand that Argentina desired to adhere to the League as soon as the formal means of doing so were available. Alvear replied that this was indeed the interpretation that he wished to have placed upon his words.[2]

This was certainly displaying enthusiasm for the internationalist idea. Yrigoyen also had the satisfaction of beating the Brazilians out of first place, as Argentina became a founding member when the League formally entered into existence on 10 January 1920, while the Covenant was not actually ratified in Rio de Janeiro until 16 January. There was only one snag. Yrigoyen never referred the Covenant to Congress. Argentina's membership was therefore not legal in terms of Argentine constitutional law. Neither was its membership unqualified, whatever Yrigoyen might have said or Alvear implied. Yrigoyen himself made this clear when he told Wilson that Argentina accepted the League 'in principle', but could not adhere to any international organization which distinguished in any way between former belligerents and neutrals.

It was thus to be expected that the Argentine delegates would try to transform the League into an organization which it would

[1] *La Presna,* 13 July 1919
[2] Seviri, *La Ligue de las Naciones, su origen y la obra realizada en la Republica Argentina,* 1928, B.A., p. 504

be safe for their own country to join. What was not anticipated, however, was the brutal nature of the methods that Yrigoyen adopted. He tried against Geneva the same peremptory techniques that had worked so satisfactorily against Berlin and Washington. Congress had agreed on 30 September 1920 to send delegates to the First Assembly of the League, even though it still had not been asked to ratify the Covenant. Pueyrredon and Alvear were instructed that the world body would have to accept the principles of universality and the absolute equality of nations. Pueyrredon presented the Argentine requests on 17 November. He asked directly that all sovereign states should be allowed to become members of the League automatically and to be free to withdraw from it when they chose; that all members of the Security Council should be elected by a majority vote of the Assembly, instead of having five places permanently reserved for the Great Powers; and that a Permanent Court of International Justice should be established on the principles of compulsory arbitration and complete jurisdiction.[1]

These were by no means ideas to be lightly dismissed, as the historian of the League records. Nor was the venture entirely without hope of success. The Council was in fact already considering the establishment of a World Court, as Pueyrredon well knew; the challenging second proposal really involved no serious change in the existing situation, as it provided quite inconsistently for the permanent re-election of the Great Powers to the Council; and the principle of universality expressed in the first proposal was calculated to appeal to neutral and defeated nations alike. Chile indeed promptly gave its support, claiming that the principles of discretionary membership and election to the Council would give the world body 'an American character, consecrated to the truly democratic nature of the Continent, against an oligarchy of the Great European Powers'.[2] This, of course, meant that Brazil could hardly hold out. The Brazilians were in any case themselves worried about the implications of the 'European Oligarchy', even though they were equally concerned not to jeopardize their own

[1] League of Nations, *Records of the First Assembly*, (1920) p. 87.
[2] J. C. de Macedo Soares, *O Brasil e a Sociedade das Nacios*, Pedone, Paris, 1927, p. 93

chances of success in the League by alienating those same oligarchs. They accordingly compromised by endorsing the idea of equality within the Council.[1]

Pueyrredon had thus gained a real diplomatic success. He had created an unforgettable sensation; he had won real and valuable support; and he had whipped Chile and Brazil into line behind an Argentine initiative. But he had no chance of actually getting his demands accepted. In the first place, it was an unsuitable time to start re-drafting the Covenant. In the second, the Great Powers naturally preferred to believe that the interests of the world body required that their own control over its development should remain unchecked. The Argentine proposals were accordingly referred to a Committee for study and report. The question was what to do next. Acting Foreign Minister Torello cabled from Buenos Aires that Pueyrredon and Alvear were to withdraw unconditionally from the League if their proposals were rejected or adjourned 'for any reason whatever'.[2] Pueyrredon had had enough drama for the moment, however. He accordingly sent back reassuring and misleading reports that : ' . . . our wish will in point of fact be realized: the Argentine theory is triumphing in the world conscience'.[3] Yrigoyen's mind was, however, made up : Argentina should adhere only to a League based on Argentine principles. Accordingly, on 6 December, the Assembly listened, amazed, to a statement from Pueyrredon that :

'Our country saw in the proposed League the birth of a new and beneficent instrument for peace . . . and in the [Argentine] amendments to the Covenant it saw the prospect of co-operation in perfecting the Constituent Charter of the League . . . The chief aim of the Argentine Government was to co-operate in the work of drawing up, by means of amendments to the Covenant, a charter which it was hoped it would be possible to embody the ideals and principles which Argentina has always upheld in international affairs and from which she will never deviate. When once this aim has disappeared, owing to the postponement of the amendments, the moment has arrived for

[1] ibid., p. 94
[2] Ministerio de Relaciones Exteriores y Culto, *Boletin de la Liga de las Naciones,* 1920, no. 2, p. 159.
[3] Pueyrredon to Torello, *Memorias,* 24 November 1920

Argentina's co-operation in the work to cease . . . For the above reasons . . . I have the honour to inform the Assembly that the Argentine delegation considers its mission at an end.'[1]

Pueyrredon then led his colleagues out of the Assembly Hall. There was no denying that he achieved a great dramatic success. Nor was there any doubt that he had thereby set a precedent which could be absolutely fatal to the authority and the very existence of the world body. As Lord Robert Cecil prophetically remarked : 'If every Member of the Assembly were to take the line which the Argentine Delegation has taken, no progress would have been possible.'[2] The other Latin States hastened to disassociate themselves from the now failed initiative. Brazil described Pueyrredon's action as a desertion. The Chileans attributed it simply to wounded gaucho self-esteem. But it was not entirely unappreciated. The defeated Central Powers assumed that Argentina had been generously trying to facilitate their own entry into the League, even though Pueyrredon himself explained that he had not been trying to assist Germany to join the League, but to force it to do so, so that it could be the more easily supervised by other countries.[3] Hipolito Yrigoyen's name was honoured with a standing ovation in the German Reichstag, and in September 1921 the Germans at last fulfilled their promise to salute the Argentine flag when the sky-blue-and-white was ceremonially raised on board the German cruiser, *Hannover*, in Kiel Harbour during a reception given to the new Argentine Ambassador.

Meanwhile, there remained very general confusion as to what the Argentines had actually done. It was quite obvious that they were not agreed upon this themselves. Minister Torello tried to evade the issue by stating that Argentina was now 'not with anybody, or against anybody, but with everybody for the good of all'.[4] Pressed for a direct answer, he said that Argentina had not left the League because it had never belonged to it.[5] However, Pueyrredon himself claimed that the issue was perfectly clear. Argentina had left the Assembly, but it remained a member of

[1] League of Nations, *op. cit.*, pp. 276–277
[2] League of Nations, *op. cit.*, p. 278.
[3] *The Times*, 9 December 1920
[4] *La Presna*, 7 December 1920
[5] ibid., 15 December 1920

the League.[1] Yrigoyen for his part managed to make things totally obscure when he told Congress that he was merely trying 'to assure and consolidate the personality of Argentina in the international order by placing it in a temple of honour, right, and justice'.[2]

There was at least no doubt as to what this meant in practice. Yrigoyen had already made the world feel the gaucho whip when he ruthlessly halted grain exports at a time of world famine, pending the imposition of new export taxes.[3] He then challenged the League again by refusing to forbid Germany to sell arms to Argentina, contrary to the provisions of the Treaty of Versailles, on the grounds that Argentina had no concern about the provisions of a treaty between foreign countries.[4] He completed his work of goodwill by repudiating the ABC Treaty, asserting that nothing could be more dangerous than the creation of such regional arrangements 'establishing differences and giving offence'.[5]

Yrigoyen was thus preparing to hand over to Alvear a nation of booming prosperity and no friends. By contrast, Brazil and Chile had worked hard to establish themselves as good neighbours in the world community. Brazil had assisted Belgian recovery by granting that country a credit of 280 million Francs with which to buy raw materials. Chile sought to ingratiate itself with the United States by upholding the supremacy of the Monroe Doctrine against the League on 7 September 1921, and with Brazil by proposing twelve days later that Brazil and Spain should be appointed permanent members of the Council of the League. Chile also prepared to host the Fifth Pan-American Conference in Santiago in January 1923. Meanwhile, Brazil sought and obtained a naval mission from the United States to assist in overhauling the Brazilian Fleet,[6] and even attempted to repair relations with Argentina by proposing that the ABC Treaty should be revived. Yrigoyen rejected this curtly on 6 December on the grounds that it would arouse suspicion among other Latin countries.[7]

[1] ibid., 18 December 1920
[2] *La Presna,* 31 December 1920
[3] *The Times,* 8 June 1920
[4] *La Presna,* 19 February 1921
[5] ibid., 18 March 1921
[6] *The Times,* 7 November 1922
[7] *La Presna,* 7 December 1922

President Alvear was not committed to the same technique of displaying universal friendship by giving offence to everybody. He accordingly sent Foreign Minister Angel Gallardo to Rio to placate the offended Brazilians. But the Pan-American Conference in the New Year precipitated the most serious rupture yet among the Latins. Alvear attempted to head off the challenge of Brazilian naval re-armament by instructing Pueyrredon to propose reductions in all military establishments. The Conference handled his initiative badly, mainly because of intervention by the United States, which cautioned Brazil and Chile against committing themselves to total disarmament. The Argentine proposal was accordingly submerged in a vague and unsatisfactory report; and Pueyrredon had for the second time in three years the satisfaction of disassociating himself from the work of an international assembly, and of ridiculing the incoherent arguments of those who had the temerity to disagree with him.

This, however, was not entirely the effect that Alvear had hoped to achieve. He therefore made approaches to the League of Nations. Angel Gallardo claimed on 7 March that Argentina was still a member of the world body, using the rather dubious argument that Argentina had 'acceded' to the League, even if it had not 'adhered' to it. On 17 May, Alvear asked Congress to regularize Argentina's relations with Geneva by paying its arrears of membership dues. These approaches were welcomed neither in Geneva nor in Buenos Aires. Drummond rejected Gallardo's sophistry; and Congress rather surprisingly refused to ratify the Covenant, although it agreed to introduce a budget item to pay for the outstanding membership dues.

This was perhaps the one thing that could have complicated Argentina's relations with Geneva still further. Meanwhile, good internationalists Chile and Brazil rushed on to unprecedented humiliation and disaster. The political stability of both countries was already weakening under the impact of a world-wide fall in commodity prices. Bloody fighting had broken out in the southern-most state of Brazil, Rio Grande do Sul, where gaucho traditions of family honour and blood feuds gave a quality of intensity to local politics frequently lacking in Rio itself. The Chilean and Brazilian Governments desperately tried to redeem their domestic failures by striving for success on the international stage, uniting in a claim that America deserved a larger representation in the Council, as the American Republics had anticipated the hopes of the League by effectively disarming already. The most convincing answer to this boast came in November 1923, when the Argentine Congress appropriated $100,000,000 for a massive rearmament programme intended to make the armed forces of the gaucho republic the most formidable south of the Rio Grande.

This was really the end of Chilean and Brazilian attempts to find a worthwhile international place in the League of Nations. They had both worked hard and contributed greatly, Brazil's achievement being naturally the more impressive. Brazil had become by far the most important of the non-European members of the world body, except Japan. Epitacio Pessoa had done little himself to make his nation's mark on the Covenant of the League itself, having sat in complete silence throughout the whole of the drafting process. Raoul Fernandez, however, the Brazilian jurist, had been largely instrumental in drafting the statute of the International Court of Justice; Ruy Barbosa had been among the first judges appointed to the Court; and between 1920 and 1926, Brazil had been represented in forty meetings of the Council of the League, which was more than any other country not actually a Great Power, apart from Spain and Belgium. This was the superb record of distinguished service that Epitacio Pessoa, now unfortunately President, began to gamble away in 1924, as Brazil's external trade figures fell from a combined figure of $1,027,000,000 in 1920 to less than $800,000,000, and revolts against his rule spread throughout the great state of São Paulo. On 14 September 1924 Raoul Fernandez reaffirmed the sentiments that inspired Brazil 'in its sincere co-operation with all the forces which . . . work for the foundation of world peace'.[1] Then he got to the point. Germany had been offered a permanent seat in the Council by the Western Powers as part of its price for accepting the terms of the Treaty of Locarno which guaranteed the existing boundaries of France, Belgium, Germany, and Italy. Fernandez explained that Brazil would support Germany's claim to a permanent seat only if it were granted one itself.

[1] Macedo Soares, *op. cit.*, p. 112

Pessoa undoubtedly had something of a case. The Locarno Agreement was the supreme example of the 'European Oligarchy' at work. It was strictly a system of regional defence, conceived solely in terms of the interests of Western Europe and the Treaty of Versailles, though there was no denying that these were important considerations. Nor was there any denying that Pessoa was primarily concerned with achieving a diplomatic coup to prop up his own foundering regime. Not even the other Latins were prepared to support such a cause. Chile might have done so to preserve its traditional links with Brazil; but Chilean political and economic viability alike were collapsing in a welter of distress and humiliation. In September 1924 a military coup by Altaminaro brought an end to the most promising Latin tradition of representative government. Then in 1925 the Republic of the Andes endured the attentions of four successive Heads of State. In such conditions no coherent external or even domestic policies were possible. Interest in the League was also fading among the other Latin countries. In December 1924, Costa Rica had given formal notice of withdrawal from the League, pleading difficulty in paying its membership dues. In 1925, Uruguay disregarded the principles of the Covenant of the League, naturally with Argentine support, by breaking off diplomatic relations with the Soviet Union, on the grounds that the Russians had been using their embassy in Montevideo to disseminate Communist propaganda in Latin America.

All this helped to make the position of the Brazilian Government still more difficult to defend, for the defection of the biggest of the Latin American countries was bound to destroy completely the much-vaunted 'American character' of the League. Pessoa, though, was incapable of seeing beyond the narrow limits of Brazilian domestic politics. In circumstances described reasonably as among the most distressing in the history of the League, Afranio de Mello Franco tearfully presented once more the hopeless Brazilian case.[1] The best he could do was to suggest that the American character of the League could be maintained by reserving a permanent seat in the Council for the United States,

[1] Manual Perez-Guerrero, *Les Relations des Etats de l'Amerique Latine avec la Societe des Nations*, Pedone, Paris, 1936, p. 21.

and allowing it to be occupied by Brazil in the absence of the North Americans. All that this achieved was of course to have Brazilian pretensions repudiated by the very Latin countries that Brazil had once hoped to lead.

The Brazilian humiliation was gleefully reported and commented on in the Argentine press. On 12 June 1926, Mello Franco served formal notice of Brazil's withdrawal from the League, after a last despairing claim that Germany ought not to be counted among the Great Powers since the other Great Powers had pledged themselves to keep it permanently disarmed. This argument of defencelessness was exactly the one that he had formerly urged in support of a greater American representation in Geneva. All that Mello Franco's words achieved was to indicate how difficult it was to justify what Pessoa was doing. Mello Franco did at least gain the personal success of having all the other speakers in the Assembly express the keenest sorrow at losing the valued co-operation of their Brazilian colleagues. Honorio Pueyrredon had received far different treatment. Even this slight consolation to Brazilian pride was lost in the wake of Pessoa's next gaffe. On the same day that Mello Franco was serving notice of withdrawal in the Assembly, Pessoa announced that the United States Ambassador in Rio had congratulated him on the position being adopted by Brazil. The American Ambassador, however, immediately denied that he had ever discussed the matter with the Brazilian President at all, and the United States representative in Geneva communicated with Drummond formally disassociating his government from Pessoa's statement.[1] The international prestige of Brazil had reached its nadir.

It had done so at a time when Alvear was initiating the steps to give Argentina a position of unchallengeable material strength in the continent. In September 1925, Congress had agreed to expend a further $200,000,000 on a naval rearmament programme designed to give Argentina the sixth-largest navy in the world. The Brazilian challenge was effectively answered.

This might well have seemed a most appropriate time for the powerful and prosperous gaucho republic to reassert its influence in world affairs. So at least it appeared to Alvear, but it did not

[1] *New York Times,* 20 June 1926

appear so to Congress, which still refused to ratify the Covenant; to the rapidly growing body of Argentine electors who wished to bring back Yrigoyen to office; or to Honorio Pueyrredon, who was achieving his greatest distinction by walking out of international conferences. Indeed, in February 1927, Pueyrredon disobeyed Alvear's orders by refusing to sign the Convention on the Organization and Purposes of the Pan-American Union unless it incorporated a declaration in favour of liberalizing world commodity trade. Alvear overcame this difficulty by simply replacing Pueyrredon with a diplomat more amenable to taking orders. He was, however, unable to persuade Congress to regularize Argentine relations with the League, even when the world body tried to recover some Latin American character by inviting Argentina to send delegates to the Committees on the Reorganization of the Council and on Arbitration and Security. All that Alvear could manage was to have Torres le Breton sent to Geneva as an Observer. However, he did succeed in initiating talks in Buenos Aires between Bolivia and Paraguay, disputing over the territorial division of the Chaco Boreal; and he provided Pueyrredon with an opportunity for another dramatic perform-ance at the Pan-American Conference in Havana, where he rallied the support of the other Latin Republics for his attack on United States intervention in Nicaragua: 'The sovereignty of states lies in their absolute right to full domestic autonomy and entire external independence ... Diplomatic or armed intervention ... is an attack against the independence of these states.'[1]

Surprisingly, this burst of diplomatic activity initiated by Alvear did not come to an end with Yrigoyen's second accession to the Presidency. It was merely the tone that changed. Argentine diplo-mats addressed themselves anew to the agreeable task of defying the United States. Yrigoyen's spokesmen even carried the assault into Europe, where Ambassador Uriburu claimed in Brussels that the Monroe Doctrine meant only 'America for the United States'.[2] It was a telling phrase. The opportunity soon came to repeat it. Having failed to entice Argentina back to Geneva, the League now made advances to Costa Rica. The Government of that country replied by requiring the League to define formally what

[1] *New York Times,* 13 March 1927
[2] *New York Times,* 1 March 1928

it understood the Monroe Doctrine to imply. The gravamen of Costa Rica's concern was the very reasonable fear that the Doctrine was being interpreted on both sides of the Atlantic in a way which left the Latin Republics unable to appeal to the League for protection against United States aggression. Obviously the last thing that would serve the interests of the League was a confrontation with Washington. Brazil might have found some solution partially agreeable to everyone but the Brazilians compounded their folly of 1926 by rejecting an invitation from Geneva to change their position and remain within the world body. The way was open for Buenos Aires. In August 1928 Angel Gallardo hastily announced that Argentina had completed all the formalities necessary for membership of the League, and that its adhesion was irregular only from the point of view of Argentine constitutional law.[1] This aspect would be cleared up when Congress ratified the League Covenant and agreed to pay its membership dues. Congress was still reluctant to do either, though it did agree to designate Jose Maria Cantilo to succeed Torres le Breton as Argentine Observer to the Ninth Assembly of the League, which at least cost little, and at the same time it assured Argentina of a voice if not a vote in Geneva.

Cantilo was equal to the occasion. United States Marines had already begun to withdraw from Nicaragua in November 1928. The immediate cause of Latin concern over the Monroe Doctrine was thus already being liquidated. However, Chile, Colombia, and Peru were still pressing for a formal interpretation of the Doctrine by Geneva, along with Costa Rica. It was an opportunity for making a gesture of a kind that the Argentines could never resist. On 10 December, Cantilo formally objected 'in the name of historical truth' to Article 21 of the League Covenant for its error in 'presenting the Monroe Doctrine as a regional arrangement when it is a unilateral political declaration which has never been specifically endorsed by the other American countries'.[2] The Argentines followed up this attack by rejecting an invitation to attend the Washington Conference on Conciliation and Arbitra-

---

[1] Ministerio de Relaciones Exteriores y Culto, *Memoria sobra la Ligue de las Naciones*, 1928, p. 3
[2] *La Presna,* 11 December 1928

tion, despite their erstwhile enthusiasm for such an idea; offering
the coolest of welcomes to Presidential candidate Herbert Hoover,
and making the point more obvious by following it with an
effusive invitation to the French President; and deliberately
leaving vacant their embassy in Washington. The final gesture of
Yrigoyen-type diplomacy came when the former Argentine
chancellor at Washington, Liborio Justo, contemptuously stated
that Argentina would be withdrawing from the Pan-American
Union as this had become merely a United States institution, and
Argentina did not intend to remain within a United States institution when it had not been prepared to remain within a world
one. He added that United States economic sanctions against
Argentina merely had the effect of strengthening Argentina's ties
with Britain.[1]

The Argentines undoubtedly had some excuse for their
behaviour. Their prosperity had continued to mount during the
whole of the first post-war decade. Argentine exports had
increased in value 50 per cent between 1923 and 1928. By 1929,
it had become the seventh largest trading nation in the world and
the second largest exporter to the United Kingdom. Then the
commodity market collapsed again. Argentina's trade was affected
more seriously than that of any other major exporting nation.
Recovery was partly impeded by the introduction of the ferocious
Hawley-Smoot tariffs in the United States, to which the
Argentines replied by imposing punitive restrictions on American
fruit exports. It was not surprising that gaucho frustration and
despair sought release in attacks on Yankee imperialism which
were shown to be largely unjustified by the very fact that they
could be delivered with impunity.

What was far more serious for the Argentines themselves was
the fact that Yrigoyen was now quite obviously incapable of
carrying out the functions of his office. His always remarkable
remoteness and obscurity had developed into undeniable insanity.
This in itself had not been a serious objection to his re-election in
1928, but even his most ardent supporters hesitated to entrust the
destiny of the Argentine Republic in the time of its greatest
national crisis to a man who could no longer read state papers

[1] ibid., 22 August 1930

himself, nor understand them when they were read to him. The appropriate steps were accordingly taken. General Jose F. Uriburu marched his troops from the Campo de Mayo outside Buenos Aires to the Casa Rosada, relieved Yrigoyen of the responsibilities which he scarcely any longer knew that he possessed, and installed himself as provisional president. A great tradition of representative democracy had temporarily come to an end. It was just in time.

Uriburu's coup could be only a brief interruption to the history of Argentine constitutional government. The General himself, behind his magnificent uniforms and moustachios, was only a plain-thinking, straightforward Fascist with no ambitions to be a popular Caesar. He was therefore of no use to the Conservative interest. Argentina's general staff could easily produce an eminently suitable political candidate. General Augustin P. Justo, portly, jovial, with a remarkable sensitivity to changes in the political atmosphere, was in many respects Argentina's answer to Franklin D. Roosevelt. The only problem was to get him elected. An Argentine electoral law had sought to safeguard the expression of the popular will by providing for universal suffrage and secret ballot. Such obstacles were, however, merely an exciting challenge for Justo and his campaign managers. Every imaginable technique of distorting electoral returns was employed to engineer his advance to the Casa Rosada. The most effective was probably the simplest. Armed guards warned electors suspected of Radical or Socialist sympathies away from the polling booths, while inside, the votes of the dead were safely recorded in the Conservative interest. Democracy returned to Argentina in November 1931 when Justo was inaugurated triumphantly as constitutional President. It was indeed none too soon for the Republic of the Pampas to find a leader again. The supreme hour of Argentine history had already arrived. The great triumphs of gaucho diplomacy were about to begin.

Chapter II

THE WINGS OF THE DOVE
(1931-1939)

I

The hour of destiny had indeed arrived nearly three years before in 1928 but Yrigoyen had been incapable of taking advantage of the situation. Despite attempts by both Buenos Aires and Washington to settle the Chaco dispute by arbitration, Bolivian troops had continued to advance through the region and had begun to construct a series of forts to mark their furthest line of advance. The northern defences of this line were attacked by the Paraguayans on 5 December 1928. Bolivia retaliated by bombing the Paraguayan town of Bahia Negra. This attack was the first aerial bombardment of a town in the American hemisphere. Its military effect was considerably lessened, however, by the fact that none of the bombs actually exploded.[1] Dud bombs were not going to deter the Paraguayans. The Bolivian Government accordingly prepared for serious fighting by importing arms. Its attempts to do so were impeded by the Argentines, who seized a shipment of machine-guns destined for Bolivia by way of the Pilcomayo River. La Paz then demanded that consignments of weapons should be allowed to pass through Brazilian territory, citing on behalf of its position the 1920 Treaty of Commerce and Navigation.

The Brazilians were in an awkward situation. Economic exigencies required that they should make the most of every opportunity to sell or tranship anything to anybody. On the other hand, they were also well aware that Washington was desperately anxious to

---

[1] B. Wood, *The United States and Latin American Wars, 1932–1942*, Colombia University Press, N.Y., 1966, p. 21

avoid a serious revolt in the Chaco. Moreover, Argentina was clearly interesting itself in the affair, and the Brazilians were anxious to restore good relations with their powerful and touchy neighbour.[1] Rio characteristically tried to evade the basic issue, adopting the convenient principle that strict neutrality required that the arms should be allowed to pass, as long as the same freedom to import war materials was offered to Paraguay.

Buenos Aires was in no position to precipitate a showdown either, as it happened. Yrigoyen in turn released the shipment impounded on the Pilcomayo. Peace talks continued inconclusively in Washington and Buenos Aires. Then on 15 June 1932 the dispute acquired a new dimension with the opening of a major Bolivian offensive. This was no longer merely an irritating squabble over an indefinite area of the Green Hell of the Chaco Boreal. Paraguay's existence as a sovereign state was at stake. The implications of this were limitless and horrifying. The last time Paraguay had fought for its survival, in the War of the Triple Alliance, more people had died than in almost any other war of the nineteenth century since the defeat of Napoleon.

It was for long fashionable to decry the Chaco War as a peculiarly unprofitable and irrational exercise in bloodletting. There is no doubt that it would have been difficult to find two countries anywhere in the world worse placed to afford the luxury of fighting each other. Paraguay was the least populous and one of the most underdeveloped of South American Republics, with a population of barely one million, at least 80 per cent of whom were illiterate, and a national income of about $100 per head. Bolivia had over three times the population, but had the same level of illiteracy and a national income per head less than half that of Paraguay, making it the most poverty-stricken country in the Americas. In simple terms, Paraguay was almost the smallest country in the world, and Bolivia almost the poorest. Between them, they managed to fight the third deadliest war in the history of the American Hemisphere.

The obvious question is why; and the answer is that the issues involved in the Chaco War were very far from trivial. Bolivia had

---

[1] Jayme de Barros, *A Politica Exterior Do Brasil, 1930–1940,* Departamento de Impresna e Propaganda, Rio de Janeiro, 1941, p. 111.

been cut off from the Pacific since 1879 as a consequence of Chilean aggression. It therefore had a real and practical interest in seeking an unimpeded outlet to the Atlantic by gaining control of the waterway of the Pilcomayo River. Anything that could improve the economic prospects of Bolivia might well be deemed worth fighting for in La Paz. If Bolivia were to seize the north bank of the Pilcomayo though, Paraguay would become cut off from access to the sea in its turn, and become little more than a dependency of Bolivia. It was not likely that the people who had fought so heroically against the combined forces of Argentina, Brazil, and Uruguay seventy years before would passively yield their independence to Bolivia, a nation even poorer than their own. Nor was it possible to find a solution compatible with national pride by arbitrating on the basis of original title, since no clearly defined boundaries could be discovered in the hopelessly confused Spanish colonial archives.

The aspirations of two such poor and primitive nations were not the main factor in the case. What had to determine the outcome of the situation was the fact that Paraguay could resist a Bolivian attack successfully only if it were helped to do so by Argentina. Buenos Aires could not stop Asuncion from fighting, but it had absolute power to determine whether it would fight for victory or defeat. The truth was that the passionately independent Paraguayans were in reality helpless and ruthlessly exploited satellites of Argentina. Argentine capital dominated the Chaco itself; Argentine interests owned 75 per cent of the Paraguayan Central Railroad; 80 per cent of Paraguay's external trade was carried by the Argentine shipping line, Mihanovich; Argentina controlled Paraguay's only import industry and was by far Paraguay's best customer; and Paraguay was dependent for the survival of its people upon receiving supplies of Argentine bread and wheat.

The key to peace thus necessarily lay in Buenos Aires. In any case the other Latin Republics were in no mood to dispute Argentina's right to a controlling interest in the affair. Chile had been granted a period of comparative political stability under Alessandri between 1927 and 1930, but this had been followed by two years of total anarchy, during which trade figures fell by 84 per cent and the presidency in Santiago changed hands ten times. Brazil's experiences had been even more demoralizing. External trade fell from $940,000,000 in 1928 to only $284,000,000 in 1932. In that year, full-scale civil war broke out as the establishment of São Paulo rose against the rule of the gaucho president from Rio Grande do Sul, Getulio Vargas. The Paulistas declared their independence of the government in Rio, enlisted volunteers to augment their highly-trained state militia, and announced that they were not fighting with any intention of seceding from the Brazilian Union, but simply to give all Brazilians the opportunity of determining their own destinies under constitutional rule. What they were fighting for, of course, was the opportunity to continue to govern Brazil in the interests of the state of São Paulo itself, and more particularly to set up a regime which would be able to do more to improve the price of coffee in the world market than Vargas had managed to accomplish so far.

There was no doubt that the achievements of the Paulistas were genuinely inspiring, even if their motives were not. The great commercial and mining establishment displayed brilliantly all those qualities which had enabled it to dominate Brazil for so long. Enlistment had to be stopped temporarily at 60,000 men for lack of equipment to arm the volunteers who had rushed to the Paulista cause; Paulista forces repeatedly and successfully took the offensive against the disorganized and far less enthusiastic federals; and rumoured or actual uprisings throughout Brazil seemed to confirm the rebel boast that Vargas had lost control. Even his own gaucho state of Rio Grande do Sul threatened to join with the distant miners and frontiersmen of Minas Geraes in support of the Paulistas, thereby creating the most improbable alliance in Latin history. The Paulistas increased their enlistment to 200,000 men, developed their own factories to produce arms, ammunition, and defences, and even began a series of air raids on Federal cities, dropping leaflets and, where appropriate, flowers. The biggest of Brazilian wars developed unchecked, despite Vargas's pleas for peace, and a pause came only when both sides observed a truce in memory of the aviator Alberto Santos-Dumont, who died in São Paulo on 25 July. However, Vargas skilfully retained his authority over the other states of his enormous country; the ambitions of Rio Grande do Sul were satisfied by the appointment of gaucho General Goes Monteiro as chief of the Federalista forces; Minas Geraes hesitated to commit itself to the rebels; and by the end of September the great revolt was over.

Vargas and his gaucho allies remained as cool after victory as they had been during the war. Goes Monteiro assured the Paulistas that they had merely been deceived in what they had done. There was not a man in Brazil who did not share their desire for a return to constitutional government; they had fought heroically, as had indeed been their duty; and the Federal Government had no desire to humiliate the brave people of São Paulo. He was even better than his word. Vargas agreed to Monteiro's proposal that a general amnesty should be granted to civilians who had taken part in the revolt, and that the Paulista soldiers should be treated as civilians in this respect, apart from a few responsible officers, who should be deported. In all, only seventy-six Paulista leaders were eventually sent into exile.[1] It was one of the gentlest suppressions of rebellion in history, carried out by men with the fiercest traditions in Brazil.

What the rebellion had of course effectively accomplished was the financial ruination of Brazil. It necessarily resulted in the indefinite postponement of a massive programme of naval rearmament which Vargas had proposed in June to counter the Argentine challenge. It certainly meant that for three critical months there was no government in Latin America which could presume to challenge Argentina's right to supervize the settlement of the Chaco dispute. Fighting had become general with the Bolivian offensive in July 1932. Both La Paz and Asuncion appealed to Geneva. The League responded at first merely by reminding both contenders of their obligation under the Covenant to settle disputes by peaceful arbitration. This had no visible effect. Then as the Paulista rebellion flared and armies began to march across Latin America from the Andes to the Atlantic, Getulio Vargas appealed directly to Justo to use Argentina's paramount influence in Paraguay to bring the fighting to an end. Buenos Aires had received as a free gift diplomatic leadership of the Latin American world.

[1] *New York Times,* 3 November 1932

There was no doubt that Paraguay's barefoot army, out-numbered five to one, could not resist the Bolivians without Argentine support, but the Argentines were already doing some-thing about that. Two million rounds of small-arms ammunition as well as clothing and blankets were rushed across the Pilcomayo to strengthen the Paraguayan defence. Justo was clearly not going to act as a mere agent of the League, and he could afford to wait until he received a completely free hand. He accordingly insisted to Vargas that the matter should be left to the jurisdiction of a Commission of Neutrals established by the United States.[1] The North Americans themselves, fully appreciating the situation, duly appealed to Justo in their turn. Buenos Aires was now prepared to act. The Argentines presented in the other American capitals the draft of an ABCP Manifesto, under the terms of which responsibility for mediation would be transferred from the Com-mission of Neutrals to the ABC Governments and Peru. Mean-while, they assured Paraguay that what the Neutrals really wanted was to leave negotiations entirely to Justo himself. With a triumphant flourish, the new Argentine Ambassador in Washing-ton, Felipe A. Espil, handed to Secretary of State Stimson, along with the ABCP Manifesto, the draft of a new Anti-War Treaty, prepared by Argentina's Minister of Foreign Affairs, Carlos Saavedra Lamas.[2]

One anti-war pact was already in force, the Kellogg-Briand Pact, which had quite literally made war illegal. Espil explained to Stimson, however, that the Anti-War Treaty would strengthen the Kellogg-Briand arrangement by adapting it to the Covenant of the League of Nations. Stimson replied tactlessly that this was an unexpected initiative from a country which was one of the few in the world not to have ratified the Kellogg-Briand Pact itself, and which moreover had not co-operated with the League since its opening session, and was for all practical purposes not even a member now. He then added a further insult by suggesting that the Treaty seemed to have been rather hastily drafted. These were unsympathetic remarks to make about a document which was already being hailed in Argentina as 'a great international

---

[1] White (memo) *Foreign Relations of the United States*, 25 July 1932
[2] 1878–1959, Minister of Justice 1915, Minister of Foreign Affairs 1932–38

triumph, with a doctrine of no recognition of territory acquired by force'.[1] In any case, Espil had an effective reply to any such Yankee discouragements. This was to make it quite clear that peace in the Chaco depended on Argentine goodwill, which would be available at Argentina's price; and Argentina's price was simply that Buenos Aires should get all the credit for any peace settlement that might eventually be achieved. It was easy to couch this demand in the traditional language of the Argentine sovereignty theory. Espil warned the Chairman of the Commission of Neutrals that Argentina 'would not go along with the Commission . . . in any act which, extending beyond the limits of good offices and the moral influence of the opinion of all the continent, might approximate to an intervention, even though it should be merely a diplomatic one, inasmuch as such an attitude would be contrary to Argentine traditions and doctrine'.[2]

This effectively destroyed from the outset any hope of an international solution to the Chaco dispute. It could therefore be resolved only by the contenders themselves, either as the result of one side's gaining an outright victory over the other, or if they invited some third party to mediate. This made the chances of an early peace sufficiently remote, even if things were left to La Paz and Asuncion themselves. This was clearly not going to be the case. Eamonn de Valera had already pointed out in Geneva that Bolivia and Paraguay could not manufacture arms themselves. They could therefore only fight at all if they were allowed to obtain munitions from outside. There was thus every prospect of the conflict developing into an enormously dangerous international confrontation. This fact was fully appreciated in Washington. American diplomats, concerned above all else to prevent the concept of Pan-American solidarity collapsing in international war, hastily sought to meet the Argentine demands. Assistant Secretary of State Francis White accordingly assured Espil that if 'Argentina plays the game . . . so that we get a settlement, we will discuss ways in which the [Anti-War] Treaty could be modified in order to make it worthwhile signing'.[3] And from Buenos Aires, Ambassador Bliss assured his superiors that

[1] *La Presna,* 5 August 1932
[2] Espil to White, *F.R.U.S.,* 18 October 1932
[3] White (memo) *F.R.U.S.,* 22 December 1932

Argentine aspirations to diplomatic pre-eminence were merely the natural yearnings of a proud, young, ambitious people; and that Saavedra Lamas was not really anti-American, but just happened to see the United States as the chief obstacle in his path.

This was undoubtedly true, but the United States was not the only obstacle that Lamas found in his way. Chile had nothing like the same economic interest in Bolivia as Argentina had in Paraguay. Chilean capital did however represent the third largest foreign investment in Bolivian industry after Britain and the United States. Chile's only claim to real international significance depended on its ability to unite the other Andean Republics into a Pacific Association corresponding to the old Viceroyalty of Peru, or even to the approximate boundaries of the Inca Empire; and any country which had just had six presidents in one year needed all the external diversions it could get. The shrewd old Chilean Foreign Minister, Cruchaga Tocornal, accordingly tried to forestall Lamas by presenting his own formula for mediation to La Paz and Asuncion. It was immediately accepted. This seemed a favourable opportunity to halt a war which had already cost 10,000 casualties, but Lamas refused to consider the Chilean offer and was supported by the Brazilians who were desperately anxious to conciliate their now far stronger neighbour, especially when that neighbour seemed to be favoured by Washington. Tocornal duly withdrew his own formula and agreed to co-operate with Lamas in drafting a new one, the Act of Mendoza. In the meantime, however, the Bolivian offensive had gathered impetus. La Paz accordingly rejected the new formula. Espil promptly overcame his former objections to foreign intervention and asked President Roosevelt to assist Justo in enforcing the terms of the Act of Mendoza upon the belligerents. He also suggested that economic blackmail by the United States might prove particularly persuasive.[1] However, Roosevelt was about to follow in the steps of his Republican predecessors by getting rid of the tradition of Yankee interventionism and proclaiming the policy of the 'Good Neighbour'. There was, accordingly, nothing that he wanted less than to inaugurate his first term of office by employing the Big Stick already associated with the name of

[1] White (memo) *F.R.U.S.*, 28 February 1933

Roosevelt to avert a Paraguayan defeat and save the face of Buenos Aires.

The Argentines were thus left to their own resources, and these were more than adequate to achieve the desired ends. Two factors helped to encourage a bold initiative. In May 1933, Argentina's export crisis was partially ameliorated by the provisions of the Roca-Runciman Treaty, under which Argentina retained guaranteed access to the United Kingdom market for its primary products in return for granting preferential access to the Argentine market for British manufacturers. This was admittedly directed primarily towards securing the interests of the conservative farmers who were Justo's most important supporters. It was also directly damaging to the United States, but this in itself gave Justo another counter to bargain with in his dealings with Washington. In the same month the Brazilian Government opted out of the Chaco situation by declaring its complete neutrality.[1] Justo then announced his intention of leaving mediation to the League, closed the frontier of the Pilcomayo River between Argentina and Bolivia, thus cutting off supplies to the Bolivian armies and bringing their advance to a halt, and rushed supplies of munitions to re-equip the Paraguayan forces for a counter-attack.[2] As the Paraguayans rallied, the League appointed a Commission to mediate in the Chaco, then agreed to transfer its mandate to the ABCP combination. Lamas, meanwhile, at last persuaded Congress to approve Argentine membership of the League in the cheapest possible way by voting one year's membership fees, making as he did so a jovial reference to the United States :

'The Monroe Doctrine is only a unilateral declaration . . . Sad to say, international law has no sanctions, but there is an enormous gendarme who strides over the face of the ocean, and gives effect to this theory by assuming of its own accord a posture of defence.'[3]

This almost complimentary manner of speaking was made possible by Washington's evident willingness to co-operate with

[1] Decreto: 22,744 of 23 May 1933
[2] *Current History,* November 1933, p. 215
[3] Diario de la Camera de Senadores, pp. 1337–1358 of 25 September 1933

Buenos Aires as far as it possibly could. Roosevelt's Secretary of State, Cordell Hull, had already supported Justo's decision to leave mediation to the League. He had done so in the hope of securing Argentine co-operation at a Pan-American Conference which was due to be convened before the end of the year. Meanwhile, Justo and Lamas visited Rio, where they secured Getulio Vargas's adherence to the Anti-War Treaty. The other major Latin nations followed suit. Relations with the United States were imperilled again in November when Argentina introduced a system of import licensing, under which imports were to be admitted from any country only up to the value of Argentine exports which that country had purchased in the relevant year. Its effect was to slash the United State's share of the Argentine market from 25 per cent to less than $7\frac{1}{2}$ per cent.

Lamas accordingly awaited his meeting with Hull in Montevideo with considerable apprehension. He indeed repeatedly implied that he would not attend the Pan-American Conference which the Argentine press duly began to denounce as yet a further example of Yankee imperialism. The chorus of doubts and abuse grew more vociferous in Buenos Aires as Hull's party approached their destination, but there was no way that Lamas could avoid a meeting. He had, in any case, one great incentive to attend : all the evidence suggested that the Americans were prepared to give him anything within reason that he wanted. He, for his part, was prepared to give them nothing. The confrontation with Hull could thus hardly fail to be an Argentine triumph.

This did indeed prove to be the case despite the total absence of any personal accord between the two men. Hull, tall, dignified, handsome, self-righteous, his chief relaxation playing croquet, found his temperamental opposite in Lamas, small, dapper, bristling, chain-smoking, enormously knowledgeable, enormously pedantic, and as convinced of the unchallengeable rectitude of his own ideas as a man could be. Hull knew exactly what Lamas wanted, and was prepared to let him have it. He assured the Argentine Foreign Minister that the United States also would sign the Anti-War Treaty. In return, he attempted to interest Lamas in his own concept of multilateral, non-discriminatory trading arrangements as a means of restoring the vitality of the world economy. Hull explained that such methods of conducting international trade would positively help to realize the principles of the Anti-War Treaty, while discriminatory or autarchic economic systems and rearmament led directly to war for they involved an uneconomic use of resources which necessarily resulted in a loss of purchasing capacity within the country practising them. This led inevitably to poverty and dissatisfaction which could only be alleviated by wars of aggression. It was perhaps hardly to be expected that these principles would be accepted willingly by the Argentine Government, which was both applying economic discrimination and also rearming massively, but Lamas raised no objection. Smiling faintly behind his moustachios, he told Hull that the United States and Argentina would 'become the two wings of the dove : you the economic, and we the political'.[1]

It was a magnificent phrase, linking the White House and the Casa Rosada in a common endeavour for peace. The North Americans unquestionably made serious efforts for their part to get the bird of peace off the ground : United States forces were withdrawn from Nicaragua; financial control was relaxed over Haiti and Cuba; and modifications were introduced into the Treaty with Panama covering control of the Canal Zone. The Argentine wing, however, refused to flap. Lamas did lead a delegation from Buenos Aires triumphantly back to Geneva armed with the Anti-War Treaty, but as the Paraguayan advance continued in the Chaco and the weakest and poorest of South American peoples expended their exiguous resources in the greatest set battles that the hemisphere had known since Gettysburg, Lamas refused to place any pressure on Asuncion for a ceasefire, and left attempts at mediation to a Committee of Inquiry sent urgently by the League to Montevideo. He had his own reasons for expecting its efforts to be fruitless. The Committee reported back to Geneva in March 1934 that Bolivia and Paraguay were both 'using up-to-date material – airplanes, armoured cars, flame-throwers, quick-firing guns, and automatic rifles'; that 'both continue to obtain arms and war material without any difficulty'; and that these weapons 'are not manufactured locally, but are supplied to the belligerents by American and European countries'.[2]

[1] Hull, *Memoirs,* Hodder and Stoughton, London, 1948, p. 329
[2] League of Nations, Doc. C.262, M.iii, 1934, VII

Nor could there be any possible doubt as to the routes by which
the material in question was reaching Paraguay and Bolivia. Hull
nonetheless hastened to reassure Lamas by congratulating him on
his 'splendid efforts for the pacific settlement of international
disputes'.[1] This assurance of United States goodwill encouraged
Argentine Under-Secretary of State for Foreign Affairs, Jose
Cantilo, to proclaim that Argentina had been observing sanctions
against the sale of arms to the belligerents ever since such measures
had been called for by the League,[2] while French military aircraft
flew with Argentine pilots from Argentine airfields to assist the
barefoot Indian armies of Paraguay, and Buenos Aires secretly
put pressure on Montevideo to do nothing to impede the flow of
arms across the Pilcomayo.

Meanwhile, Hull continued to throw the influence of the United
States behind the Argentine initiative of the Anti-War Treaty.
He assured the Scandinavian governments in June of his own
'sincere belief in the efficacy of the Pact and our hope that the
other nations of the world will become signatories . . . '[3] Lamas
for his part suddenly announced the following month that he had
devized a new conciliation formula, 'after laborious explorations',[4]
but he insisted that mediation should be carried out only by
Argentina, Brazil, and the United States. The Brazilians demurred,
alarmed at the exclusion of Chile, which would leave them facing
what appeared to be something of a Washington-Buenos Aires
Axis. Lamas promptly threw responsibility for peacemaking back
to the League again, confident that that body could not 'draw
up at a distance a text [for conciliation] which it had proved
impossible to draw up on the spot',[5] and happily described the
attitude of his own government as one of passive observance
awaiting failure.[6]

This absolute intransigence seemed positively to enhance
Argentina's standing in the world community. A retiring British

---

[1] Hull to Weddell, *F.R.U.S.*, 28 April 1934
[2] *La Presna*, 17 May 1934
[3] Hull to United States Legation in Copenhagen, *F.R.U.S.*, 21 June 1934
[4] Weddell to Hull, *F.R.U.S.*, 13 July 1934.
[5] League of Nations, *Journal Officiel*, XIV, no. 5, p. 107.
[6] *ibid*

Ambassador congratulated the Argentines on their capacity to defy the Yankee colossus; an incoming French one described Argentina as one of the really great powers of the world; and in Buenos Aires Cardinal Goma y Torres proclaimed an enchanting new world role for Argentina when he hailed the reality of *Hispanidad*, a transatlantic community which 'includes all those, regardless of race, who live under Spanish culture and religion', but which excluded, among others, masons, liberals, protestants, communists, and socialists.[1]

The year 1935 brought more intransigence and more triumphs. As Lamas had predicted, the Committee of Inquiry abandoned its efforts. Santiago and Buenos Aires accordingly resumed their own negotiations with La Paz and Asuncion in January, but these were not likely to produce quick results simply because they were not backed by any form of sanction. Chile was no less to blame in this respect than Argentina. The Chilean Foreign Ministry, indeed, admitted in December 1934 that it regarded sale of arms to a belligerent and mere transit of arms as two entirely different matters. The presumption therefore was that Bolivia was certainly receiving arms by way of Chile, even if not actually from Chile. Any remaining doubts as to the ability of Paraguay to obtain all the arms it required in defiance of League prohibitions were dispelled when that country triumphantly left the League, claiming that no sanctions against it could be effective unless they were observed by Argentina and Uruguay, which were not observing them. In this situation, the vaunted cordiality between Argentina and Chile began to dissolve.[2] The Brazilians warned Cordell Hull that Lamas had wanted the Chilean approaches to Bolivia to fail because he wanted to get all the credit for stopping the war himself. Lamas for his part told Ambassador Weddell that it was the Chileans who wanted mediation to fail. More serious disagreements soon developed. In March, the Chilean Government complained that Argentina was trying to block a proposed economic treaty between Chile and Peru. Alessandri then added further insult by claiming that the Argentinians were deliberately prolonging the Chaco War for their own ends, and that there was

---

[1] *La Presna,* 12 October 1934
[2] Frederick B. Pike, *Chile and the United States,* Notre Dame, 1963, p. 231

accordingly no point in his meeting with Justo to discuss further conciliation measures.[1]

Alessandri's charges were substantially justified, but there was still considerable speculation as to why he had chosen to make them in such a forthright manner. The answer was obvious enough. Chilean international prestige had been virtually destroyed by the economic and political chaos of the past decade. Alessandri had attempted to salvage some credit by restoring good relations with Bolivia and Peru, victims of Chilean aggression in the War of the Pacific,[2] but Chile had been unable to provide military aid for Bolivia on a scale sufficient to avert defeat by the Argentine-backed forces of Paraguay.[3] The proposed economic arrangement with Peru could only exacerbate relations with Argentina, since one of its effects would be to give Chile 70 per cent of the Peruvian wheat market, of which half was then being supplied by Argentina. The fact that the treaty between Chile and Peru was exactly the sort of arrangement which Hull had recommended at Montevideo was obviously going to make no difference. Hull had nothing to gain by backing Chile. He had everything to lose by estranging Argentina.

Alessandri accordingly backed down. He explained that his remarks had been intended merely as 'an energetic call to action', but action was the last thing that Buenos Aires had anticipated. With the Chileans subdued again, Lamas generously proposed to Vargas that the eventual peace talks on the Chaco should take place in Rio. A Brazilian historian described this initiative as 'a gesture of supreme courtesy, worthy of a Talleyrand or a Metternich'.[4] It was indeed. Lamas was perfectly safe in offering to have the peace talks anywhere, since he could guarantee that they would fail, and he succeeded in placating Brazilian pride. The great nations of the American hemisphere accordingly sat back to let events take their course. This, in effect, meant waiting to see how far the brilliant new Paraguayan counter-offensive would go

---

[1] *La Presna,* 4 March 1935
[2] Conrado Rios Gallarder, *Chile y Peru,* Editorial Nascimento, Santiago, 1959, *parsim.*
[3] *New York Times,* 16 October 1934
[4] Jaime de Barros, *op. cit.,* p. 142

before it outran its lines of communication as the Bolivians had done before. The attack lost impetus in May, but the Bolivians, totally out-fought and having no resources except Indian conscripts, were quite incapable of taking any advantage of the situation. Asuncion and La Paz accordingly now turned at last to Justo to 'kindly beg' him to ask the mediatory powers to convene the long-awaited peace conference. The Chaco War thus ended because the two belligerents concerned had grown tired of fighting each other. The total result of three years of active and generous diplomacy by the United States was that Argentina had been allowed to prolong into 1935 a war that could have been stopped by a Chilean initiative in 1933.

II

Nor had Hull so far received anything in return. Justo's answer to United States pleas for multilateral trade had been to impose a savage 20 per cent surcharge on government contracts with countries with which Argentina had an unfavourable balance of trade. This was not merely discriminatory. It was in fact clearly directed against Argentina's fellow-partner for peace. Buenos Aires was still, however, prepared to make a gesture to Europe which it would not make to North America, especially if it cost nothing. On 20 April, Cantilo concluded a Non-Aggression Treaty with the countries of the 'Little Entente', Yugoslavia, Greece, and Rumania. He described it as an act of homage both to peace and to the precious links between Argentina and the Entente states. In fact, it was hard to imagine any countries in the world between which a non-aggression pact was less necessary, as the contracting parties could hardly have reached each other to commit acts of aggression even if they had wanted to. The main purpose of the treaty was simply to remind Europe of Argentina's existence and its espousal of the cause of world peace.

The American Hemisphere did not need to be reminded of Argentina's existence. The difficulty was to convince anyone that the Republic of the Pampas was as sincerely committed to peaceful co-existence as its spokesmen claimed it was. Fighting in the Chaco had stopped at last on 14 June 1935. Peace talks began in Buenos Aires on 1 July. Lamas had got his much-desired conference after all, but the difficulty seemed to be that he was neither competent to chair the conference effectively himself, nor prepared to delegate its direction to a more able peacemaker. Cruchaga Tocornal complained furiously after the opening session that Lamas had no constructive ideas of his own and was refusing to listen to those put forward by anybody else.[1] He then lapsed into aggrieved silence. Any position of influence which Chile might still have aspired to was undermined by Alessandri's admission on 6 July that Chile had never participated in the arms embargo against Bolivia and that Peru had followed Chile's lead.[2] The maleficent Peruvian dictatorship tried to improve its own standing in Washington by warning the Americans that Argentina was determined to dominate the Peace Conference, which was obvious enough to everybody, and that it would be unwise to put too much emphasis on the Inter-American Conference scheduled to be held in Buenos Aires at the end of the following year, as this would show a lack of confidence in the peace talks themselves. The logic was not entirely clear, but what the Peruvians were really concerned about was the fact that too much emphasis on the talks in Buenos Aires in 1936 might detract from the importance of the next round of talks in Lima in 1937. The regime of President Benavides needed all the *éclat* it could get.

Anything like serious consultation on peace was clearly impossible in this cauldron of conflicting and unappeasable vanities. The situation was made worse by the increasingly unconciliatory attitude of the great conciliator himself. In September, Lamas accused the Bolivians of having infiltrated 2,700 square miles of Argentine territory in the Jujuy Province, just as they had formerly done in the Chaco.[3] The Bolivians protested in return that Argentina was denying them the transportation facilities across the Andes which had been guaranteed by the treaty of 4 July.[4] Lamas then professed to have lost hope in the peace talks, and proposed that a conference of all American states should be called, to 'avoid the ignominy of having the question go back to Europe'. However, he recovered his

[1] Weddell to Hull, *F.R.U.S.*, 2 July 1935
[2] League of Nations, Doc. C.257(d) M.129 (d) 1935, VII
[3] *La Presna*, 18 September 1935
[4] *ibid.*, 14 November 1935

confidence sufficiently to have a speech delivered over the C.B.S. network in New York on Armistice Day, referring in laudatory terms to his own 'Argentine initiative' of the Anti-War Pact, and warning enthusiasts of the League of Nations that 'modern internationalism cannot create a police under the form of a super-state . . . because this would weaken sovereignties'.[1]

Lamas had sufficient reasons for distrusting the pretensions of the League. It had been his most persistent, if quite ineffective, rival in the Chaco affair. A matter of more immediate concern, though, was the dispute between Italy and Abyssinia, which had developed into open war at the beginning of October. Massive Italian immigration since the end of the First World War had given that power probably more intimate links with Argentina than any other nation. The dilemma of reconciling sympathy with Italy with a show of respect for the League was admirably resolved by Enrique Ruiz-Guinazu, who bore the responsibility of chairing the meeting of the Council which first considered the dispute. The Council at first sought to avoid a confrontation by exonerating both parties. When this technique failed, Ruiz-Guinazu refused to 'consider the path of conciliation finally closed', and proposed that the entire Council should form itself into a conciliation committee, affirming at the same time the traditional friendship between Italy and Argentina. Argentina nonetheless imposed a ban on the sale of arms to Italy on 28 October and followed this by becoming the first country to impose 'second-line' sanctions on the sale of petrol, coal, steel, and iron to the aggressor on 25 November. This did not, in fact, affect Argentine trade with Italy greatly, as none of these items had figured in commerce between the two countries; and Justo established bases of agreement with an Italian Trade Mission in January 1936 as soon as normal economic relations could be resumed.

Ruiz-Guinazu had played the conciliatory role in Geneva with the utmost credit and the least cost. Matters back in the hemisphere were less tranquil. Argentina had experienced a year of most promising economic recovery. The Republic of the Pampas now ranked eighth in the world in ownership of cars, tenth in the size of its commercial air fleet, and tenth in its holdings of gold and

[1] *New York Times*, 12 November 1935

foreign exchange, with total reserves of £49,000,000 compared with £3,500,000 for Chile, and only £2,800,000 for Brazil. This extremely satisfactory position for Argentina had been the result largely of a complete transformation of Argentina's commercial transactions with the United States. Between 1934 and 1935, Argentine exports to the United States had risen in value by over 153 per cent, while imports had risen by only 13 per cent. By comparison, Brazil had increased its exports to the United States by 10 per cent and its imports by 8 per cent, while Chilean exports and imports had both risen by 10 per cent. Justo nonetheless refused to lift the discriminatory 12·5 per cent surcharge on imports from the United States, while Lamas warned Ambassador Weddell that Argentine attitudes towards Pan-Americanism might change completely if the United States did not amend quarantine regulations affecting the importation of Argentine meat. On 6 December, Peru in its turn received a flick of the gaucho whip when Justo raised duties on Peruvian petroleum by 50 per cent until such time as Peru agreed to accept Argentine wheat on the same terms as it accepted Chilean wheat under the treaty inspired by Cordell Hull.

In these circumstances, it was a trifle difficult for Ambassador Weddell and his colleagues to continue 'in our efforts to convince . . . [Lamas] that he can have all the credit' for bringing peace to the Chaco,[1] but there was nothing else to do. Argentina had now gained a completely free hand. Lamas had refused even to let the League accredit an observer to the peace talks; Chile and Peru had been reduced to silence by economic bullying; Uruguay was supinely echoing Argentine initiatives; and Vargas of Brazil was far too concerned with the overriding urgencies of domestic strife and economic distress to become involved in unrewarding and exhausting foreign entanglements. Indeed the talks seemed to be making some progress at last. A peace treaty was actually signed in Buenos Aires between Paraguay and Bolivia on 22 January 1936. It was ratified by the Congresses of the two former belligerents on 11 February. On 17 February, however, the Government of President Ayala was overthrown in Asuncion by a military coup led by Colonel Franco, who had repeatedly professed

[1] Weddell to Hull, *F.R.U.S.*, 6 February 1936

himself dissatisfied with the terms of the peace settlement. Justo hastened to send his two magnificent new Italian cruisers on a goodwill visit to Rio de Janeiro, when Argentine Ambassador Angel Carcano assured the Brazilians of the growing strength of Pan-American solidarity, and told them that 'while the rest of the world sinks, America becomes optimistic'.[1] The next manifestation of this optimism, however, was Colonel Franco's declaration of a totalitarian, one-party state in Paraguay. He was followed in Bolivia by Colonel Toro, who similarly seized power and proclaimed a similar ideology. Meanwhile, Vargas himself had moved further towards eliminating democratic institutions in Brazil by declaring a state of siege to enable him to deal more effectively with pressing social and economic problems. He attempted to avert foreign criticism at the same time that he advertized Brazilian international impotence by remarking jovially in a speech to his people:

'Our foreign policy? We have no international problems. Our policy is simple: peace and friendship with all nations.'[2]

So restrained and self-effacing a policy was not necessary for Argentina. Justo had already warned that his government would be spending more on defence, as Argentina's international interdependence had become accentuated. While Argentine exports boomed and the Brazilians desperately prepared to burn 37,000,000 bags of coffee, a third of their entire unsaleable crop, in a holocaust that came to symbolize the bankruptcy of orthodox economic methods in the era, Justo ordered a further seven destroyers from Britain, and Jose Cantilo summarily reminded the League that Argentine co-operation had its limits:

'If American ideas cannot be harmonized with the manner of applying the Covenant . . . if the attempt to secure the practical universality of a principle of justice might create a danger to peace . . . the Argentine Republic would be obliged to reconsider the possibility of continuing its collaboration.'[3]

Both sides of the Atlantic responded to the Gaucho spur. In July, Ambassador Weddell praised the similarity of the traditions of the

[1] *La Presna*, 3 March 1936
[2] *New York Times*, 12 June 1936
[3] League of Nations, *Monthly Summary*, vol. XVI, no. 6, June 1936, pp 154–155

two republics of Argentina and the United States, which he said had, in great international questions, arrived by different routes at the same position.[1] The following month, all the American Republics accepted an invitation from Justo to attend a Pan-American Conference in Buenos Aires in December. In September, Carlos Saavedra Lamas was appointed President of the Assembly of the League of Nations. This was not the first of the awards of international recognition which made him perhaps the most widely honoured statesman of his generation. Adolf Hitler had already approved his being decorated with the Star of the German Red Cross for his services to peace in the Chaco. Lamas attributed his new distinction to 'a recognition of Argentina's fidelity to international morality', and claimed that Argentine mediation in the Chaco had been designed 'to give to the activities of the League a universal character'.[2] This was at least an arresting description of a policy of which the primary objective had been to exclude Geneva from having any role in settling the dispute at all. Equally interesting was Lamas's denunciation of 'a disquieting international symptom, namely, the increase in armaments',[3] expressed just as Justo was completing contracts for a ship-building programme which would give Argentina the sixth most formidable fleet in the world. Lamas was by now far out of the reach of any critics. In a dinner given in his honour in Paris, French Foreign Minister Yvon Debos saluted him as 'the legislator who since 1908 has been so actively dedicated to the public welfare; the professor who has so brilliantly taught sociology, political economy, and public law; and most particularly the democrat who is seized with the concept of social progress . . . finally, the statesman, who, as president of the Chaco Peace Conference, has powerfully contributed, by his personal activity, to bring an end to the conflict which for three years has ensanguined the American Continent. But your activity is not limited to American affairs,' Debos continued. 'You have comprehended that a great nation like yours, a member of the League, must contribute to the general work of peace . . . the non-aggression pact to which your name is

[1] *La Presna,* 8 July 1936
[2] League of Nations, *Monthly Summary,* vol. XVI, no. 9, September 1936, pp. 252–253
[3] *ibid.,* no. 10, p. 284

attached is an initiative which has had the greatest impact in all countries.'[1] Still more was to come. On 24 November, Lamas was actually awarded the Nobel Peace Prize, after a campaign waged on his behalf with relentless energy by Cordell Hull.[2] He modestly attributed this honour not to his personal worth, but to the high standards of the foreign policy of his country, and warned the audience that 'the achievement of the supreme objective of peace should not be based in any way on narrowness and egotism'.[3] On 1 December, Lamas became Permanent President of the Inter-American Peace Conference at Buenos Aires, with Ambassador Espil as Secretary-General. President Roosevelt himself arrived to attend the Conference and was greeted with an unreserved welcome by the delighted *portenos*, contrasting impressively with the studied discourtesy accorded President-elect Hoover in 1928.

The Conference did not fulfil the hopes entertained either in Washington or in Buenos Aires. Justo, indeed, struck an optimistic note with a speech of welcome which contained every possible distortion of the truth appropriate to the occasion :

'The foreign relations of the Argentine Republic have always been motivated by high standards of international justice and by lofty principles of human brotherhood from which it has never departed . . . This continent is the land of freedom, as the constitutions of all the nations of this sisterhood affirm . . . This has invariably been Argentine doctrine.'[4]

Nobody was of course tactless enough to mention that political realities did not always correspond with written constitutions. The truth about the land of freedom was that only three of the republics of South America could be described as democracies in any sense, and none of them as a representative democracy in the Anglo-American tradition. Peru had suffered for three years under the authoritarian rule of General Oscar Benevides, who had outlawed the indigenous reform party Alianza Popular Revolucionaria Americana, or APRA, driven most of Peru's

[1] *Le Temps,* 21 October 1936
[2] Hull, *op. cit.,* p. 497.
[3] *New York Times,* 30 November 1936.
[4] *La Presna,* 2 December 1936.

foremost intellectuals into exile, and had established the most elaborately repressive system of government in Latin America, thereby earning the commendation of German Ambassador Schmitt that 'Peru is a country whose form of government does not differ from ours'.[1] Venezuela had just emerged from twenty-seven years of unbelievably psychopathic tyranny under the illiterate and presumably insane Juan Gomez, and had progressed to a constitutional, non-party dictatorship under General Eleazar Carderas. Paraguay and Bolivia were both totalitarian, one-party military dictatorships. Ecuador, with twelve presidents in ten years, could hardly be termed a polity at all in any significant sense of the word. Brazil was a dictatorship, with constitutional rights suspended for clearly specious reasons. Alessandri in Chile was ruthlessly maintaining a conservative order by crushing strikes and suppressing the Left. Colombia had democratic electoral processes but no political parties. Uruguay's democracy was a marvel of proportional representation under which the minority party theoretically retained a grossly disproportionate number of seats; but Uruguay had, in any case, been since 1931 under the dictatorial rule of Gabriel Terra, who had arrested the Professor of Philosophy at the University of Montevideo for daring to say that agents of the totalitarian countries were plotting against the interests of Uruguay. Only Argentina preserved a recognizable form of representative government by democracy. Even there Justo had not yet restored all the constitutional privileges suspended by Uriburu, and had come to power himself by an electoral procedure designed to thwart rather than facilitate the expression of the popular will. It was, of course, true that South America was hardly less liberal than Europe, but it was still not quite the land of freedom.

The Conference was unquestionably a failure for United States diplomacy in any event. Hull had hoped to unite the American Republics in a binding agreement to act together against any threat to their institutions or territorial integrity presented by Nazi penetration. He attempted to achieve this by a moderate proposal that the republics should undertake to consult together in the event

---

[1] Schmitt to Weizsacker, *Documents on German Foreign Policy*, 4 June 1938.

of a foreign war which might menace the peace of the hemisphere. Lamas and Espil refused to agree, however, despite a typically dramatic warning by Roosevelt himself against 'others who, driven by war madness or land hunger, might seek to commit acts of aggression against us . . . '[1] They insisted instead that the final Convention should merely require the Republics to act in the manner proposed, 'if they so desire', which they had presumably always been free to do anyway. All that Hull and Roosevelt had succeeded in doing was to establish a procedure for consultation. They had no guarantee that it would be adopted. Nor was the Chaco Conference making any headway. Lamas had finally consented to delegate the immediate task of mediation to a Committee of Three, consisting of Cruchaga Tocornal, Jose Carlos de Macedo Soares, the Brazilian Foreign Minister, and the American, Spruille Braden, but the efforts of the Committee were impeded by the fact that they were permitted to make progress at all only if they could at the same time persuade Lamas that they were not really making any. It was not an ideal situation.

Braden in particular felt this to be the case. His frustrations found a reasonable but undiplomatic outlet. He approached Justo behind Lamas's back and urged the need for prompt action. All this accomplished was to make Lamas so furious that he refused to say goodbye to Hull when the Americans returned to Washington. The Peace Prizewinner then pronounced his own epitaph on the Conference he had destroyed : 'Now we shall have to arm to the teeth.' Indeed the failure at Buenos Aires was followed by a most rewarding exercize in Big Stick diplomacy on Argentina's part. As Hull and his advisers sailed home, Justo suddenly sent seven destroyers from his magnificent new fleet on a goodwill trip to Peru. The sight of the dreaded blue-and-white flags sailing past their indefensible coastline threw the Chileans into the desired panic. Alessandri promptly disrupted his own plans for economic recovery by approving expenditure of 100,000,000 pesos on a bomber squadron and ordered two more cruisers for the Chilean Navy, but these were only fringe benefits for the Argentinians. The most fruitful response came from Lima, as had been planned. In February 1937, the Peruvians agreed to

[1] Hull, *op. cit.*, p. 501

annul the main provisions of their economic arrangement with Chile, which were so gratifying to Cordell Hull, and to allow imports of 10,000 tons of wheat duty-free from Argentina in return for that country's according similar treatment to Peruvian oil. In March, Argentine Under-Secretary for Foreign Affairs, Ibarra Garcia, hailed in memorably inappropriate words the architect of this unbroken tide of gaucho success:

'Every time during the last few years that an effort for the maintenance of peace has struggled to the fore, whether in America or in Europe, one name has stood out, a name that is a symbol of pacifism, the name of Carlos Saavedra Lamas, the Argentine Foreign Minister.'[1]

These were about the last words of public enconium that Lamas would hear. There was no doubt that he had merited some kind of praise. His personal success in his profession was almost unequalled. No diplomat had ever gained more and given less. He had also demonstrated remarkable skill in preventing others from attaining the goals that he had himself set them; and he had, for what it was worth, managed to defy with impunity the wishes of both the League of Nations and, more impressively, the United States, in an area dominated by the most formidable power on earth. The question was exactly what all this had achieved.

Lamas's policy cannot be dismissed as merely the product of a limitless personal vanity. In the first place it was not a purely personal approach to international relations. Lamas pursued traditional Argentine objectives by traditional Argentine methods. These objectives were neither irrational nor wholly unworthy. It might be asserted as a general rule that the most important service that the diplomats of any small- or middle-sized country can render to the rest of humanity is to show how the will of a superpower can be defied with impunity, but there were also more tangible issues involved. Hull was certainly not merely seeking United States domination in Latin America: he was seeking to align the Latin states with Washington in international affairs, and to persuade them to practise a form of international trade which might well have been to their own advantage, but which would also have tended to increase their commercial dependence

[1] *La Presna,* 12 March 1937

on the United States. The fact was that Argentina's most important trading relations were not with the United States at all but with the United Kingdom under the terms of the Roca-Runciman Pact, and with Continental Europe, under the terms of the various barter and exchange deals that could be negotiated with those countries. These arrangements were not compatible in principle with the concept of multilateral trade advocated by Hull. It might well have been better for everyone if all nations had practised traditional multilateral trading methods. But the fact was that the nations with which the greater part of Argentina's external trade was transacted did not do so. Moreover, there was an undeniable flavour of hypocrisy about the protestations of the United States. The country that sheltered the most valuable markets and the most efficient industries in the world behind tariffs and restrictions higher than those imposed by any other industrial nation was in no position to preach economic liberalism.

Hull himself undoubtedly rated economic considerations as secondary to political. The political aspect arose from the fact that he equated the interests of the United States with the cause of world peace. World peace was most conspicuously being endangered by the expansionist policies of Japan, Italy, and Nazi Germany, but it was not nearly so obvious that Nazi or Fascist aggression was likely to be deterred by the cessation of trade with those regimes or that such aggression constituted any meaningful threat to South America. Indeed, on all the evidence, it simply could not. There was no way in which the Germans or Italians could break out into the Atlantic as long as the barriers of the French Army and the British Navy remained in their path. Nobody could have rational grounds before May 1940 for expecting that those barriers could be broken or bypassed. The threat of aggression from across the Atlantic against which Roosevelt and Hull were warning the Latins simply did not exist for reasonable men. What did exist was a possibility that United States influence in South America might be replaced or counter-balanced by Nazi and Fascist influence. Even then, it was not feasible to assume that this European influence could be imposed upon the Latins against their will, nor that it would necessarily be wholly inimical to their interests if it did become predominant in the hemisphere. Indeed, in certain ways Nazi and Fascist intervention could seem a positive advantage. The Germans and Italians could not dominate the hemisphere by force themselves, but they might be able to deter the North Americans from doing so. Such a countervailing role would certainly constitute a threat to United States interests. It did not follow that it constituted any threat to the interests of even a relatively liberal Latin American Government. As we have seen, the number of relatively liberal Latin Governments was considerably smaller than that of those which were not only similar in ideology to the Nazi regime, but were also, from every practical point of view, notably less beneficent, liberal, or humanitarian. It could only seem an unfortunate anomaly to policy-makers in Washington that in 1938, as in 1917, it was precisely the worst of these governments that constituted the most reliable allies of the United States in its struggle with Germany for predominance in Latin America.

Lamas could thus have argued on many grounds that the East-West links between Argentina and Europe were worth preserving even at the expense of the North-South relationship proposed by Hull. There were, however, two obvious objections to his technique. One was that the ties proposed by Hull were really too light to have affected Argentina's relations with the world outside in any significant way, and that a country whose exports had risen by 107·7 per cent in the past twelve months, while its imports had risen by only 16·3 per cent, could afford to sacrifice a little of its bargaining power anyway, in the interests of goodwill and good faith. The other objection was that the patience of the United States was not inexhaustible. The North Americans had been prepared to concede Lamas almost anything in return for economic and political harmony in the hemisphere. He had given them the exact opposite. Argentina had successfully frustrated the attempts of other Latin nations to liberalize trade with each other; it had consistently resorted to a discreet but effective use of economic and military intimidation against its own weaker neighbours; and it was making a positive contribution to maintaining international tension in the Chaco. There was always the possibility that North American displeasure at these methods might take some tangible form. Force, admittedly, was not likely to be used, though Argentina could have no answer if it were. The Argentines had played for the past twenty years a uniquely brilliant diplomatic game against an opponent of vastly greater material strength, but they could continue to play it only so long as their giant opponent voluntarily refrained from using his strength.

The North Americans were, indeed, prepared to continue this soft approach. Braden was not allowed to threaten. Instead he used other methods. At a special dinner given in Buenos Aires in May 1937 he again approached Justo and assured him that as far as any settlement in the Chaco was concerned, 'Buenos Aires was the playing field', and that direct personal intervention by the President himself held the best hope of gaining a quick solution. Justo was flattered but non-committal. He was also attracted by the idea of giving Lamas enough rope to hang himself. He accordingly passed Braden's suggestion on to his Foreign Minister, who naturally disagreed completely with any idea that action by the President could be more profitable than what he was doing himself.[1] Justo himself hardly encouraged belief in his pacific intentions when he administered another turn of the screw against Chile by staging a massive military exercise just across the border from that country.

The whole structure of power relationships in the Americas was about to be subjected to more shock waves from across the Atlantic. The German press suddenly provided some support for North American warnings of impending sabotage and aggression when it proclaimed the unity of all Germans in a common *Deutschtum*. The *Deutsche Volkzeitung* announced the decision of the Fuehrer that :

> 'We are united by a common destiny and we shall never cease to be united. We are brothers. Our cradles are on the banks of the Rhine, the Danube, and the River Plate.'[2]

Stirring words of this kind did not, of course, make the extension of actual German political control across the Atlantic any more of a practical possibility than it ever had been, but there were certainly disturbing grounds for believing that this might be envisaged in Berlin as one of the later stages of the Nazi programme. German interest in Latin America had been almost

[1] Braden to Hull, *F.R.U.S.*, 7 May 1937
[2] *Deutsche Volkzeitung*, 21 July 1937.

as longstanding as British. Brazil had been a major target for German emigration ever since 1824. German publicists had been wont to refer to that country since the eighties as a predestined area for German colonization. Of its total population of 40,500,000, Brazil numbered 900,000 citizens who spoke German as their native tongue, and about 1,500,000 of mixed German-Brazilian stock. Argentina's population mix was only slightly less potentially dangerous, with 236,000 German-speakers in a total of 12,800,000. Lamas attempted to distract attention from both the Chaco fiasco and this new factor by floating yet another peace initiative, characteristically formed by submerging somebody else's ideas in a more pretentious structure of his own. Spanish Republicans had sought refuge from Franco in the Chilean Embassy in Madrid. Chile had appealed to the Nationalist authorities on their behalf. Lamas now inflated Santiago's protest into a multilateral treaty dealing with the whole question of diplomatic asylum in missions. It was shrewdly conceived, as it appealed to a principle which the United States had always been loath to accept, but the North Americans refused to rise to the bait. Braden reported discouragingly that the Chaco Conference was still as ineffective as ever thanks to Lamas's determination to preserve, above all, his personal reputation as the Great Peacemaker, as well as Argentine domination of the Chaco.[1] Justo's brutal show of force against Chile also back-fired. The Brazilian Government, alarmed alike by Argentine and German pretensions, asked if the United States would assist in strengthening Brazil's national defence by leasing six decommissioned destroyers to the Brazilian Navy until the new ships under construction were ready for service.[2] A challenge had at last arisen to Argentine military predominance south of the Rio Grande.

Hull had already formed a favourable impression of Brazilian readiness and ability to assist in the creation of hemisphere co-operation, especially by comparison with Argentine. He accordingly circulated a note to United States diplomatic missions in Latin America informing them that the United States 'will make available on equal terms to all of the American Republics possessing naval forces the facilities referred to . . . should they

[1] Braden to Hull, *F.R.U.S.*, 4 August 1937
[2] Hull to Key Pittman, *F.R.U.S.*, 5 August 1937

desire to avail themselves of them . . . the contract will contain a recapture clause, making it possible for the United States at any time to obtain the return of the destroyers so leased . . . The United States will declare it to be its policy that it will in accordance with the provisions of such clause request the immediate return of such vessels in the event that hostilities should break out between the republic leasing such destroyers and any foreign government with which the United States is at peace.'[1] Nothing could have been much more innocuous. The ships were to be leased to the Latin Americans only, and were to be used only against a country with which the United States was itself at war. Apart from certain misgivings about how the United States proposed to get the ships back, the arrangement could mean only that American naval power would be deployed to head off the dangers of a Latin arms race. More specifically, the United States would counter Argentine power in South American waters. It was thus not surprising that Lamas immediately denounced the proposal as 'a bad business, prejudicial to United States policy in the Americas', and suggested instead that Brazil should look to all the American Republics for its defence, especially to Argentina, whose financial resources were very great at the time.[2] More important, the British Ambassador in Washington warned Hull that the project would violate Article 22 of the Naval Treaty and would have serious repercussions in Europe.

It was difficult to see how any European Government could really be perturbed, unless it were contemplating aggression against the Americas. The Brazilians and Chileans certainly had no misgivings.[3] However, Brazil was still sufficiently intimidated by Argentine strength to be prepared to withdraw its request for destroyers if Washington accepted the protests of Buenos Aires.[4] The Argentines for their part took an unusually conciliatory line, explaining that they were merely offended at not having been consulted beforehand. Brazil was indeed 'availing itself of a legitimate right in order to meet an equally legitimate need', which

[1] Hull, *F.R.U.S.*, 9 August 1937
[2] Weddell to Hull, *F.R.U.S.*, 10 August 1937.
[3] Scotten to Hull, *F.R.U.S.*, 12 August 1937; Philip to Hull, ibid., 18 August 1937
[4] Scotten to Hull, *F.R.U.S.*, 13 August 1937

'cannot but awaken in Argentina the desire to lend our co-operation . . . we would support such an increase [in Brazilian naval strength] with all our will if it were necessary'.[1] The British Government formally told Washington that they viewed 'with much apprehension the serious consequences which might result for all concerned in the event of such a practice becoming at all general. The whole balance of naval power might be upset and it might become impossible to calculate the effective strength of the fleet of any given country.'[2] This again was not easy to see, as there could be very few fleets in the world in 1937 which had more ships than they required for their own needs; the British objection appears peculiarly ironic in view of the destroyer deal of 1940, under which the Royal Navy obtained the use of fifty United States destroyers, thereby indeed upsetting in its own favour the existing balance of naval power. The Americans did, however, yield to British pressure and abandoned the idea. They also politely declined to adhere to Lamas's proposal on diplomatic asylum, considering that this would involve 'an extension of traditional immunities and privileges enjoyed by diplomatic representatives'. Lamas responded to this by proposing that the Chaco Peace Conference be abolished, leaving himself as the sole mediator. Things were back to square one. But not for long. Rivalry between Argentina and Brazil for predominance in the continent was about to take on a quite new dimension. A new pattern of hemisphere leadership was developing.

III

It made its appearance in the most unpromising shape of what seemed to be an extension of the Fascist Revolution to the American Hemisphere. Following the destruction of the Communist Popular Front, President Vargas had sought the assistance of the indigenous Fascist Integralistas, or Green Shirts, including particularly his Chief of Staff, General Goes Monteiro, in forming a new authoritarian state.[3] On 1 October, he had persuaded the

[1] Weddell to Hull, *F.R.U.S.*, 20 August 1937.
[2] Weddell to Lamas, *F.R.U.S.*, 2 November 1937
[3] J. M. Bello, *A History of Modern Brazil, 1887–1964*, Stanford University Press, 1966, p. 296

Brazilian Chamber to agree to his declaring a state of war for ninety days following the discovery of an alleged Communist plot. Then, on 10 November, he dissolved by decree all existing legislative assemblies in Brazil, claiming that 'universal suffrage had become an instrument in corrupt hands'; denouncing the threats of 'regional mobsters'; and explaining that he had discovered that political assemblies should be of a corporative nature, as all other systems were inoperative.[1] Vargas himself described this new development as 'the consecration of authoritarian government' in a nation which had traditionally been hostile to dictatorship in any form. However, Foreign Minister Macedo Soares hastened to assure Ambassador Caffery that the coup had been carried out merely because the Government was facing an electoral campaign which would have led to revolution; that a new constitution would be presented shortly to the Brazilian people for ratification by plebiscite; and that Vargas had no intention of persecuting individuals, and had no imperialistic designs, but desired to maintain cordial relations with the United States, and to attract foreign capital to Brazil. Macedo Soares also insisted that the Integralistas were 'only clowns in the political circus, and had played no part whatever' in the coup, although Goes Monteiro had clearly been involved, and fellow-Integralista Justice Minister, Francisco Campos, was to claim that 'the Integralista doctrine provided the basis for the Estado Novo'; that 'neither the democratic regime nor the parliamentary system is affected', (in point of fact, both had been abolished); and that the new Government expected to receive the collaboration of friendly nations on whom it counted for sympathy and unaltered friendship.[2] The first gesture of sympathy and friendship came from Nazi Germany, where Brazil was hailed as 'the vanguard of the fight against the Red Pest'.[3] Hull cautiously told Caffery that it did not appear that the Brazilian coup had been inspired by the European dictatorships, and that he had no great anxieties himself, although it was important not to underestimate the effect

[1] And that 'the country was in imminent danger of being submerged under a tidal wave of Communism'. F. Hambloch, 'The New Regime in Brazil', *Foreign Affairs,* vol. XVI, no. 3, April 1938, pp. 484–493.
[2] Caffery to Hull, *F.R.U.S.,* 10 November 1937
[3] *Berliner Zeitung,* 10 November 1937

of Nazi and Fascist propaganda in Brazil.[1] The constitution of
the Estado Novo which Vargas outlined to the Brazilian people
certainly sounded like a textbook example of Fascism in action.
The President was to be the supreme authority of the state, with
the power to dissolve Congress, decree laws, and succeed himself.
A National Economic Council was to be formed, made up of
representatives of industry and unions recognized by the State.
The death penalty was to be introduced for crimes against public
order; strikes and lockouts were to be declared antisocial; marriage
was to be made indissoluble; and censorship of all communications
media was to be carried out by the *Departmenta do Impresna e
Propaganda,* or DIP. As a final safeguard, a state of emergency
was proclaimed, allowing the President to suspend all
Congressional immunities.

Vargas told Caffery that it was 'laughable to think that the
Germans, Italians, or Japanese had any connection whatever with
the recent movement. Nor had the Integralistas in any way. The
new Constitution is in no way Integralista or Nazi or Fascist, and
my Government has absolutely no connection with Rome, Berlin,
or Tokyo.'[2] This seemed about as reliable as a statement of international goodwill from Buenos Aires. The Integralistas had been
connected with the movement, and the new constitution was
basically Integralista in doctrine. However unsatisfactory it might
be to attempt a comprehensive definition of Fascism, it would be
difficult to withhold that term from a revolutionary dictatorship
supported by the armed forces, erected upon a corporative
economic and social structure, and aggressively illiberal,
nationalistic, and anti-communist. The German press intelligently
pointed out that Vargas would be certain to reject any Nazi overtures of friendship because of Brazil's relations with Britain and
the United States, but the mere fact that a regime might be
anti-German did not make it non-Fascist. At the same time, the
Brazilian genius for moderation did give the new regime some
redeeming features. Vargas's slightly-smiling face appeared on
hoardings everywhere, but there was no melodramatic cult of
personality as was the case with the European autocracies; the

[1] Hull to Caffery, *F.R.U.S.,* 12 November 1937.
[2] Caffery to Hull, *F.R.U.S.,* 13 November 1937

visible trappings of authoritarian rule were almost completely absent; repression was carried on unobtrusively without spectacular purges and vendettas; the conduct of foreign affairs was left in the superbly deft hands of the most engaging of Gauchos from Rio Grande Do Sul, Oswaldo Aranha; and the dictator did not have even the organized backing of a mass party. The only blemishes on the tranquil face of Brazilian politics were that constitutional processes had been abolished and individual liberty had ceased to exist.

This, of course, did not matter as far as Brazilian-United States relations were concerned, as long as the Brazilian tyranny remained anti-German. First indications were contradictory. A Decree Law of 22 December indeed banned Nazi activities in Rio Grande do Sul, but on the very next day, Vargas's newly-formed Ministry of Justice and Internal Affairs asked the German Government to display its Anti-Communist Exhibition in Brazil to help in the fight against Communism.[1] In fact bad relations with Nazi Germany were virtually guaranteed by Vargas's own Fascist orthodoxy. Fascist nationalism can scarcely tolerate the claims on its own citizens of an alien Fascism. On 4 January, Vargas outlawed all cultural or recreational societies in Brazil, unless they were fully equipped to carry out an approved programme. This meant officially that they would have to own their own gymnasia, swimming pools, and parks. His target was the allegedly cultural or sporting clubs established by the Italians and Germans which in reality served primarily and sometimes solely as agencies to disseminate Fascist or Nazi propaganda. This development was undoubtedly disturbing for the European autocrats. Far more portentous was the announcement on 10 January that eighteen people had been arrested after a fight between Integralistas and the Brazilian Police. It appeared, extraordinarily enough, as if Vargas was cracking down even on domestic Fascists.

At the beginning of 1938, the situation in Brazil was thus as obscure and disturbing as it could be. That in Argentina seemed, however, to have changed immeasurably for the better, at least as far as the United States and the forces of democracy were concerned. Crafty old Justo had come to the end of his term of office. He had arranged his succession in a manner remarkable

[1] Ritter to Weizsacker, *D.G.F.P.*, 27 December 1937.

even by the high standards of Argentine political engineering. Himself a former Radical turned Conservative to gain the approval of Uriburu, he now arranged with the Radicals to stay out of the Anti-Conservative front so as to allow his nominee, Roberto M. Ortiz, to be elected, on the understanding that the new Conservative President would betray his own party and help the Radicals to come to power. The most extraordinary thing about this memorable example of Argentine democracy in action was that it provided the Argentine people with the most liberal and enlightened leadership that they could have hoped for. This big, handsome, wealthy, bespectacled corporation lawyer, a millionaire servant of foreign interests, was to be literally the last best hope of Argentine democracy. It was perhaps the greatest single tragedy of the hemisphere that he did not live long enough to complete his work.

Ortiz did not look like a dying hope in February 1938. He looked instead like a new dawn in United States-Argentine relations. These had deteriorated again with the news that the Chief of Staff of the Argentine Air Force, General Armando Verdaguer, was being feted in Nazi Germany, and had persuaded his government to agree to the establishment of a German aircraft factory in Cordoba, to produce aircraft for the whole continent.[1] Ambassador Weddell reported incredulously to Hull that Ortiz had promised him 'whole-hearted co-operation' in ending the Chaco War.[2] The Roosevelt administration responded immediately and appropriately. On 20 February, Roosevelt sent six Flying Fortress B-17 heavy bombers, probably the most formidable and certainly the most impressive military aircraft in the world, on a spectacular flight from Miami to Buenos Aires to provide an airborne guard of honour for Ortiz's inauguration. This provided the double function of countering any undesirable impression made on Verdaguer by Hermann Goering's Luftwaffe, and of doing honour to Ortiz in the most conspicuous way possible. As the six great aircraft circled Buenos Aires in the brilliant sunshine, escorted by the Pursuit Group of the Argentine Air Force, Ortiz read a cable from Roosevelt assuring him that: 'Our two republics, nurtured with similar ideals, have lived peace-

[1] *New York Times,* 7 February 1938
[2] Weddell to Hull, *F.R.U.S.,* 18 February 1938

fully in a troubled world for over a century, and it is my hope that they will continue to co-operate efficaciously and wholeheartedly for the preservation of peace.'[1]

None of this was missed anywhere. Ortiz's first act after his inauguration was to respond to Roosevelt's expressions of goodwill by abolishing the remains of the system of censorship imposed by Uriburu and retained by Justo. This was a gratifying step in the direction of liberalism. Even more gratifying to Washington was a new step in the direction of oppression which Getulio Vargas hastened to take. On 25 February, Caffery reported that he had been told by Brazilian Foreign Minister Brandão that the Army had decided to suppress completely all Nazi and Fascist activity in Brazil. To that end, they had arrested Ernest Dorsch, the Nazi leader in Rio Grande do Sul. The implications of this course of action were emphasized by Brandao when he told Caffery that the German Ambassador, Ritter, had told him that he was primarily a representative of Hitler and the Nazi Party; that Brazil was the only country in the world where such a campaign was being carried on; and that the arrest of Dorsch was a direct slap against Hitler. Brandão assured Hull nonetheless that the anti-Nazi programme would be carried out relentlessly.[2]

Fascist-type repression in Brazil could suit the ends of the United States at least as well as a new birth of freedom in Argentina. Roosevelt conveyed to Vargas his appreciation of the Brazilian dictator's confidence. He told him that the United States was confronted with much the same kind of Nazi problem, and promised to keep the Brazilian Government informed of any new developments in the United States. The Vargas regime then began to move more severely against the Integralistas, six hundred of whom were rounded up on 19 March. The German official press referred with understandable concern to the 'regrettable and very strange measures' being taken in Brazil, but attempted to explain them away by expressing the views that Vargas could not be in complete control, as it was known that he by no means approved such action.[3] Vargas was, however, in complete control. Aranha

---

[1] *New York Times*, 22 February 1938
[2] Caffery to Hull, *F.R.U.S.*, 25 February 1938
[3] *Diplomatische Korrespondenz*, 21 March 1938

dismissed the German comment by saying that the less said about
it the better, and told Caffery that the tactics of Hitler had
irritated Brazilians so much that they might lead to physical
attacks upon Germans in Brazil.[1] The increasing warmth of
United States-Argentine relations in any case guaranteed that the
anti-German campaign would be intensified. Justo's infallible
political instincts had warned him already that there was no
electoral profit to be gained from stonewalling in the Chaco any
longer. Moreover, as retiring President, he could safely advocate
a policy of action, since he would not be responsible for carrying
it out. He accordingly proposed to Weddell that the six major
American neutrals should combine to force Paraguay to come to
terms. Meanwhile, the Argentine Government, duly impressed by
the performance of the Flying Fortresses, asked for instructors in
military aviation to be sent by the United States War Department
so that Argentine flyers would be able to operate United States-
built warplanes. This had the attraction for Washington that it
would discourage the Argentines from flying German aircraft.

Roosevelt accordingly prepared to send flying instructors to
Argentina as well as the three naval officers already acting as
instructors with the Argentine fleet. The reaction in Rio was
immediate and varied. Aranha began questioning Caffery
anxiously about the extent of United States-Argentine military
co-operation; Vargas placed orders with Italy for submarines and
with Krupps for arms, and ordered the construction of three new
destroyers and five minelayers for the Brazilian Navy; and the
campaign against political activity of all kinds in Brazil moved
into a new area of repression. German, Italian, and Polish schools
had already been assimilated into the state system in Rio Grande
do Sul and Santa Catharina. This action could at least be partially
justified on the grounds that the foreign schools were scarcely
training their pupils to be Brazilian citizens. Ambassador Marion
de Pimental told Hull that only twenty out of 2,845 German
schools in the repressing states taught Portuguese. The somewhat
excessive remedy adopted by the Vargas regime was to forbid the
teaching of any language other than Portuguese. This was still
only the beginning. Decree Law 383 of 18 March savagely

[1] Caffery to Hull, *F.R.U.S.*, 23 March 1938

declared illegal any political activity on the part of any foreign political organization in Brazil. Existing organizations falling within the scope of this measure were given thirty days in which to wind up their affairs and put themselves out of existence.

It was impossible for the European Fascists to pretend any longer that what was happening in Brazil was other than a deliberate pogrom against their activities, conceived and executed by Vargas for purposes of his own. The only choice open to them was acquiescence or confrontation. The Italians characteristically chose the former, responding with Latin dexterity to a Latin challenge. Italian diplomats arrived on the same night at a gala operatic performance in São Paulo in formal evening wear, conspicuously devoid of Fascist emblems or uniforms, and congratulated their hosts on Brazil's neutrality during the Italian-Abyssinian War, promising them in return that proletarian Italy would always march with its friends against plutocracy. This gesture certainly achieved a further slackening of the already moderate campaign against Italian schools and organizations. The Germans, of course, got the full treatment. On 22 April, a further Decree banned all German propaganda in Brazil. Vargas then broadcast to the world, claiming that this action should remove any doubts as to the nature of the new regime in Brazil. He also explained that the abolition of all political activity, domestic or foreign, in the country meant that the Brazilian people were now able to practise true democracy free from the conditions existing before 10 November 1937. For example, the dissolution of political parties meant that people could approach the government freely, without having to go through intermediaries.[1]

Arguments of this kind made sense only in terms of Fascist ideology, but it was the very orthodoxy of Vargas-type Fascism that made it fully compatible with United States policy. Vargas might indeed be implementing what *La Presna* smugly termed 'a comedy played after the model of European Fascist dictators';[2] but he was most certainly not 'under the thumb of Germany and Italy', as Carleton Beals claimed.[3] He was, indeed, embarked on

[1] *New York Times,* 23 April 1938
[2] *La Presna,* 12 November 1937
[3] C. Beals, *Current History,* vol. XLVII, no. 4, April 1938, p. 30

a policy which could hardly lead other than to head-on collision with the nation in all the world least likely to brook provocation. The prize was the restoration of the unwritten alliance with the United States.

Vargas admittedly did not exactly choose the moment of confrontation. This was done for him by disaffected domestic Fascists, apparently without any assistance from outside. The Integralistas had found themselves subject to arrest, disbanded, and forbidden to wear their uniforms and regalia by a regime that was increasingly putting their own doctrines into practice. On the evening of 10 May they joined with elements of the Navy in a singularly complex and amazingly inept *putsch*. The Ministries of War and Marine were besieged, together with the Post and Telegraph Office, while an armed attack was made on the Guanabara Palace itself, aided by most of the Presidential Guard. The attack was pressed with such little enthusiasm, however, that Vargas, his daughter, and five servants were able to hold the Palace, revolver in hand in the best gaucho style, until relieved by the Army, who had waited down the street to see how things developed. A final touch of absurdity was provided by the fact that the only occupant of the Palace wounded in the fray was the arch-Fascist Minister of War, General Enrico Dutra, who was potted by a fellow-Integralista in the garden.[1] The whole farcical business was over by morning. Twenty people had been killed and Vargas was entrenched in power more firmly than ever. This was not how the Paulistas had fought in 1932.

The foreign implications of this domestic black comedy were evident immediately. Roosevelt sent off a telegram to Vargas at once, congratulating him on having escaped with his life. German Ambassador Ritter, however, rather tactlessly commented that the affair should indicate to the Vargas regime that it was impractical for them to continue to show so little understanding of German interests. German interests were challenged more directly than ever when Vargas allowed his reptile press to issue reports charging Germany with having assisted the rebels, and followed this up with the arrest of six Germans living in Brazil.

[1] *The Times,* 12 May 1938

Meanwhile, he replied to Roosevelt in terms of emotional comradeship:

> 'I take satisfaction in thanking you for the terms of your message, Eminent Friend, who well interprets the spirit of solidarity of American nations at the moment when the advocates of foreign doctrines attempted a coup against Brazilian democracy.'[1]

Even a government more phlegmatic and forbearing than that of Nazi Germany could scarcely have ignored this extraordinary provocation. The German press warned that the Reich could not tolerate any further Brazilian annoyances and chicanery, which were interpreted in Berlin as either a reaction against the growing power of National Socialism, or as an attempt by Vargas to find a scapegoat to divert public attention from the 'deeply resented and ever-increasing economic penetration of Brazil by the United States', which he had condoned. Meanwhile, Ritter hastily repudiated a brutal suggestion by Ribbentrop that there might have been 'bungling or mistakes by persons of German origin or by elements', which might have excused the attitude of the Vargas regime, but recommended in any case that Germany should break off relations with Brazil.[2] The Germans had other worries. An ill-conceived order by the Nazis that German consulates and embassies should compile registrations of Germans living overseas had led to active co-operation between the Brazilian and Argentine Governments on the whole question of German activities. In Europe, Germany was finding itself faced by a common front of Britain, France, Russia, and Czechoslovakia. The Nazi Government accordingly followed the prudent advice of von Thermann, the German Ambassador in Argentina, and ordered their organizations in Latin America to avoid open activity, and concentrate on less obtrusive and offensive internal indoctrination as the Italians were doing.[3] A showdown seemed to have been avoided.

The Brazilians would not be placated. Alarm over the entente between Buenos Aires and Washington had by now made even

[1] Caffery to Hull, *F.R.U.S.*, 15 May 1938
[2] Ritter to Weizsacker, *D.G.F.P.*, 18 May 1938
[3] Thermann to Weizsacker, ibid.

Aranha quite irrational. On 19 May he protested to Caffery that a change had occurred in United States policy which was forcing Brazil to look after its own interests without any help from Washington.[1] This only made his position even more undignified. Justo cheerfully invited Vargas to line up with Argentina, and offered Brazil the use of three new destroyers being built for Argentina in British dockyards, conveniently forgetting the furious protests that he himself had made when Cordell Hull had tendered a similar offer the previous year. Hull himself merely replied irritably that Aranha 'consistently appeared to believe that the United States should accord facilities to Brazil and deny them to Argentina'.[2] For a few days it looked as if the desperate Vargas dictatorship was in fact going to turn towards the European Fascists. Ambassador Moniz de Arigão told German officials in Berlin that the attacks on Brazil by the German press had not been justified, but that there was no evidence of German complicity in the failed *putsch*. The grateful Nazis welcomed this statement as being in line with the well-known far-sightedness of the Chief of State of the great South American Republic. Yet on 4 June, Vargas unconditionally suspended exports of cotton from Brazil to Germany on the grounds that the Germans were reselling part of their imports of Brazilian cotton for gold at a higher price than they had paid themselves. Then, on 25 June, a *Volkdeutsch* leader named Kopp was arrested by the Brazilian police and subsequently died in their care, after they had allegedly found in his possession plans for an Integralista revolt in Santa Catherina and Rio Grande do Sul.[3] On 28 June, Vargas halted barter trade between Brazil and Germany entirely, claiming that Brazil had sold goods valued at 87,000,000 marks to Germany, and had received only 73,000,000 marks' worth in exchange. The Germans responded by suspending purchases from Brazil, and denounced Vargas's action as a further example of the economic encirclement of Germany as practised by the plutocratic rulers of the United States.

Vargas had challenged the might of the most feared nation on earth. Meanwhile, Ortiz continued to enjoy a honeymoon with

[1] Caffery to Hull, *F.R.U.S.*, 19 May 1938
[2] Hull to Caffery, *F.R.U.S.*, 20 May 1938
[3] Ritter to Weizsacker, *D.G.F.P.*, 27 June 1938

both the Argentine electorate and the Roosevelt administration. In May he had promised the return of the secret ballot, while crowds of young people marched cheering through the streets of Buenos Aires, chanting: 'Democracy, yes! Fascism, no!'[1] He then told Weddell that it was 'absurd and anomalous' that there was no trade agreement between Argentina and the United States to the advantage of both countries. Throughout May and June, Argentine diplomats stepped up the pressure on Franco's regime in Asuncion. Their objective was to get the peace treaty signed in time for the great Argentine national holiday on 9 July. They did not quite make it in time, so Argentina had two national holidays that year, but the Chaco Peace Treaty was duly signed at last, in Buenos Aires, on 21 July, while 200,000 students paraded behind units of the Argentine armed forces in a pageant unmatched outside Continental Europe, down the widest street in the world, the great Avenida Nuevo de Julio, specially constructed for such occasions. The third deadliest war of the American Hemisphere had finally been halted to make an Argentine holiday. The country which had done more than any other to make the war possible in the first place and to prolong its duration, had duly received all the credit and glory for stopping it. Peace certainly had its victories, and Argentina had won them. A further happy historical coincidence helped to underline Argentine predominance in the continent. On the day before the celebrations in Buenos Aires, Rio's resistance to German economic pressure collapsed. Barter trade was resumed for all significant products between Brazil and Nazi Germany. Hitler had won the second round.

But the carnival was over in Buenos Aires as well. A Conference in Lima was the price for peace in Buenos Aires, and there was no doubt that Hull would renew his demands for some effective declaration of Pan-American solidarity against external aggression. Ortiz himself was barely prepared to change a hundred years of Argentine tradition in foreign policy. His Conservative colleagues certainly were not. Cantilo had already tried to postpone the Conference for a year. The Peruvians, acutely aware of the growing Argentine preponderance in the region, urgently

[1] *New York Times,* 26 May 1938.

pressed for the proposed meeting. Foreign Minister Concha, in perhaps the most incongruous statement to come out of any Latin capital, reminded Hull that the American Governments had 'a lofty duty to fulfil towards all men and all peoples', in the way of serving 'noble impulses of fraternity'. He remarked truly that the Peruvian Government could not add lustre to these noble impulses, but insisted that it would 'reflect the purity of American sentiments'. Meanwhile, just to be on the safe side, the Peruvians had responded to the flight of the Flying Fortresses to Buenos Aires by ordering 88mm. anti-aircraft guns from Germany to demonstrate to their North American visitors that Lima was not defenceless even against the United States Army Air Corps.[1] In Brazil, the Vargas dictatorship renewed its efforts to strengthen the bridges between Rio and Washington. Vargas himself proved as moderate with the defeated Integralistas as he had been with the far more courageous Paulistas. There were no executions, but 208 Integralista leaders were quietly shipped off to a penal colony near Pernambuco. This agreeable impression was reinforced by the decision to take advantage of Ambassador Ritter's absence from Rio at the Nuremberg rally to declare him *persona non grata*, at the very moment of the greatest international tension over the second Czech crisis.

The Brazilians had chosen a particularly favourable time to be defiant. Not only was Ritter out of the country, thereby making it possible to avoid any personal unpleasantness and complications, but the United States had already made quite unmistakable its determination to defend the whole hemisphere from a trans-atlantic attack which nobody could reasonably expect to be imminent. On 18 August, Roosevelt had told an astonished and enraptured Canadian audience at Kingston, Ontario, that the United States would not stand idly by if anybody were to attempt to conquer Canada. Nobody could ever have imagined that the Americans would stand idly by in such circumstances, but the timing of his assurance made it unusually significant. So did his decision a fortnight later to re-constitute the Atlantic Squadron of the United States Navy, with a nucleus of seven of the newest and most formidable 10,000-ton cruisers in the world, with

[1] Schmitt to Weizsacker, *D.G.F.P.*, 26 March 1938

attendant destroyers. Hull then implicitly denounced the Munich Settlement, telling Concha that: 'Events in other parts of the world have emphasised recently the extent to which some nations have wavered from the orderly and friendly relations which should prevail between neighbours;'[1] and Roosevelt himself disparaged it later as an example of 'peace by fear' which had 'no higher or more enduring quality than peace by the sword'.[2]

Meanwhile, the Germans furiously responded to this latest Brazilian exercise in defiance from a distance by sending Arigao back to Rio. On 3 October, Nazi Germany formally broke off diplomatic relations with the United States of Brazil, the most severe means, short of war, by which one national government can express its disapproval of another. This was followed by a warning from Roosevelt to the European autocracies not to meddle in the affairs of the American hemisphere. Far stronger words yet were to be spoken. On 7 November, a Third Secretary of the German Embassy in Paris was shot and fatally wounded by an *émigré* Polish Jew. The assassination was followed by the most ferocious organized pogroms yet carried out in Nazi Germany, commencing on 10 November. Five days later, Roosevelt told the American people, in an address drafted initially by Hull but amended in more vigorous and provocative terms by himself, that he could 'scarcely believe that such things could occur in a Twentieth Century civilization', and that he had therefore ordered 'our Ambassador in Berlin to return at once for report and consultation'. On the same day, the President also announced that American military preparedness would have to be developed in order to be able to assume responsibility for the defence of the twenty Republics and Canada; and his Secretary for Defense called for a quadrupling of United States aircraft production to match that of Nazi Germany. The battle-lines were drawn for a struggle for world power. They were made even more explicit within forty-eight hours, when a new Trade Agreement was signed between the United States and Britain which was hailed by the press in both countries as a proof of the solidarity existing between the two greatest democracies in a world threatened by

[1] *New York Times*, 11 September 1938.
[2] ibid., 27 October 1938.

aggressive dictators. Meanwhile, Hitler recalled the German Ambassador from Washington. Diplomatic relations between the two great powers were not formally severed, but neither Government accredited an ambassador to the other again. For all practical purposes, only an overt act of war could make relations between the United States and Nazi Germany worse than they obviously were already.

Brazil and the United States were thus solidly in the same camp. Both had effectively broken diplomatically with Germany, Brazil more formally and the United States more provocatively. Both were in consequence committed to Pan-American solidarity for hemisphere defence. On 10 November, Vargas, after somewhat tactlessly congratulating himself on having brought an end to 'farcical parliamentarism' in Brazil, stated that the programme of his country would be to obtain a peaceful bloc of nations to defend the interests of the American continent without hostility to anybody. Hull could not have wished for more, but he was obviously not going to get it. The basic problem of United States diplomacy in the hemisphere remained unchanged. Pan-American solidarity depended upon the willingness of Argentina to compromise its diplomatic independence, and Argentina was as unwilling as ever to do this. On 23 November, Cantilo warned that although Argentina desired to maintain complete co-operation with all Pan-American prospects it could not turn its back on Europe. It would continue its traditional policy of assisting sister nations, but it would find it difficult to subscribe to pacts which gave the impression of drawing away from friendly European nations.[1] Hull solemnly warned the delegates while on his way to Lima that the existing international situation 'requires the nations of America to strengthen their traditional ties and endeavour to create new kinds of solidarity which would . . . safeguard them from the propagation on their soil of extra-Continental disputes'.[2] He proposed to this end that the American Republics should 'make effective their solidarity' in any case where 'the peace, security or territorial integrity' of any of them were 'threatened by acts of any nature that may impair them'.

[1] Tuck to Hull, *F.R.U.S.*, 23 November 1938
[2] *New York Times,* 26 November 1938

They would in such a situation 'co-ordinate their respective sovereign wills by the procedure of consultation . . . using the measures which in each case the circumstances may make advisable'. This was not really asking much. However, Cantilo flatly opposed anything akin to a collective security pact which might involve the Latin countries' breaking away from Europe and relying on the United States exclusively. He accordingly presented an alternative draft, making no reference to co-operation against aggression, and insisting that any procedure of consultation agreed upon should be implemented by the individual countries concerned 'only when they deem it advisable'.[1] Back to square one again.

Aranha now introduced a new element by warning everybody that Brazil might be forced to take a stand diametrically opposed to that of Argentina, but this was not what Washington wanted either. Under-Secretary of State Sumner Welles cabled that what was hoped for at Lima was harmony, even if it might not be all that the United States and Brazil desired. Indeed, it was obvious that even those Latin countries most disposed to endorse any United States proposal were not entirely clear as to why they were doing so. Peruvian Minister Concha astounded Hull by telling him confidentially that he understood that the United States was in physical danger, and asked what help it needed. Meanwhile, Cantilo made interminable and obfuscating speeches: Argentina wanted to co-operate with the United States in every way, but it also wanted the greatest flexibility in its external affairs because it had special relations with Europe; it did not want any part of a military alliance; and its main concern was with foreign activity in Argentina itself. Rising to the formidable heights of eloquence always available to an Argentine Minister seeking to obscure a situation, Cantilo proclaimed:

'American solidarity is a fact which must never be placed in any doubt. All and each of us are determined to retain and to prove such solidarity in the face of any danger, come whence it may, which might threaten the independence or the sovereignty of any state in this part of the world. For that we do not need pacts. The pacts are already made in our history.'[2]

[1] Scotten to Welles, *F.R.U.S.*, 1 December 1938
[2] *La Presna*, 11 December 1938

In that case, why not sign one? Hull again warned ominously about a shadow that 'falls athwart our continent'. But Cantilo refused to see any shadow. Nor was he alone. Uruguay, satellite Paraguay, and even Bolivia joined with Argentina in insisting that their economic liberty depended upon their retaining free access to the markets of Europe. They were, therefore, unwilling to become involved in diplomatic arrangements which might have the effect of closing those markets to them. Again the United States had to back down after failing to isolate the Argentines. Aranha was requested at the last moment to avoid a confrontation with Cantilo. The Argentines responded by presenting a new draft, slightly more conciliatory than their original form of wording, but still insisting on the 'only when they deem it advisable' principle. Hull then asked for a guarantee that the American Republics would not 'permit any non-American state to assist or abet in the fomenting of internal disorder in any American Republic'. Cantilo rejected this. He agreed, however, that the American Republics should 'reaffirm their determined will to maintain democratic principles inherent in their institutional regime against foreign intervention or any act that might threaten them'. He insisted on eliminating any anti-European implication by explaining that Argentina understood the Spanish word 'extrana', used to translate the English 'foreign' in this context as meaning both inside and outside the American hemisphere. Welles vigorously insisted that 'extrana' unquestionably implied extra-continental acts or interventions, but he could hardly argue with Cantilo on the correct meaning of a Spanish word. Cantilo was, by now, determined to concede nothing further. The United States would have perforce to be satisfied with an expression of a will on the part of the Latins to resist Yankee as well as European interventions, or to abandon even the appearance of Pan-American solidarity. The latter was something that Washington was never prepared to contemplate. It would also have been diplomatically disastrous. Nothing would have been more liable to force Argentina and its allies into the arms of Europe than any suggestion of pressure against them from the United States and other Latin countries. Aranha was accordingly warned off again; a hurried conversation between Ortiz and Vargas helped to preserve some appearance of amicable co-operation; and yet another United States delegation left for home, having to accept the total frustration of their policies by the diplomats of Argentina. There was a further turn of the screw to increase the forebodings of pessimists in Washington. As the Americans sailed north, the Seventh Naval Division of the Italian Fleet put into Buenos Aires. The purpose of the visit according to its Commodore was 'a testimony of the feelings of sympathy and friendship of the Italian Nation for the great Argentine Republic'. Hull's jeremiads had been fulfilled more swiftly and dramatically than he had imagined to be possible. A shadow from across the Atlantic had fallen over half the continent of South America. There was now no hope in Washington that it could be lifted. The initiative was with Buenos Aires again. It was up to Argentina.

Chapter III

SHADOW ATHWART A CONTINENT (1939-1941)

There was certainly no question of Brazil's asserting effective leadership in Latin diplomacy. Vargas admittedly did his best. In a New Year's Day address to the Brazilian people he called for unity against all foreign ideologies. This show of defiance only provoked a curt reminder from Berlin that Germany was prepared to buy coffee only from countries that were prepared to buy German goods. Since there was no doubt that Brazil needed to sell coffee, Vargas duly hastened to abolish the last restrictions on Brazilian-German trade, although he accepted at the same time Roosevelt's invitation to send Aranha to Washington to discuss trade, development, debts, and national defence. Aranha pleased his hosts by referring to the American people as true friends of Brazil, and claiming that all friendly people had to fear Germany. The effect of these remarks was rather spoiled by the news that Vargas had just extended a barter agreement with Germany for a further six months, and was sending his son to that country to study. However, relations between Washington and Buenos Aires remained at least equally confused. Finance Minister Groppo had told American diplomats that there was an excellent basis for a trade agreement between Argentina and the United States, as Argentina was officially not interested in bilateral deals with Germany because one could never tell what Germany had in store for the future. He also promised that Uruguay would follow Argentina's lead in trade policy.[1] Within a week, however, Ortiz

[1] Tuck to Hull, *F.R.U.S.*, 10 February 1939

89

drastically curtailed imports from the United States by 40 per cent, down to the level of three years previously. The Argentines explained that their foreign trade had fallen by $39\frac{1}{2}$ per cent in 1938, and that they had enjoyed favourable balances of trade of $46,000,000 with Britain and $5,000,000 with Germany, but had an unfavourable balance of $46,000,000 with the United States. This was not reasonable. Argentina could hardly expect to have favourable trade balances with everybody. In any case the United States had had an unfavourable balance of almost equal proportions with Argentina in 1937. However, the North Americans tried to placate Ortiz again by proposing a triangular trade agreement with Brazil and Argentina. The only response from Buenos Aires was to conclude an enormous barter deal with Nazi Germany involving 1,500,000 tons of wheat, 100,000 tons of which were to be exchanged directly for railway equipment. An agreement was reached between the United States and Brazil which involved a United States credit of $120,000,000, said by Aranha to prove that the American dollar was a greater force for peace than American arms. Even the effect of this was spoiled for Washington by Vargas's decision to send Brazilian Air Force officers to Germany to take lessons from the Luftwaffe. The high tide of Nazi success in dealing with the Latins reached a new peak when Ribbentrop took leave of Argentine Ambassador Eduardo Labougle, congratulating him on his country's refusal to be intimidated by pretended dangers of extra-continental invasion. Ribbentrop said that only idiots could imagine such an invasion. He also assured Labougle that only the lack of foreign exchange prevented Germany from buying still more goods from Argentina. All that was needed was for Germany to strike gold, and then it could buy all the Argentine goods it wanted.[1]

The Germans were not having everything their own way. Their relations with Argentina itself were suddenly called in question in much the same way as their relations with Brazil had been the previous year. A document was published in Buenos Aires on 30 March purporting to be dispatched from the Counsellor of the German Embassy in Argentina to the Colonial Office of the Reich, and claiming that the annexation of Patagonia was a basic

[1] E. Labougle, *Mision en Berlin,* Editorial Guillermo Kraft, B.A., 1944, p. 227

objective of Nazi policy. Nazi chief Alfredo Mueller was immediately arrested, along with five other Argentine Nazis. However, the Ortiz administration reacted to this situation in a manner very different from that adopted by the Brazilians in comparable circumstances. Jose-Maria Cantilo insisted that there was no break in Argentina's friendly relations with Germany, in spite of Ortiz's expression of regret at the tone of German comments and his failure to send an Ambassador to replace Labougle. Cantilo indeed promised a full juridical and legal investigation, but again softened the effect of his words by stating that such a procedure would be the best way of serving the cordial relations existing between Argentina and Germany. The document proved in the end to have been merely a forgery by a German *émigré*, Heinrich Jurges, whose wife had died in a concentration camp. Jurges was himself arrested, and Mueller released. However, the investigation had revealed that Nazi activity in Argentina was widespread and probably dangerous. There was accordingly another brief rapprochement between Buenos Aires and Washington. Ortiz told Congress that he really did favour multilateral rather than bilateral arrangements, that he deplored the fact that long-standing Argentine political traditions were being replaced by ideologies tending to divide people unpatriotically into 'Right' and 'Left', and argued that Argentines should have an outlook based on attachment to the *patria*. He then decreed that all foreign societies in Argentina should be subject to regulations, and required to furnish details of membership and political objectives. Wearing of special uniforms would be forbidden.

Roosevelt, ever resourceful when it came to making a cordial gesture, responded by proposing that Argentine beef, which he described as the best and cheapest in the world, should be imported for the United States Navy, which deserved only the best. This provoked furious complaints from the senators of beef-producing states, despite his jovial assurance that he wished to impugn neither the virtue of the American cow nor the valour of the American bull. A more significant *démarche* was launched by Cordell Hull, when he circulated to Latin capitals suggestions for making some new United States military hardware available on credit terms to other American republics. Responses came promptly. Aranha replied within twenty-four hours, saying that the legislation was positively overdue, as Brazil already had guns under construction for destroyers it had not been able to build. Tyrannical Benavides gave his approval the following day. So, within the next week, did twelve other Republics. Hull then asked Armour to try to expedite a reply from Argentina, apparently preoccupied with a barter deal valued at 460,000,000 lire each way with Fascist Italy. Buenos Aires seemed to have no objections. The Ministry of External Affairs explained at enormous length that it had 'examined with interest the memorandum . . . The proposals for co-operation, in view of the extreme situation they contemplate, and the sense of continental solidarity they reflect in the face of problems arising from the political and military situation of the Old World, are consistent with the position publicly adopted by the Argentine Republic in the Lima Conference of 1938 . . . The Argentine Chancellery takes note of the project transmitted to it, as a further expression of that policy of good-neighbourliness and co-operation.'[1]

This unfortunately did not mean that the Argentine Chancellery was going to do anything about it. Hull could only wait. In the meantime the political and military situation of the Old World deteriorated beyond hope of recovery. Vargas replied to the mounting crisis with more repression, aimed at insulating Brazil from the infection of any foreign doctrine not approved of by the regime. Foreign periodicals were allowed to appear only if published in Portuguese, and children were allowed to be sent abroad only if accompanied by parents or guardians. The Chileans hopefully sought to provide some distraction by again appealing to the American Republics to rescue the refugees still seeking sanctuary from Franco in the Chilean Embassy in Madrid. All diplomatic initiatives were, however, interrupted by the outbreak of the European War on 1 September. The struggle for the world had moved into the shooting stage.

There was no uncertainty about the initial responses of the American Republics. Roosevelt invoked the Neutrality Act as each belligerent in turn went to war. Argentina followed his example

[1] Armour to Hull, *F.R.U.S.*, 10 July 1939

on 4 September. So did the other Latin Governments. Although Ortiz sent an Argentine military mission to Brazil to reaffirm the will of the two great Latin nations to live in serenity and friendly association, the prospects of real co-operation between Rio and Buenos Aires were as remote as ever. Hull had told the Latins that the outbreak of the European War constituted a potential menace to peace which justified the resort to the procedures of Inter-American consultation envisaged in the Conference of Buenos Aires.[1] Aranha and Vargas agreed on the spot,[2] but Cantilo could see consultation only as a further attempt to erode Argentine sovereignty. He secretly told the Italian Ambassador, Preziosi, that any conference would have to be strictly juridical, with each nation's sovereignty rigorously preserved, and that Argentina's attitude in this respect would be supported by Brazil and Uruguay, and probably by Chile and Peru. In any case, his immediate concern was with the decision of the Western Allies to include food for civilian populations as contraband, despite previous Argentine rulings on this point. Indeed, even the comparatively liberal Guani in Uruguay agreed that his position was the same as Cantilo's on the question of contraband.[3] Cantilo renewed his assurances to Preziosi a week later, promising that Argentina would co-operate with Brazil and Uruguay to preserve Latin neutrality; that the Bolivians had been told secretly that the proposed Conference would have to exclude anything relating to political or military arrangements;[4] and that Argentina would retain its links with all European countries.[5]

For once, even a German diplomat managed to understand the situation. Freytag explained to Weizsacker that Argentina would lead the ABC Powers against any military pact, on the grounds that this would debase Latin neutrality into something like a preliminary state of war. On the other hand, the Central Americans would be forced by economic dependency to yield to pressure from Washington since they lacked the strength to resist.

[1] Hull to Armour, *F.R.U.S.*, 3 September 1939
[2] Caffery to Welles, ibid., 5 September 1939
[3] Preziosi to Ciano, *Italiani Documenti Diplomatici,* Nona Serie, vol. 1, 195 of 13 September 1939
[4] Preziosi to Ciano, ibid., 241 of 16 September 1939
[5] ibid., 386 of 22 September 1939

It was accordingly necessary for Germany to take exactly the same position as Argentina, as had been done in 1917, and to promise to stop goods listed as conditional contraband only if they were destined for the armed forces of the enemy.[1]

This was being unusually perceptive for the Germans, even if they had apparently failed to realize that the ABC no longer existed, in view of the impossibility of Argentina's ever drawing Brazil out of the orbit of the United States. Cantilo's calculated indiscretions kept Axis diplomats well informed about the Latin situation. The furious diplomatic exchanges between Buenos Aires, Rio, and Montevideo were not hard to construe in any event. The Argentines were obviously determined to maintain and exploit their neutral position as far as lay within their power.[2] They were also convinced that the United States intended to replace Britain, Germany and Italy as the main industrial force in Latin America, and they were anxious not to let this happen both because they feared the consequences of becoming exclusively dependent upon the Yankee colossus, and because they doubted that the North Americans would prove an adequate substitute for the displaced belligerents.[3] Argentina had accordingly flatly rejected a proposal from Roosevelt that it should co-operate with Brazil and the United States in patrolling the Atlantic jointly from the Mar de la Plata to the 49th parallel.[4] On the other hand, there was no desire for a German victory, except among a few intellectuals in the Army or in business circles, as most Argentines believed it would mean the end of democracy in Latin America. There was also universal sympathy for France, even if there was little for Britain. The Latins were thus effectively on nobody's side. The war held the gravest implications for them, whoever won it. The best hopes for Axis propaganda, therefore, lay in the ability of the Italians to convince their fellow-Latins that Mussolini's sole concern was to limit the European conflict, not extend it.[5]

Two vital factors at least had been fully comprehended by the Axis diplomats. One was that the Latin countries individually

[1] Freytag to Weizsacker, *D.G.F.P.*, 23 September 1939
[2] Meynen to Weizsacker, ibid., 28 September 1939
[3] Preziosi to Ciano, *I.D.D.*, 494 of 28 September 1939
[4] Hull to Welles, *F.R.U.S.*, 29 September 1939
[5] Preziosi to Ciano, *I.D.D.*, 548 of 30 September 1939

stood in very different positions. The other was that Argentina's position was different from that of any other Latin republic. The factor providing the main differentiation was simply economics. In general, the Latin Republics in 1938 had transacted 33·7 per cent of their total trade with the United States, 14 per cent with Great Britain, and 18 per cent with Germany and Italy. Individually, however, the countries deviated wildly from this pattern. Brazil, for example, transacted 23·9 per cent of its total trade in 1938 with the United States, 14 per cent with Britain, and 27 per cent with the Axis. Comparable figures for Chile were 21·7 per cent, 16 per cent and 22·8 per cent; for Peru, 31 per cent, 26·5 per cent, and 19 per cent; For Uruguay, 7·9 per cent, 23·3 per cent, and 26·6 per cent; and for Argentina, 13 per cent, 26·5 per cent, and 17·7 per cent. Dependence on the United States increased as one moved north into the Banana Belt. Thus, Colombia transacted 54·4 per cent of its total trade with the United States; Panama, 73·4 per cent; Honduras, 74·3 per cent; Mexico, 62·6 per cent; and Cuba, 73·4 per cent. These figures admittedly need a little explanation. Countries which transacted over half their foreign trade with the United States were obviously in no position to quarrel with American policies, even if their geographical position had not made it acutely necessary for them to co-operate with Washington in any event. But the three nations, Brazil, Uruguay, and Chile, which had the Axis for their major trading partners, were not thereby committed to favouring the cause of European Fascism. Brazil had a Fascism of its own; it was traditionally committed to an alignment with Washington through fear of Argentina and motives of prudence; and its heavy purchases of German military equipment were positively encouraged by Roosevelt and Hull, who preferred to see German weapons in Brazilian hands rather than in German. Uruguay was struggling back to democracy, and was in any case more disposed to co-operate with Argentina, which was near, than with the Axis, which was far away. Chile's Aguirre Cerda was enjoying, for the time being, the support of his country's Nazis, even if only because sixty-two of them had been shot by his even more reactionary opponent, Alessandri, to whom they had given themselves up on the understanding that their lives would be spared. In any case those Latin countries which had developed important trading links with Germany found these links severed abruptly by the British blockade. Germany at war could offer neither trade nor aid for the time being. They were thus forced back upon the United States by the fortunes of war, as Brazil was by fear of Argentina.

Fear of Argentina was indeed a more potent factor in Latin politics in 1939 than at any previous time in history. The professed devotion to the cause of peace of Lamas and Cantilo did not disguise either their readiness to defy ruthlessly and with impunity the wishes of every other American Republic nor the thoroughly alarming growth of Argentine power. Argentine diplomatic predominance among the Latins both at home and in the League remained quite unchallengeable. So did Argentine economic predominance. The Republic of the Pampas provided by itself 33 per cent of total South American trade; its national income of $2,657,000,000 was over 25 per cent greater than that of its far more populous but much less developed rival, Brazil; its standard of living was by far the highest south of the Rio Grande, and its foreign exchange and gold reserves of $481,000,000 accounted for nearly 80 per cent of the total reserves of all Latin American countries put together.[1] What was even more disconcerting to the other South American governments was the apparently unmatchable striking force that Buenos Aires could deploy. No one doubted that the Argentine Army was far better trained, equipped, and more formidable generally than any other in the Continent, even Brazil's, which was twice the size but reputedly less efficient, probably less reliable, and certainly far more widely dispersed. Similarly, the strength of the Argentine Air Force was variously estimated at from 161 to over 600 aircraft, but it was invariably adjudged the largest and the best in the continent, whatever its actual numerical strength. The power of the Argentine Navy at least could be assessed with complete certainty. The only other Latin country with a fleet to be reckoned with was Brazil; and Brazil's two ancient battleships, one cruiser, and one destroyer were hopelessly outmatched by the two

[1] International Monetary Fund, *International Financial Statistics*, 1948; United Nations, *National and Per Capita Incomes, Seventy Countries*, 1949

modernized battleships, three splendid new Italian cruisers, and sixteen destroyers of Argentina.

There was therefore still every reason in the world for the United States to continue to seek an accommodation with Argentina and for the other Latin Republics to wait to see what form such an accommodation would take. The concomitant of this policy was that Brazil might have to endure further diplomatic humiliations. Initially, no serious differences on external policy seemed likely to arise among the Americas. The main concern of the Latins was simply to find means of compensating for the loss of their German trade, which had amounted in 1938 to 13·7 per cent of all South American external trade. The Argentines took the initiative on 17 October, when they reached an agreement with the British to use blocked Sterling balances for Britain to purchase imports of 170,000 tons of beef and 30,000 tons of mutton. Central Bank Manager Alfredo Louro enthusiastically aligned Argentina's trade policy with the Western Allies, announcing that : 'All requests for exchange for importations from other countries of merchandise that can in some form be acquired in Great Britain will be refused.'[1] His reasons were simple. The Allies would be able to buy goods from Argentina only if Argentina continued to buy goods from them. In any case Argentina could not buy goods satisfactorily from Germany any longer. Barter talks with the Germans involving the exchange of wheat and wool for rolling-stock and other transport equipment broke down on 29 October because the Germans were unable to guarantee delivery. One country which was able, of course, to sell to Argentina all the goods it could possibly want was the United States, whose exports to Argentina had fallen by 21 per cent, while purchases had risen by over 62 per cent, but it was highly unlikely that the Latins would do anything willingly to accelerate a process by which the United States would add Germany's share of their trade to its own.

Economic considerations had not yet become all-important. The Latins could still afford the luxury of empty ideological gestures. One on which they could all agree was condemnation of the Russian attack on Finland on 30 November. This was, indeed,

[1] *La Presna*, 19 September 1939

the ideal occasion for a Latin *démarche*. It was a manifest violation of sovereignty; it was being committed by Communists; and it was taking place at a safe distance from themselves. Argentina once more arrogated the place of distinction to itself. Other League members were positively startled by the fury of Cantilo's verbal assaults on a nation which had long been the paladin of collective security. The trouble was that the odium being reaped by the Russians was to some degree attaching to their German treaty partners. Some of the more vulnerable Latin states accordingly began to disassociate themselves from the Argentine attack. Uruguay, abruptly warned by Germany about the dangers of excessive criticism of the Nazi regime, refused to support and denounced as useless Cantilo's suggestion that the Latins 'unite their efforts in the common aim of considering giving effect to the guarantees of peace and security inscribed in the Preamble to the Covenant [of the League of Nations]'.[1] Chile also disassociated itself from Cantilo's next bombshell, that the Latins should form a common front against Communist propaganda, 'which constitutes a serious threat to which those people cannot be indifferent who care about life, conscience, and human liberty'.[2] Santiago warned that any joint front against Russia would be contrary to its doctrine of avoiding all European entanglements.

Cantilo stormed on regardless. On 12 December, he stated that Argentina was determined to oppose the decay of moral values by defending international rights against the brutal use of force.[3] His country would therefore not consider itself a member of the League as long as the U.S.S.R. could claim that title. He was, indeed, successful in achieving the expulsion of Russia in what has been termed the 'last courageous gasp' of the League of Nations.[4] Argentina thus managed to take a triumphant leading role in the last act of an organization at whose commencement it had performed so spectacularly and which it had managed to dominate so impressively during the previous decade.

[1] *La Presna*, 5 December 1939
[2] *ibid.*, 6 December 1939
[3] *La Presna*, 13 December 1939
[4] Telford Taylor, *The March of Conquest*, Edward Hulton, London, 1959, p. 85

The last Argentine *démarche* in the League had not, of course, been much more fruitful than any of the others. The only real effect of expelling Russia from the League was to leave the United Kingdom and France as the only two Great Powers in what had once been a world body. In any case, the Latins had problems nearer to home. While Cantilo fulminated in Geneva, the war came to South American territorial waters. The German 'pocket battleship', *Graf Spee*, broke off an action with three British cruisers to take shelter in the Uruguayan port of Montevideo, thereby compelling Foreign Minister Guani to reconcile the provisions of international law with the pressures being applied to him by both the Western Allies and Germany. This, in fact, was not a particularly serious problem. The fate of the *Graf Spee* had been sealed, practically speaking, from the moment its captain broke off action, having failed to destroy or deter the British squadron. The battleship was then too short of ammunition to be able to fight another prolonged engagement; damage to its galleys and fresh-water supplies made the prospects of a dash through tropical seas uncomfortable, to say the least; and shell-holes in the forepart of the ship made it unseaworthy for the North Atlantic, even if it were able to get that far.[1] Nothing could be done about the shortage of ammunition; and by the time the *Graf Spee* had been made seaworthy, the British would have been able to assemble a new squadron too strong for it to deal with. Since the Germans could thus neither fight nor run, Guani had little difficulty in dealing with the situation. He could safely plead on behalf of the Germans that international law provided that a belligerent ship might take refuge in a neutral port, so that 'repairs sufficient to ensure seaworthiness may be carried out – provided always that her fighting strength is in no way increased';[2] and at the same time happily tell the British and French diplomats that 'he was on the point of aligning all the nations of the American Continent against Germany'.[3] What the nations of the American Continent were really united about was the need to avoid situations of this kind in the future. The main diplomatic consequence of the *Graf*

---

[1] *Graf Spee 1939, The German Story,* H.M.S.O.
[2] Ministry of Foreign Affairs, Diplomatic, 1464/939-3659 of 16 December 1939
[3] Millington-Drake to Foreign Office, 16 December 1939

Spee affair was yet another demonstration of continental leadership by Argentina, and yet another setback for Brazil.

Aranha and his Anglophile Foreign Secretary, Mauricio Nabucco, had from the outset expressed their eagerness to co-operate fully with the State Department in all aspects of the affair. They accordingly recommended that the *Graf Spee* should be defined as an aggressor and therefore interned for the duration of the war. In point of fact the Germans had not committed the first or the most serious violations of South American neutrality. The British had, for example, seized the German ship, *Dusseldorf,* only twenty miles off the Chilean coast, well within the 200-mile wide neutrality zone. The Chileans were admittedly not in a strong position to protest, as they had themselves attempted to placate the Germans by denouncing the neutrality zone concept as a capricious violation of international law, but there was always one Latin country prepared to take a doctrinaire stand on somebody else's position. Cantilo recommended to Hull that the American Republics should make a strong declaration, protesting to the belligerents about violations of Latin neutrality, and referring to British as well as German transgressions. He was also prepared to initiate the necessary consultation to strengthen the system of protection in common, and to prevent belligerent ships from supplying themselves in American ports when they had committed warlike acts in the Neutrality Zone.[1] Aranha attempted to discredit the Argentine proposal by claiming that he could not imagine why Cantilo dragged in the British actions off the Chilean coast when the Chileans themselves had made no objection :[2] but the Chileans had; they had objected to Buenos Aires. Hull, in turn, rejected Aranha's over-enthusiastic suggestions about internment, advising all the American Republics to support the Argentine proposal.[3]

Anything like collaboration between Washington and Buenos Aires was still as impossible as ever. The Argentines were strong enough to exact concessions. They were too weak to grant any.

[1] Armour to Hull, *F.R.U.S.*, 16 December 1939
[2] Caffery to Hull, ibid., 17 December 1939
[3] Hull to all Chiefs of Mission, ibid., 18 December 1939

At the very moment when the foreign policy of Argentina was in many respects more gratifying to Washington than the vagaries of the Brazilians, Ortiz again unleashed an economic offensive which was about as injurious to United States interests as anything he could have done. He could not even plead necessity. The Latins in general had weathered the economic dislocations of the first year of war quite satisfactorily. Argentina, Brazil, and Chile had all reduced their imports and raised their exports from the 1938 level. Argentina's reserves of gold and foreign exchange had indeed risen by nearly 14 per cent, from $423,000,000 to $481,000,000. This had been due mainly to enormously increased sales to the United States. On 6 January 1940, Cantilo called off the talks on a United States-Argentine Trade Agreement, accusing the Americans of 'persistence and aggravation of a postwar protectionist policy'.[1] His own predilection for protectionist measures was shown a fortnight later when he imposed a ban on all imports of cotton textiles from Brazil on the eve of Aranha's arrival in Buenos Aires for a new series of trade talks. This, of course, meant that the Brazilians had to grant concessions to get the new ban lifted before they could even begin on the original basis for discussion. Cantilo then departed still further from the ideals of liberal trade which he had blamed the United States for disregarding, by completing a 100,000,000 lire barter deal with the Italians on 21 January. An Argentine Trade Mission then crossed the Pacific to conclude a most-favoured-nation agreement with Japan, valued at $7,000,000 each, which was intended to have the effect of trebling commerce between the two countries. A similar agreement with Brazil had already provided for each country to grant credits to the other for the mutual purchase of surpluses. It had been one of the most remarkable trading campaigns in history.

One of its side-effects was to severely injure, indeed eliminate, United States trade with Argentina in some 2,000 items. Washington could not dream of retaliating as long as Argentine foreign policy continued to be generally acceptable to the Allies. The German attack on Denmark and Norway evoked a response from Buenos Aires which completely overlooked the fact that

[1] *La Presna,* 7 January 1940

British ships had been laying mines in Norwegian territorial waters in the north at the same time as German ships began the assault on Oslo in the south. Cantilo denounced only the German aggression, recalling Honorio Pueyrredon's attack on foreign intervention at Havana thirteen years previously.[1] He affirmed that Argentina did not recognize territorial conquest by force, and would therefore continue to recognize the Danish and Norwegian diplomatic representatives in Buenos Aires.[2] Ortiz followed this up by recalling the Argentine military mission from Germany, while Cantilo began to talk in terms of a Latin American front against Germany, in the same way as he had previously put forward the idea of one against Russia. The Chileans, obsessed with the problems of defending their indefensible land and sea frontiers, once again wanted no part of a front against anyone. Again, it was left to Argentine diplomats to assume the moral leadership of the continent in phrases fully worthy of the occasion. Quoting Ruy Barbosa to the effect that one could not be impartial on a question of right and wrong, Cantilo told the European diplomats that: 'Neutrality cannot be indifference, cannot be insensibility, cannot be silence', and announced that Argentina would be sending Norway 20,000 tons of wheat on credit, as it had previously sent 50,000 tons to Finland.[3]

This was generous and inspiring, but it was only a partial solution. The aggressors were not going to be deterred by sales of wheat on credit to their victims. Aranha accordingly tried to take advantage of the visit of General Marshall to Brazil to recover the ground lost by his *Graf Spee* fiasco. He explained to Marshall that Brazilian national defence was complicated by the necessity of keeping forces concentrated in the south against the danger of an Argentine invasion. He was, therefore, prepared to offer the United States the use of bases in the northern part of the country around Natal to be used to keep the Atlantic sea lanes open. Welles was sufficiently intrigued to ask Caffery to find out exactly how the Brazilians proposed to make sure that any such bases were

[1] See p. 37
[2] Serena to Ciano, I.D.D., 66 of 13 April 1939
[3] ibid., 259 of 30 April 1940

not seized by the Germans.[1] His inquiries were given an unexpected urgency by the development on 10 May of the most portentous crisis of modern times. The war in the west, already distinctly active in Norway, took on a new dimension as the Germans gambled for victory in an offensive aganst France and the Low Countries. Its outcome was in doubt for the first few days. During this time, the chief reaction of the Latin Governments was one of fury at the loss of still more European markets. Cantilo repeated the principle that Argentina could not recognize territorial conquest by force.[2] Ortiz sent his sympathy to the Dutch and Belgian monarchs, and proposed that the Latin countries should reconsider their position as neutrals, adopting a policy of 'co-ordinated vigilance for the purely juridical purpose of neutrality'.[3] This was endorsed by Guani, who agreed that all the Latin Republics should make a declaration on the new German violations of neutrality.

The situation had by now gone beyond the stage of mere declaration. By 13 May, it was evident that the Western Allies had been heavily defeated. By 15 May, the French front had been broken and the Dutch forced to surrender. The probability was that Germany had won the war, and that would mean that the American Hemisphere would be open to attack by an enormously stronger European aggressor.

The Roosevelt Administration recognized the danger with an intensity that approached panic. Their anxiety was not difficult to comprehend. On the most favourable reading, the defeat of Britain and France would mean that the United States had lost the race for world leadership. It would be confronted with a Europe controlled and organized by a Germany whose resources would be far greater than those available to the United States.[4] The Americas would be living on German terms under the German gun, and this would be so even if the masters of the New Europe were people of moderate ambitions, with no designs on

[1] Welles to Caffery, *F.R.U.S.*, 8 May 1940
[2] Serena to Ciano, *I.D.D.*, 375 of 11 May 1940
[3] ibid., 392 of 12 May 1940
[4] Pickersgill, *The Mackenzie King Record,* University of Toronto Press, 1960, p. 123

anyone outside their own continent. There was certainly no evidence to assume that the Nazis fitted either description. The dangers implicit in a German desire to dominate the Americas by force simply could not be exaggerated. The United States did not possess the military capacity to guarantee its own security let alone that of any other American Republic. Its Army, equipped largely with First World War weapons, was about the same size as that of the Belgians, which had been forced to surrender after seventeen days. Its air striking force was outnumbered twenty to one by the Luftwaffe. It was true that the Germans had to get across the Atlantic, and the Americans possessed almost the largest and probably the most formidable Navy in the world, but their naval strength would have to be deployed in two oceans against the Japanese in the Pacific as well as against the Germans and their allies in the Atlantic. American naval power was simply not up to the task, however one reckoned the odds. Against America's fifteen battleships, the Japanese could deploy ten, the Germans two, with two more being built, and the Italians, who would presumably soon be entering the war on Germany's side, a further six. These odds might be partially offset if the United States could count on the co-operation of the Latin navies, though nothing could offset the odds that would be presented if the Germans were able to get their hands on any of the five French and fifteen British capital ships. The United States Naval Air Service was undoubtedly the best in the world, but it was barely sufficient to contain the Japanese. It could certainly not stop the Germans from getting their own air power across the Atlantic.

Moreover, the bases were there for them already. Hitler had boasted in 1938 that he did not need land armies to win Brazil by force of arms. Invisible weapons would suffice 'to make of that continent of half-breeds a great German dominion',[1] but not all German weapons in South America were wholly invisible. Extremely conspicuous were the forty-nine aircraft of the nine German or German-controlled airlines, which covered some 23,750 miles of air routes along the whole Atlantic coastline of Brazil, Uruguay, and Argentina, and traversed the continent from

[1] H. F. Artucio, *The Nazi Octopus in South America,* Robert Hale, London, 1943, p. 43

Rio to Lima and from Buenos Aires to Santiago. This mileage exceeded by about 10 per cent that covered by the combined routes of United States airlines in South America.[1] More importantly, the routes of the German airlines were not selected for their commercial significance, but were chosen deliberately to familiarize their air crews with the strategically significant parts of the continent, and to communicate between the rallying points of Nazi sympathizers in the various Latin states.[2]

All this was as evident to the Latin Governments as it was to the Roosevelt administration. It was not surprising in the circumstances that the framework of hemisphere co-operation fell apart. What was, perhaps, surprising was the firmness with which Buenos Aires aligned itself with Washington in this moment of supreme crisis. Roosevelt had sought the views of the Latin Republics on the expediency of seizing the American colonies of countries conquered by the Axis. The immediate problem was presented by the Dutch colonies in the Antilles and Surinam. Both Brazil and Chile expressed the fear that American action against these territories to forestall German occupation might provoke their own German and Italian populations. Chile was also acutely anxious about the Japanese in the Pacific. Argentina was not affected by these considerations. All that mattered to Buenos Aires was to keep the war away from the American Hemisphere. For the first time in history Argentine diplomats endorsed the principle of the Monroe Doctrine, arguing that the Dutch possessions should be occupied by the United States as the representative of all the American Republics, since it would violate the Monroe Doctrine if the Western Allies were to seize these areas themselves.[3] For once, Buenos Aires was giving Washington the green light.

The Argentines seemed inclined to go even further. Cantilo had already recommended that the Republics should reconsider their neutral position. He now persuaded Guani to float an idea for a

---

[1] Royal Institute of International Affairs, *Survey,* 1938, Oxford University Press, 1940, p. 676
[2] Melvin Hall and Walter Peck, 'Wings for The Trojan Horse', *Foreign Affairs,* December 1940, pp. 347-369
[3] Boscarelli to Ciano, *I.D.D.,* 428 of 15 May 1940

joint declaration on the invasion of the Low Countries. Hull naturally endorsed this gladly, and Aranha of course had no option but to do the same, though Chile felt itself too vulnerable to risk doing anything that might irritate the Germans.[1] The Argentines themselves found their moral issues compromized by an enormous barter deal with Italy involving 350,000 tons of maize, which was then nearing completion.

Guani's motion was accordingly lost, and Latin America sprawled in diplomatic disarray while the Germans swept on to victory in France. Only Peru, repressive, friendless, and desperately in need of North American support, plumped unreservedly for talks on hemisphere defence. Even Aranha was by now prepared to co-operate with the United States only for mutual defence, and then only subject to the reservation that any North American military mission to Brazil should be dressed inconspicuously in civilian clothes. His attitude changed slightly when the British averted total defeat and gained an unpredictably long breathing-space for the democracies by successfully withdrawing the bulk of their army from Dunkirk: he told Caffery that Brazil was prepared to co-operate with the United States in the defence of Uruguay and Argentina as well as itself.[2] The United States had no equipment available for that purpose. The British had left nearly all their own heavy equipment in France, and Roosevelt and Marshall had agreed to supplement them with enormous sales of artillery and small arms from United States arsenals. This left the North Americans with stocks available to supply only 1,800,000 men, which was not enough for their own defence, let alone that of any other American Republic as well.

Brazil in fact was still buying arms from Germany because of the inability of the United States to supply them. As Vargas pointed out to Caffery, the Americans held conversations but the Germans sent guns. This would clearly complicate Brazil's position if the United States were to intervene in the European war. Even the increasingly urgent American demands for bases in Brazil were not easy to meet, partly from traditional fears that it might be difficult to get the Americans out of Brazil once they

[1] ibid., 441 and 442 of 16 May 1940
[2] Caffery to Wells, *F.R.U.S.*, 7 June 1940

had moved in in force, and mainly from a justified fear that backing the United States would mean backing the losing side.

For it now seemed certain that the British could not possibly survive the summer. On 10 June, Italy entered the war, thereby deploying against the British an army of 1,000,000 men, an air force of about 1,500 first-line aircraft, and a navy of 700,000 tons. The British, already outnumbered three to one in the air and ten to one on the ground by the Germans, were now faced in Africa and the Mediterranean by Italian land forces three times as numerous as their own, and by a superb fleet which matched their own battleship strength in the area and outnumbered them by approximately two to one in cruisers, three to one in destroyers, and six to one in submarines. On the face of it, all the Italians had to do was to employ their air force and heavy units to cover their enormous torpedo striking force to drive the British from the Mediterranean within a week. The Axis had, to all appearances, won the war.

The Americans responded predictably. North of the Rio Grande, Roosevelt, moved to fury and desperation by the worst news in United States history since Valley Forge, disregarded a speech prepared for him by Hull and denounced the Italian aggression with the words: 'On this tenth day of June the hand that held the dagger has struck it into the back of its neighbour.' In Buenos Aires, a Public Safety Bill was passed providing for a state of national emergency, and Cantilo asked United States military advisers just how the United States proposed to defend the South American continent in the event of a British defeat, even if it were disposed to do so. In Rio, Vargas, also reckoning the odds against democracy, cleared the way for alignment with his fellow-Fascists across the Atlantic. He told the Brazilian people:

'We and all humanity are passing through an historical moment of great repercussions arising from rapid changes of values . . . old systems and antiquated formulas have entered a decline. It is not however the end of civilization as the pessimists and die-hard conservatives claim, but the tumultuous and fruitful beginning of a new era . . . The era of improvident liberalism, sterile demagoguery, and useless individualism has passed. There is no longer room for regimes founded on privilege and class distinction . . . It is necessary to understand the new epoch and remove the rubbish of dead ideas and sterile ideals. Vigorous people for life must follow the route of their aspirations.'[1]

There could be no possible doubt that what Vargas was doing was hailing Fascism as the force of the future. His words could not bear any other meaning. The affirmation of Fascist slogans at a time of Fascist triumph does not leave room for misunderstanding. And nothing could have shown more clearly how little independence in foreign policy the Brazilians had left themselves by their wooing of the United States than the fact that Vargas now found himself compelled to explain that his words had not meant what they did mean, and to embark still further on a policy which he had clearly intended to renounce. It was of course his misfortune that he had not read Roosevelt's 'stab in the back speech' before delivering his own. The timing of his address was thus as inopportune as it possibly could have been. Even Cantilo had the satisfaction of being able to say that the views of the Brazilian President differed from those of his own government. Aranha hastened to place the blame entirely upon Vargas by telling Caffery that no one in the Brazilian cabinet had known anything about the speech. Vargas himself tried to reassure the alarmed Roosevelt by telling him that he had not read Roosevelt's speech before making his own, which was true; that there was nothing in his address contradictory to Roosevelt's, which was manifest nonsense; and that it was still his intention to co-operate 100 per cent with the United States, which was the only safe thing to say in the circumstances.

It was clearly not yet time for Brazil to break with its traditional policy and disassociate itself completely from the United States. Apart from anything else, it was quite impossible to predict what the North American reaction might be to such a move. Roosevelt and his advisers, obsessed with their own vulnerability and driven to desperation by the fear of seeing the French and British Fleets fall into the hands of the Axis, were grasping at anything that

[1] *Correio da Manha*, 12 June 1940

might offer them some measure of security. No men certainly ever had a more difficult problem to solve. They could neither afford to let the British be overwhelmed through lack of United States support nor let vital equipment be sacrificed in an unavailing defence of the Home Islands. Their dilemma was made more intense yet by Churchill's refusal to provide the guarantees of the fate of the British Fleet, which alone would justify the Americans in letting him have some of their own urgently needed ships. It was not one of the more inspiring moments of Anglo-American diplomacy. In an attempt to force the United States to enter a war which it had neither the will nor the means to fight, Churchill was prepared to deny his own country the destroyers which he believed to be necessary for its survival. The Americans for their part deferred letting the British have the ships until they had demonstrated their ability to survive without them.

All that Roosevelt could think of in the meantime was to offer the Latins the opportunity to buy any United States military equipment that might became available, so that they might at least have arms for their own defence. Vargas accepted the offer gladly as an opportunity to demonstrate a devotion to hemisphere solidarity which he obviously did not feel, and explained eloquently that his speech was 'only a warning, a call to reality, addressed to Brazilians, and which might cause surprise only to persons devoted to routine, not to a far-seeing mind like Roosevelt's, who is liberal-minded, progressive and forward-looking . . . and who knows that Brazil will not fail him in loyalty'.[1] The important clause was the last. Ideology had no bearing on the relationships between the United States and the Latin Americans. Fascist Brazil and tyrannical Peru were sure to give assurances of support which could not be expected from representative Argentina and democratic Uruguay. But such assurances still meant nothing in practice. Rossetti in Santiago might proclaim that Chile would defend itself and any third country to the utmost if attacked, and would aid to the utmost the United States and any third country that the United States wished to defend.[2] Chile, however had no capacity to defend itself or anybody else, and no

---

[1] *New York Times*, 16 June 1940.
[2] Bowers to Hull, *F.R.U.S.*, 10 June 1940

intention of getting into any situation where it would have to. Guarantees relating to hemisphere defence from any quarter depended on a provision that did not exist, that of continental solidarity. The Argentines made sure of that. Cantilo had shifted his position by the end of the month from questioning the capacity of the United States to defend the southern continent, to questioning the existence of any threat against which defence would be necessary. He told Armour that he could see no such threat in the future himself, but that he would welcome any data from Washington that might indicate the existence of a potential menace. This sounded fatuous, but the implications were sensible. The dangers of neutrality are nothing compared with those of joining the wrong side. Every indication was that the Axis was going to win. Germany and Italy did not need Argentina on their side so Buenos Aires had nothing to fear from that quarter as long as it did not make the fatal mistake of joining the losers. This went for Chile as well, and Paraguay and Uruguay could still be relied upon to follow the Argentine lead. There was thus no possibility of a united Latin anti-Axis front, and therefore nothing risked by professing devotion to such a front.

Brazilian or Chilean assurances thus rested on the safe foundation of Argentine intransigence. The North Americans had now come to the conclusion that they could not risk alienating any Latin Republic by coercive measures. Hull said frankly that an overt split would be tragic.[1] If the United States was not prepared to punish its enemies, it could still reward its friends. Aranha's tireless cultivation of the North Americans suddenly showed signs of paying off. On 27 July, the American Export-Import Bank approved credits to Brazil amounting to $60,000,000, to be made available at the rate of $5,000,000 per month, and Hull announced the new United States arms policy for Latin America. The Republics were divided into four categories. Most favoured were Brazil and Mexico, which were to be provided with military aid sufficient 'to insure [their] ability to defend [themselves] against a major Axis attack from neighbouring states, or from overseas, and against internal disorders until United States armed aid could arrive in sufficient force to insure success'. Ecuador, Colombia, and

[1] Hull to Welles, *F.R.U.S.*, 22 July 1940

Venezuela were to be equipped 'to insure their ability to meet and repel any probable minor attack from overseas and to insure their internal stability'. The Central Americans would be prepared 'to insure internal stability'. Provision of military aid to Argentina and its cohorts, Uruguay, Paraguay, Chile, Bolivia, and Peru would be 'determined only after requirements of other republics have been completed and plans to supply them have been approved'.[1]

These inducements produced an immediate response. Within three days, Argentina was the only Latin Republic still overtly dissenting from United States policies on hemisphere defence.[2] This opposition succumbed to a new turn of the American screw on 2 August, when Caffery told Dutra that Brazil could at last buy some long-needed automotive equipment and aviation material from the United States. The prospect of Brazil having increasingly free access to the arsenals of the United States constituted the most serious challenge to Argentine pretensions yet, far more immediate than any remote threat of invasion from across the Atlantic. Argentina's rulers had always conceived their nation's world role as that of leader among the Latin Americans. They had hitherto been able to counter Brazil's advantage of size and population by wealth and military power. These would be lost if Brazil were to be allowed to buy United States arms with money loaned by the United States for that purpose. Buenos Aires accordingly put in a bid for similar treatment with a flurry of pro-Allied gestures made more congenial because of the very real sympathy which the Argentines felt for the British, the very real power they still exercized there, and the increasing evidence of the British capacity to resist. On 10 August, Finance Minister Federico Pinedo claimed that Britain was 'defending the rights of the world in a magnificent crusade'.[3] Minister of Agriculture Cosme Ezcurra praised the ideals of the Havana Conference and urged the development of freer trade among the Americas. The Italians momentarily hoped for a swing back to neutrality when President Ortiz, almost blind and dying of diabetes, tendered his

[1] Hull to Heads of Mission, ibid., 27 July 1940
[2] Boscarelli to Ciano, *I.D.D.*, 335 of 31 July 1940.
[3] *La Presna,* 10 August 1940

resignation in favour of the doctrinaire conservative Vice-President, Ramon S. Castillo.[1] Congress, however, not only refused by 150 votes to 1 to accept Ortiz's resignation, but also approved the appointment of Anglophile Julio Roca as Foreign Minister to succeed the equivocal Cantilo.

Meanwhile, the Brazilians had become alarmed in their turn. Roosevelt had already made a show of force in the South Atlantic by dispatching three cruisers and three destroyers on a goodwill visit to Rio. He now carried United States involvement in the war a giant step further by concluding a deal with the British, under which fifty destroyers were transferred from the United States Navy to the White Ensign, in return for the British leasing facilities in the West Indies and Newfoundland which the United States would have seized anyway, in case of emergency. This not only committed the North Americans to achieving the defeat of the Axis, but also dashed Brazilian hopes of occupying Dutch New Guinea or Surinam, and revived fears of Yankee military presence in the southern continent. Vargas accordingly set to work to revive the Pan-American idea as a precaution against further unilateral interventions by the United States.[2] This necessitated a new conciliatory approach to Argentina. On 6 October, Pinedo and Brazilian Finance Minister Souza Costa signed a treaty under which each country granted the other $12,000,000 for the purchase of surplus products from each other, and declared a ten-year truce on competitive tariffs. Meanwhile, the Argentines attempted to safeguard their own position by commencing informal military talks with the United States. These proved to be as generalized and evasive as might have been expected, but Hull professed himself delighted with even this gesture towards co-operation,[3] and the United States Treasury followed up with a further grant of $10,000,000 and a credit of $10,000,000 extended to Argentina by the Export-Import Bank.

This did not match the credits of $60,000,000 gained by the Brazilians, but it ensured that Argentina would not miss out entirely on any military aid being tendered by the North

[1] *Giornale d'Italia*, 24 August 1940
[2] Serena to Ciano, *I.D.D.*, 573 of 9 September 1940
[3] Hull to Armour, *F.R.U.S.*, 22 October 1940

Americans. In any case the dreadful crisis of the summer and early autumn had passed. Against all probability, the tide of war had swung spectacularly in favour of the British. By the middle of September the Germans, outfought in the skies and outproduced in the factories, had irretrievably lost their bid for victory in the air over Britain. This meant that they had also lost their chance of successfully invading the Home Islands. This decisive setback for the Germans had been followed by a series of British victories against their Italian ally unmatched in the history of warfare between first-class powers. The Italians had from the start shown themselves extraordinarily unwilling to come to grips with a fleet possessed of vastly less offensive capacity than their own. Then, on 11 November, the British struck at the Italian battlefleet with their Air Arm. In the most economic use in history of air power against surface ships, twenty-one of the oldest operational aircraft possessed by any air service sank at their moorings the brand-new 35,000-ton *Littorio* and two older battleships. In December, the British Army of the Nile opened a dazzlingly successful offensive against an Italian Army nearly five times its own strength. Other British Armies soon began to operate with similar success against similar odds in East Africa. By the beginning of 1941, it was possible for the British to start considering plans to reopen a continental land front by invading Sicily.

All this made an Axis victory by no means the practical certainty that it had seemed in June 1940. It also removed completely for the time being any prospect of an Axis threat against the American Hemisphere. The dreadful urgency of the third quarter of 1940 no longer existed. Latin Governments could hope again that Washington would do nothing, as Berlin could do nothing, to force them to commit themselves. In any case, Latin neutrality had acquired a new respectability. Spain had found a mission for its sister nations.

There had, of course, been some doubt during the latter stages of the Battle of Britain whether Spain itself would stay neutral. Hitler had hoped to persuade Franco to join with the Axis in a drive to seize Gibraltar and close the Mediterranean to the British. The prospect was most attractive. The last thing in the world that Spain needed in 1940 was another war, and the destruction of the French Fleet at Mers-el-Kebir, German defeats in the air, and Italian disasters at sea, in Greece and in North Africa, had demonstrated that the British could still be immensely formidable. Franco accordingly opted for neutrality in November 1940. It was still open to the Germans to march through Spain by force, but there were strong arguments against this too. Spain was a notoriously unrewarding country to invade; all available German resources would be needed for the scheduled assault on Russia; a new front in Spain would be vulnerable to British air- and sea-power; and there were obvious advantages in keeping Spain neutral, both for purposes of Intelligence and as a port through which Germany could trade with the rest of the world outside Europe. In the meantime, the Spanish themselves had hit on a way to remain neutral with dignity. On 9 November 1940, Franco announced the formation of the Grand Council of Hispanidad, to be supervised by the Foreign Ministry and to bear the obligations of 'watching over the wellbeing and interest of our spirit in the Spanish world . . . [and] of ensuring the continuation and efficacy of the ideas and works of the Spanish genius'. He explained that Spain 'is not moved by the desire for lands or riches', but was 'only wishing to return to Hispanidad the unity of conscience'.[1]

Hispanidad as a concept was neither new nor readily comprehensible to the non-Spanish mind. Its essential character was a doctrinaire Catholic opposition to everything associated with the almost equally vague concept of 'Liberalism', meaning most specifically Marxism, freemasonry, international jewry, and all philosophical and ecclesiastical heresies left of St Peter. It was the basic ideology of the Falange in Spain and provided a constellation of values which centres of Latin power across the Atlantic could share with Madrid and Lisbon.

It might well have seemed over-ambitious to the point of fatuity for a country placed as Spain was in 1940 to aspire to any kind of world role at all. In population, resources, and economic strength, Franco's post-civil war Spain ranked approximately on a level with Yugoslavia. In one sense the world crisis had rendered calculations of material strength almost irrelevant among the powers below the first rank. The most probable outcome of the European

[1] *The Times,* 10 November 1940

War would still be a world dominated by irresistible German strength, in which case any competition among other nations would have to be in the field of ideas, since military and economic power would be reserved to the Masters. Alternatively, the present Great Powers might well all exhaust themselves to such an extent that weak but intact neutrals could exercize a disproportionate influence on world events. A community of nations preserving the Iberian traditions of Catholicism, Spanish culture, and illiberalism might then conceivably have a role to play in determining the shape of the postwar world. It was a dream that could appeal to the weak. It was also an attractive rationalization for the obvious material advantages of neutrality for the countries concerned. A neutral Spain was free to trade with the world outside. It was also a means by which other neutrals could gain access through the British blockade to the enormous markets of Axis-dominated Europe. An ideology does not have to be too logical as long as it can appeal to a sufficient number of basic human emotions. Hispanidad appealed to Christian conscience, national pride, cupidity, and fear of war. It is not surprising that it found numerous and powerful adherents on both sides of the Atlantic. The real question is why it did not find more.

The answer is the United States. Latin neutrality depended in the end on the willingness of the North Americans to let the Southern Continent remain uninvolved in the war. Their willingness to do so could be expected to endure only for as long as the British could keep the Axis Powers contained in central and western Europe. This hope persisted throughout the opening months of 1941. While British armies sped to victory in North Africa, Roca forestalled a United States bid for bases on the River Plate by an agreement with Guani under which Argentina undertook to help Uruguay build bases which would later be made available to Argentine armed forces. Meanwhile, Argentina and Spain agreed on a colossal barter deal valued at $4,150,000 and involving initially the sale by Argentina of 350,000 tons of corn. This was followed by a further shipment of 500,000 tons of wheat and 1,500 tons of meat, sold, according to Foreign Minister Enrique Ruiz-Guinazu, 'to satisfy to the fullest extent the necessities of life of the Spanish people'.[1] The Spanish press in turn

[1] *La Presna,* 10 February 1941

hailed it as an example of Hispanidad in action. It was certainly an example of the advantages of being neutral. As Julio Roca smoothly told the British Ambassador : 'It is the condition of our happiness and of our future greatness that we should not ally or consolidate ourselves with the opposing parties of our day for the single and ephemeral fortune of arms.'[1]

This was all very well; but the preservation of this happy state depended itself on the fortune of arms. This changed drastically in the spring of 1941. On 2 April, the British were crushed in the Western Desert by Rommel and forced back to the Egyptian frontier. On 6 April, the Germans invaded Yugoslavia and Greece. The Roosevelt Administration responded immediately to the rapidly worsening situation across the Atlantic. On 3 April, ten heavily armed cutters were transferred from the United States Coastguard Service to the Royal Navy. On the following day, arrangements were made to refit British warships in United States dockyards. American naval and air bases were opened in Bermuda and Greenland on 7 April. On 11 April, as Yugoslavian resistance collapsed and the British began to retreat to the sea in Greece, the newly-formed United States Atlantic Fleet began to patrol all waters west of 26° West in the Atlantic, a further 1,500 miles nearer Europe than had been covered by the original Neutrality Patrol.

German victories thus effectively helped to increase the odds against Germany by accelerating the rate of American involvement. Yet there was still no certainty that even the most complete United States intervention would be sufficient to defeat Hitler. What was clear rather was that the Axis was now in a literally unassailable position in Europe. The initiative heroically won by the British in the New Year had been totally lost. No imaginable combination of British armies and American material could now challenge Hitler in Continental Europe. The only question was where he was going to strike next.

There were four options open to the Germans : they could make a renewed attempt to invade Britain itself; they could strike through Spain and French Africa to threaten the American Hemisphere; they could drive east through Egypt into Asia, to

[1] *New York Times,* 19 December 1940

overrun the British Eastern Empire and possibly link up with the Japanese; or they could eliminate their only possible rival for continental supremacy, and cripple Russia. There was no reasonable hope that they would try the first. No invasion of Britain could be contemplated unless the Germans gained air supremacy over the home counties, and this they had lost irrevocably in 1940. The last prospect was perhaps the most agreeable for the British and Americans, in that it would give them at least a temporary respite and would align with them the one country in the world which had the manpower and the industrial capacity to overwhelm the Germans on land. If a Russian campaign contained the only foreseeable prospect of a German defeat, it also contained a very real prospect of a victory which would place under Axis control resources which would allow Hitler and his allies to dictate the terms under which the rest of the world would live. It was, from the point of view of the British and Americans, at once almost too much to hope for and almost too awful to contemplate. That left Africa and Asia. There was no doubt that the Germans had hopes of striking through Egypt, but they were contained for the moment on the frontier by superior British forces, and their chances of improving the situation depended on their ability to cripple British air and sea striking power in the Mediterranean, which it was by no means certain they could accomplish.

The easiest option was certainly a thrust into Africa across the Straits of Gibraltar, from which Germany could reach across the Atlantic to an almost defenceless South America, and to its sympathizers in the Latin Republics. Roosevelt desperately tried to shore up hemisphere defences by asking Vargas to agree to the use of Bahia and Pernambuco as bases by the United States Navy, and calling on the Latin Republics to appeal to Spain to stay out of the war. The results were scarcely satisfactory. Aranha agreed to let the North Americans have the use of bases in Brazil's terribly vulnerable north-eastern bulge, but coupled this with renewed complaints about the failure of the United States to supply arms or equipment to Brazil on terms anything like as favourable as those offered by Nazi Germany. Vargas agreed to support an appeal to Spain by the united Hispanic states only after he had made sure that no such united appeal would be forthcoming, since Peru had declared itself uninterested, Uruguay had said that no appeal would have any effect, and Chile and Argentina had failed to make any comment. The Argentine silence was the more significant because of the enormously increasing economic ties between Argentina and Spain. Five days after Welles had floated the idea of a common Latin appeal to Madrid, an agreement was reached under which Argentina exchanged a further 380,000 tons of wheat and 8,000 tons of meat for industrial goods and machinery from Spain. It was intriguing that President Benavides should himself have been in Buenos Aires at the time that the Peruvian Government disassociated itself from the appeal. Worse still, a medical committee had reported to the Argentine Congress that Roberto M. Ortiz was no longer capable of performing his official duties. Full authority thus fell into the hands of the arch-Conservative Castillo, who immediately abrogated constitutional processes in Argentina and began to rule by decree. Argentine policy had not been notably conciliatory under Ortiz. It could only get less so under Castillo.

In the circumstances, Washington could again only bargain as best it could. The Export-Import Bank promptly made a further credit of $12,000,000 available to Brazil for the purchase of arms from wherever they were available and on 12 May, Hull announced that he would again try to negotiate a trade treaty with Argentina and Uruguay. Buenos Aires was always ready to do business. Ruiz-Guinazu's assistant in the Ministry of Foreign Affairs, Guillermo Rothe, claimed immediately that the conclusion of a commercial treaty with the United States would not only be 'the most important event that could take place in Argentine international economic relations', but would also be 'a practical example of the spirit of collaboration that animates the American Republics and of the common aspiration to bind their economies by means of agreements'.[1] Meanwhile, as the British, driven again from the Continent, prepared to defend the island of Crete, United States naval forces took over bases in Newfoundland, and Hull assured the Vargas regime that: 'There is no Government anywhere with which this Government regards itself as being on more intimate terms of trust and confidence than with the Government of Brazil. ...' He also told Aranha that in his opinion

[1] *La Presna*, 12 May 1941

the Germans could never achieve victory as long as they did not obtain mastery of the seas, and this the United States would never allow them to have.[1]

It was not going to be easy to stop them. The most utterly dispiriting days of the war were at hand. On 24 May, the German battleship, *Bismarck*, blew the largest British warship, *Hood*, out of the water with its third salvo. On 26 May, the British were forced to abandon Crete to an airborne German invasion. The Americas responded appropriately. Roosevelt declared a state of Unlimited National Emergency, warning his people that it would be suicide to wait until the Nazis were in their backyard; Vargas cabled to Roosevelt, telling him 'you can count on us'; and Argentina formed its first Parachute Corps on the pattern of the German victors of Crete.

Not all Argentines felt that this was the best that they could do. Justo's infallible political antennae warned him that the time might be ripe for a change of line, just as they had done in 1938. He suddenly proclaimed that he was himself in accord with the policies of Roosevelt, as he believed the majority of Argentines were; that the tradition of Argentina had always been to support American Republics against non-Americans; and that it should not be impossible to reach some general agreement for co-operation on defence of the hemisphere. Even Saavedra Lamas surprisingly urged immediate consultations among the American Governments, 'so that an emergency would not find this hemisphere as disunited as the Balkans were'.[2]

The Great Peacemaker had certainly divined that the unity of the continent was at stake in a manner seriously disadvantageous for Argentina. Brazil was going it alone as an ally of the United States. Vargas had refused to sell strategic materials to anybody except the Americans; he had refused to let the Italians establish an aircraft tender off the Brazilian coast; and he was pressing on with the construction of bases around Natal for use by the United States. These policies had already extracted in return $100,000,000 in Lend-Lease aid and $72,000,000 in credits from the Export-Import Bank. Now, Brazil was making overtures to

[1] Hull to Caffery, *F.R.U.S.*, 22 May 1941
[2] *La Presna*, 3 June 1941

Argentina's own satellite, Paraguay, for a commercial and transportation agreement that would draw that country out of the
influence of Buenos Aires and into that of Rio. Argentine domination of the continent had suddenly been called in question.
Castillo still temporized. His eagerly-awaited address to Congress
on 15 June brought nothing but falsehoods and platitudes. He
denied that the United States had ever shown interest in bases on
the River Plate and insisted that the traditional cordiality of
Argentine relations with practically everyone remained un-
impaired, although he could not help feeling uneasy for the future.
His unbelievably uninspiring Minister of the Interior, Miguel
Culaciatti, similarly admitted to Congress that there was intense
Nazi activity going on in Argentina, but insisted that its importance was exaggerated. This interpretation was ridiculed by
Congress itself, which voted by 95 to 1 to appoint a Committee
of Inquiry into 'activities contrary to the institutions and
sovereignty of the Argentine Republic', under the presidency of
the vigorous and Anglophile young Radical, Damonte Taborda.
The Committee had scarcely been formed when the world situation underwent yet another momentous change. There had never
really been any options open to the Germans since December
1940, when Hitler had decided to eliminate Russian rivalry and
possess himself of Russian resources as a preliminary to coming
to terms with the Anglo-Americans. On 22 June, the German
forces moved east into the Soviet Union. New complications of
strategy and ideology were thus interjected into a situation already
unmanageably complex.

For the Germans did not march alone. Operation Barbarossa
indeed developed into more of a common European enterprize
than the Crusades themselves had ever been. Italy, Finland,
Hungary, Rumania, Bulgaria, and the revived Fascist formation
of Croatia shared in the campaign as full allies; groups of
collaborators joined in from every country of Occupied Europe;
and neutral Spain sent an immensely useful Blue Legion of
durable and merciless infantry. The new German venture could
thus pretend to be defending traditional European culture and
even religion in a way in which it was difficult to represent earlier
Nazi forays as doing. It obviously created difficulties for
Washington, trying to enlist Latin American support for a war in

which the United States and Britain now had for their principal partner the very source of atheistic communism. The Latins had not been happy to contemplate the prospect of a German-dominated Europe. They were even less happy to contemplate the prospect of a Russian-dominated one, supposing the Russians were to win, though there was every indication throughout the summer of 1941 that they would not. The Germans were winning the most impressive victories in the history of land warfare. The Russians were withdrawing along a front of 1,200 miles. It seemed the best time possible for any country which had the opportunity to stay neutral to do so.

Nothing could certainly have been less encouraging to Washington than the Latin reaction. The worst aspect of it was of course a sudden and savage attack by Peru on its defenceless neighbour, Ecuador, on 24 June. Even more ominous was Castillo's statement that not only was he unaware of any United States request for bases on the River Plate, but he also knew nothing of the Colonia Agreement itself, under which Argentina had undertaken to provide Uruguay with finance to build such bases for their common use. Roosevelt nonetheless performed yet another conciliatory gesture, sending Castillo a telegram on the occasion of Argentine Independence Day celebrations on 9 July, referring to the 'unity of ideals and spiritual affinity' between the United States and Argentina. However, his warning that war and aggression in other countries constituted an 'active threat' to the liberty and independence of the twenty-one republics elicited from Castillo only the usual rigmarole about Argentine determination 'to obtain the most determined and complete military defence of our country; to maintain the principle of neutrality in the good relations with all countries . . . [and] to promote continental solidarity in a constructive and farsighted form. . . .'[1] Roosevelt was still prepared to back a 'supreme call' by Castillo to Benavides to stop aggression against Ecuador and to let the Argentines have the credit for the fact that fighting stopped three days later. There was some slight comfort in the fact that Culaciatti was prepared to abolish the Supreme Council of Argentine Nationalism, and

---

[1] Enrique Ruiz-Guinazu, *La Politica Argentina y el Futuro de America,* Liberia Humuel, B.A., 1944, p. 20

even the Comite Nacional de Juventud, on the grounds of their being totalitarian bodies and therefore in contravention of the principles of the Argentine Constitution. Similarly gratifying to Washington was the arrest of thirty Argentine Nazis on 23 August; the flight from justice to Rio of all places of the Press Secretary of the German Embassy in Buenos Aires who was denounced by Taborda as the probable chief of the Gestapo in Argentina; and the unflagging zeal of the Taborda Committee itself. If the operations of the Committee were a happy augury for the future of Argentine liberalism, what they had to reveal was unqualifiedly alarming. Between 1938 and 1941, the expenditure of the German Embassy in Buenos Aires had increased over thirty-six-fold. Its outlay of 5,983,000 pesos in 1940–41 was over three times as much as the British were spending, and nearly twelve times as much as the Americans. Still more serious was the discovery that firms under Axis control accounted for 1,700,000,000 pesos, or 18 per cent of total foreign capital invested in Argentina, nearly as much as the United States contribution.[1] Moreover, Argentine commercial links with Spain had now developed to the extent that virtually the whole of the Argentine cotton crop was going to that country, as well as massive shipments of grain and meat; and there was no doubt at all where a large part of Spanish imports were going. The Iberian neutrals constituted a gap in the British blockade through which goods flooded from Latin America into Axis Europe. Total Spanish external trade increased only marginally from 1940 to 1941, but exports from Spain to Germany increased eleven and a half times, from 14,000,000 to 161,000,000 pesetas. Portuguese exports to that market rose nineteen-fold during the same period. German Ambassador von Thermann had promised Ruiz-Guinazu that Germany would become the biggest purchaser of Argentine goods in the postwar world, since Germany would be requiring imports of meat, wheat, and corn which the United States would not want as it produced these commodities itself.

Nor was Argentina the only Latin country being increasingly attracted economically into the Axis net. Even in Brazil, the Germans had actually increased their sales over the past twelve

[1] Commission Investigadora, B.A., *Informe No. 2*, 5 September 1941, p. 80

months to 3·5 per cent from 3 per cent of Brazil's total imports. The Germans were now confidently offering to sell Brazil the weapons Vargas had not yet been able to obtain from the United States, shipping them on neutral transports out of Lisbon. Contrary to appearances the Brazilians were in no sense playing a double game. Vargas had grimly resigned himself to a policy of co-operating with the North Americans, wherever that might lead him. On 1 September, Roosevelt had allowed the United States Atlantic Fleet to escort ships of any nationality across the Atlantic. On 6 September, he directly transferred American ships to carry British troops and equipment to Egypt. On the following day, during a parade in Rio which featured armoured cars and trucks newly obtained from the North Americans, Vargas told the world that 'aggression from whatever quarter will find us the greatest bloc of varied nationalities ever assembled in any definite alliance'.[1] He also assented gladly to a far-sighted proposal by Guani that any American Republic at war with an enemy country outside the hemisphere should be treated as an non-belligerent by its sister republics. In London, Arigão affirmed that the chief feature of Brazilian foreign policy was now, as always, a spirit of mutual co-operation and close collaboration with all American nations, without any pretensions to a dominant position.[2]

The unmistakable fact was that Vargas's policy of reluctant but faithful co-operation with the North Americans was raising Brazil to a dominant position among the Latins while Argentina's power base was correspondingly shrinking. Between 1940 and 1941, Brazil's total foreign trade had risen by 24 per cent and its reserves of foreign exchange by 86 per cent, compared with Argentine rises of only 2·9 per cent and 22·5 per cent respectively. Brazil was also guaranteed access to United States military equipment, while the Argentines could neither produce their own nor import any from Europe. In September, Castillo set up a national arms industry to try to fill the gap allocating it $10,000,000 a year. This was not, however, likely to be operative for years, or adequate when it did go into production. In the meantime, there were disturbing signs that the other Latin neutrals

[1] *New York Times,* 7 September 1941
[2] *The Times,* 9 September 1941

were drawing their own conclusions and preparing to change sides. Colombia began investigating Nazi activities on 16 September. On 17 September, Bolivia invited the other Republics to a Foreign Ministers' Conference to discuss an alleged campaign by the Axis to undermine friendly relations among the Latins. Castillo curtly replied that Argentina was aware of its common duty to defend the continent and that existing pacts were sufficient for that purpose. He also disassociated his Administration from anti-German statements made in Congress, at the same time that he strengthened his own position by sacking the Chief of Army Aviation and ordering loyal troops to seize two main airports, where he suspected the aviators of disaffection. He was still at pains to insist that the groups in Argentina which were enemies of the law did not form a single organization or obey a single leader, nor did they find their inspiration in the existing international situation.

Nobody believed this, of course. The most serious blow yet to Argentina's patiently-wrought predominance came when Chilean Foreign Minister Rossetti, of all people, announced unilaterally that if Brazil were menaced by an aggressor, Chile would consider that to be aggression against herself also. He also agreed to a United States proposal to pool oil resources in the hemisphere, and to let United States ships refuel at storage tanks in Chilean ports. Chile had apparently decided where its safety lay. There was naturally no question of the Chileans defending anybody. All they wanted was to be defended, and it was obvious that the countries to which they looked for their defence were Brazil and the United States. Moreover, the Brazilians themselves were now so sure of their immunity from any Latin threat that for the first time in their history they were concentrating their forces in the north-east, where the Americans wanted them to, away from their border with Argentina. Buenos Aires apparently now counted for neither a source of protection nor menace. Eighty years of authority through intimidation had been swept away in a fortnight. The heritage of Bartolome Mitre lay in ruins.

There was no mystery about it. Buenos Aires could simply not outbid Washington, though neither could Washington afford to intimidate Buenos Aires. Frustrated everywhere else the Argentines could still drive their usual ferociously hard bargain with the United States. Under the terms of a treaty signed by Armour and Ruiz-Guinazu on 14 October to replace the original 1853 Treaty of Friendship, Commerce, and Navigation, the United States agreed to reduce its tariffs on 75 per cent of Argentine exports, including cuts of 50 per cent on main items such as wool, canned meat, hides, and skins. In return, Argentina reduced from 22 to 33 per cent the tariffs on goods amounting to 30 per cent of United States exports. It was also provided that the United States was not to receive any benefits from special quotas, tariff concessions, and exchange preferences negotiated between Argentina and neighbouring Latin countries, and that Argentina would be free to discriminate against United States goods in favour of the United Kingdom until problems in dealing with sterling balances were solved, which looked like taking forever. Roosevelt bitterly saluted this one-sided arrangement in words calculated to appeal to Castillo's overactive religious conscience :

'United as we are under Divine guidance in the defence of our precious heritage in this hemisphere, we have today forged a new link in the chain of friendship, peace and good neighbour-liness which happily binds our two nations together.'[1]

The North Americans could always match the Latins in splendid and extraneous rhetoric, though it had no effect upon Castillo, who said nothing. The agreement itself, however, led to an Argentine response more fervid than anything Roosevelt could have expected. The Nazi press denounced the agreement as having made Argentina a North American colony, and referred specific-ally to Damonte Taborda as an agent of dollar corruption. The choleric Taborda, who was in Washington at the time, replied with a public address in which he asserted that the Argentine people would stand with the United States and would fight at the side of other free nations to prevent Nazi domination of the world. Castillo did not comment on this either, but that was because he had more pressing worries. Argentine domination was fading in its last and safest area. Paraguay had been kept helplessly depen-dent on Argentine-owned transport facilities by the consistent refusal of Buenos Aires to allow that country a free port anywhere

[1] *New York Times,* 15 October 1941

along the Pilcomayo. The Brazilians now offered Paraguay not only a trade agreement, but also a free port at Santos, as well as aid to construct a railroad from Concepcion to Porto Esperanca. The last outpost of the Gaucho Empire was falling.

The Brazilian net swept even more widely. Promising that Brazil 'shall not be neutral if an American nation enters the war. We have been and will stay Pan-American. We follow America and will share America's destiny', Aranha replied to Rossetti's empty promises with an appeal to Chile to abandon its posture of fearful neutrality and to follow the guidance of Cordell Hull with Brazilian assistance. He promised that a declaration of war by the United States would bring swift Brazilian support, and followed this up with the declaration at Montevideo on 23 November: 'We are at war.' Meanwhile, he urged all the Latins to press on with their defence preparations; concluded a covenant on trade and culture with Chile; and completed an agreement with Guani to construct an international bridge between Uruguay and Brazil over the River Uruguay.

The Argentines still had resources, if only they could find a policy. The trouble was that neither Ruiz-Guinazu nor Castillo could conceive principles of foreign policy more positive and explicit than the irrelevant vapourings of Hispanidad, though even partial commitments could bring some reward. On 24 October, Castillo introduced a mammoth arms budget, allocating $169,000,000 to military and $153,000,000 to naval rearmament. A military mission was sent to the United States to negotiate on the purchase of $250,000,000 worth of military equipment. It was not stated definitely whether the Argentines would be applying for Lend-Lease, but their purchases were 'to be adjusted to the continental defence programme'. This concession had one important consequence: the delighted North Americans arranged with the British to allow German arms purchased by Argentina before the war to be shipped out of Lisbon through the blockade. Castillo also rushed through a proposal to share in the development of Bolivian oilfields, reluctantly lowered tariffs on 18·2 per cent of American imports after the United States had reduced on 92·4 per cent of purchases from Argentina, and moved in to retain some measure of control over Brazilian development through the medium of an agreement. The terms of this were that the two countries would grant free entry to goods produced by newly-developed industries in each other's territory; reduce duties on non-competitive goods; and ultimately 'establish in progressive form a regime of free exchange that will permit a customs union to be reached between Argentina and Brazil'. Ruiz-Guinazu claimed that this would be 'the foundation of closer friendship and unalterable union . . . Between the Argentine Republic and Brazil there exists today complete and absolute agreement on the manner of facing problems that concern them.'[1] In fact, there was total disagreement. At the very moment that the Brazilians were endorsing the movement of United States troops into Surinam and swearing their own readiness to establish military vigilance on their frontiers, Castillo was reaffirming a policy of strict neutrality and banning a monster programme of 5,000 public meetings organized by Accion Argentina to protest against his policy of 'international isolation'. Castillo could well afford to be intransigent when even the slightest concession on his part brought gratifying rewards. The United States agreed to buy all Argentina's production of tungsten for the next three years at a rate of $1,500 per ton for up to 3,000 tons annually, and on 1 December, the United States Export-Import Bank offered a further credit of $66,000,000 to Argentina. Neutrality still had its blessings.

It also had its difficulties. These were increased beyond measure by the Japanese attack on Pearl Harbor on 7 December. Ever-reliable Panama declared war on the aggressor almost before the United States did itself. Brazil, Costa Rica, and Colombia declared their solidarity with the North Americans, and Aranha promised that he would take action to cut telecommunications between Brazil and the Axis countries. Paraguay and Argentina said that they would not regard the United States as a belligerent, thereby earning themselves warm thanks from Roosevelt. Bolivia proposed without much enthusiasm to try to form a common Latin front against aggression. These reactions were much what one would have anticipated from the traditional behaviour of the states concerned. One Latin country, however, was in a situation

---

[1] *La Presna,* 25 November 1941

in which traditional attitudes were no longer appropriate. Chile's malaise had deepened into simple panic. There was, of course, every reason for terror in Santiago. Chile had the longest and least defensible or defended coastline in the world, and it was inextricably associated with countries which had lost the command of the seas. The situation was indeed far worse than the Chileans knew. Over 7–9 December, six American and two British capital ships were sunk or put out of action in the Pacific. British naval power in the Mediterranean was soon to be crippled in three days in February with the immobilizing of two more battleships and four cruisers. For nearly six months the Allies were on the defensive at sea.

This meant that it was impossible for the United States to do the only thing that could have reassured the Chileans – guarantee them against any attack from outside the hemisphere. Argentina, as ever, was ready to fill the vacuum left by United States inaction, agreeing with Chile to renounce the Treaty of 1881 and fortify the Straits of Magellan. This did not, however, signify anything like a step away from neutrality on the part of Buenos Aires. Indeed, Castillo responded to widespread indignation in Argentina against the Japanese attack on Pearl Harbor by cancelling a meeting called by Accion Argentina to pay homage to Roosevelt, at which Armour himself had promised to speak. Ruiz-Guinazu made it clear that he had not agreed to do anything definite to fortify the Straits; he had merely discussed the possibility of doing so with Santiago. Castillo took further precautions to insulate his administration against any popular pressure by declaring a state of siege in Argentina, allegedly because of propaganda being carried on in favour of the countries which were at war with the United States. Armour irritably prophesied that nothing more rational could be expected from Buenos Aires than a 'day-to-day policy of procrastination and evasion'.[1] There was more to it than that, however. Procrastination and evasion were only two of the weapons in the extensive armoury still available to the diplomats of Buenos Aires. The basic objective remained, as ever, Argentine predominance in the southern continent regardless of any complicating considerations of morality, the implications of the world

[1] Armour to Hull, *F.R.U.S.*, 24 December 1941

conflict, or the welfare of the other Latin states. There were, however, two factors which changed things: Argentina had always been able to count hitherto on Yankee forbearance and Latin weakness, but the United States could not be expected to be patient any longer now that it was literally fighting for its life, and the smaller Latin states were now so far from being susceptible to Argentine bullying or enticements that they were openly rallying around Brazil. The most reasonable expectation was that Castillo and his advisers would abandon all hopes of Gaucho empire and align themselves with Washington along with the other Latins, but they never had the slightest intention of doing so. The battle for predominance in the hemisphere had to be fought out to the last. Success for Buenos Aires was only three years away.

Chapter IV

A PLACE OF AMBIGUITY
(1942)

There was no doubt about the way ahead for Argentina. Alignment with the Axis was utterly unacceptable and unprofitable. Alignment with the Allies meant following the lead of Washington and perhaps even of Rio. Compared with these alternatives neutrality appeared to be both rational and positive : it helped to preserve traditional links with Europe by associating Argentina's position directly with that of Spain; it held out prospects of profit by leaving Argentina free to strike the best bargains it could with whoever wanted to buy its products; and it preserved the jealously-guarded diplomatic independence of 120 years. As has been shown, neutrality as a policy made sense only under two conditions: that the United States would allow Buenos Aires to continue to pursue such a line; and that a neutral Argentina should still be able to exercize some dominant influence over other Latin states. There was, indeed, not much to worry about on the first score. The Yankees were more resolved than ever to conciliate their fellow-Americans rather than fight them. There was nothing the United States needed less than an enemy in the hemisphere in 1942. Nor was there real danger of isolation, at least temporarily. Chile and Peru might be lavish in their guarantees of continental solidarity, but neither, especially Chile, intended to do anything that might invite retaliation from an irresistible Japan.[1] The Andean Group was effectively committed to neutrality, for the time being at least.

[1] Dawson to Hull, *F.R.U.S.*, 3 January 1942

What was needed was to exploit this Andean timorousness in a way which would not alienate the North Americans too dangerously. Ruiz-Guinazu attempted to forestall any danger of a confrontation by providing ingenious arguments against any Pan-American Conference. He suggested that declarations of war by the Latin Republics would not be in the real interests of the Allies because they would only invite sabotage of essential industries by Axis agents; that there was no point in breaking off diplomatic relations without declaring war because a breach of relations would lead to war anyway; and that those Latin Republics which had already declared war on the Axis had really breached continental solidarity as recognized at Lima and Havana. Meanwhile, Castillo sought to defend Argentina's position as much as possible by shipping off a further 170,000 tons of wheat to Spain in return for Spanish investment in Argentine Electrical Company bonds; proposing an economic bloc of neutrals comprising Chile, Peru, Bolivia, and Argentina; and, most significantly, doubling the strength of the Argentine Army by retaining the 50,000 conscripts of the class of 1920 with the colours. As a further proof of neutrality, he also decreed that no foreign news reports would be allowed which expressed contempt for governments of countries with which Argentina was not at war.

This new demonstration of Argentine determination was not lost on Brazil. Aranha hastened to tell the North Americans that it would be best to let him handle Castillo himself. In his address to the delegates at the Tiradentes Palace in Rio, Vargas limited himself to defining the position of Brazil without suggesting what any other Republic should do. He gave good assurance to all that: 'Brazil will defend, step by step, her territory against any outside incursions and will not permit her lands or waters to be used as a vantage point from which sister nations can be attacked . . . All measures will be taken to prevent known or disguised enemies from finding shelter within our doors to do us harm and jeopardize the security of the Americas.' Sumner Welles insisted on bringing the position of the Latin neutrals into question. He claimed that 'the predominant issue is solely that those Republics engaged in the war shall not be dealt a deadly thrust by the agents of the Axis ensconced upon the soil and enjoying the hospitality of others of the American Republics.'

This, of course, provoked exactly the kind of show-down that Brazil and Argentina had, for different reasons, both hoped to avoid. Castillo replied indignantly that Welles was mounting a deliberate campaign to misrepresent Argentina. He said that he had given his representatives instructions inspired by 'frank, loyal collaboration . . . Our critics are misleading. They never will be able to show that Argentina is not close to the country that is fighting to defend threatened principles that are also Argentina's principles. . . .' He also repeated the argument that the United States would not be assisted materially by Latin declarations of war. Although Roosevelt himself had already come round to this way of thinking, as the United States lacked the means to defend the coasts of any of its prospective Latin allies, Castillo's parade of benevolent neutrality was not helped by enthusiastic references in the Nazi press to 'Argentina's brave South American fight for independence', or by harsh warnings from Germany and Italy to Brazil against the consequences of a hostile attitude.

Nothing could conceal the fact that the battlelines were already being drawn. Ruiz-Guinazu attempted to compromize by suggesting that the Republics limit themselves to condemning the Japanese aggression, while negotiating with the United States on questions on Lend-Lease and hemisphere defence. Welles countered this by warning that aid would be available only to republics that co-operated with Washington. This kind of talk seemed to make some impression on Ruiz-Guinazu. For a moment on 21 January it seemed possible that Argentina might agree to make a unanimous declaration with the other Republics, severing relations with the Axis, while leaving each Government to adopt the procedure appropriate to its own constitution. This formula was rejected by Castillo himself. Tom Conally, Chairman of the Foreign Relations Committee of the United States Senate, then did everything possible to make an unfortunate situation worse by denouncing Castillo as a gambler who tried to play red and black at the same time and by expressing the hope that either Castillo would change his mind or the Argentine people would change Presidents. Hull repudiated Conally's views, but considered that merely to recommend that the Republics break relations with the Axis would amount to a surrender to Argentina. This was perhaps an even more unfortunate way of putting things, since the surrender was actually made within twenty-four hours. In the interests of unanimity, the other Republics agreed to a formula arrived at by Vargas and Castillo that 'the American Republics, in accordance with the procedure established by their own laws and within the position and circumstances of each country in the actual continental conflict, recommend the rupture of their diplomatic relations with Japan, Germany, and Italy, since the first of these states has attacked and the other two have declared war upon an American country'.

Argentina had triumphed yet again. Complete diplomatic independence had been preserved once more in the most difficult situation the statesmen of Buenos Aires had ever faced. An Argentine victory necessarily amounted to a defeat for the United States. Roosevelt described himself as amazed and confused after seeing what Hull had condemned as a surrender hailed by Aranha as a triumph on the grounds that it had avoided an open breach which might have resulted in Argentina and Chile becoming foci for Axis agents.[1] Nor was Rossetti any happier at having been forced to demonstrate publicly that Chile had to line up with Argentina however much it might profess devotion to Brazil. With tears in his eyes he told a surprised Aranha that he felt that he had been personally responsible for destroying 100 years of friendship between their two countries. However, he promised to expedite delivery of two horses for Aranha's stable as a demonstration of goodwill. The clear winner was Castillo, who once again stole a march on Rio by immediately breaking off economic and financial relations with Axis-owned firms before Vargas had time to act. Santiago and Lima duly followed the lead of Buenos Aires. Brazil, the Latin country most sincerely devoted to the Allied cause, did not actually break off relations with the Axis until three days later, although the breach, when it came, was diplomatic as well as economic.

This was as far as Vargas dared go at that moment. The desperately vulnerable state of Brazil's north-east coastline became more a matter for concern as the Axis ran roughshod over its opponents. By the end of January, British troops in Malaya were retreating to the island of Singapore, and the Germans and

[1] Welles to Hull, *F.R.U.S.*, 24 January 1942

Italians had advanced 250 miles in North Africa, destroying for the second time in nine months British hopes of victory in the Mediterranean. Shipping losses in the Atlantic were increasing enormously. Only tentative Russian advances on land and British air attacks on Europe marred the picture of total Axis triumph. The most reasonable expectation for the future was that the whole of Africa would fall under German and Italian control, making possible once again direct Axis attacks on the American hemisphere. In these circumstances, the aid so far received from the United States was not going to help much. Aranha indignantly protested that the United States was just dumping a lot of trucks in Brazil; that he was being given the runaround; and that Welles could file his Lend-Lease away and forget about it. Although Hull tried to explain that Aranha's 'uncanny intuition was at fault for once', as the United States seriously intended to give Brazil all the aid it could,[1] Aranha's outburst successfully sealed the fate of the mission that Castillo had sent to Washington to negotiate the purchase of arms from the United States. Argentina was not going to get arms that were not available for Brazil. The North Americans hammered the lesson home by restricting exports of virtually all commodities to Argentina. At the same time, the Export-Import Bank made a further $100,000,000 available to Brazil to develop Amazonian rubber and the Itabira iron deposits. Once again, Argentina's limited but anxiously-guarded links with Europe offered a means of temporarily avoiding dependency on the United States, as Spain floated proposals for a $46,000,000 deal, possibly involving the replacement of Axis-controlled air communications between Argentina and Europe by a Spanish airline. Symbolically, on the day that the Argentine mission left Washington empty-handed, the Spanish vessel, *Cabo do Hornes*, arrived in Buenos Aires with equipment for a new explosives factory.

Meanwhile, Brazil was being swiftly propelled into war. German submarine attacks on Brazilian merchant ships began on 7 March. Vargas retaliated by seizing the property of Germans and Italians domiciled in Brazil, and beginning to arrest persons designated by Welles as prospective Nazi agents. The sinkings

[1] Hull to Caffery, *F.R.U.S.*, 9 February 1942

continued. Aranha cut the Italian telecommunications cable between Buenos Aires and Rio to prevent leakage of sailing information between the two capitals. At this point, indiscriminate German U-Boat attacks seemed likely to place Argentina and Brazil in the same camp, when the Argentine tanker, *Victoria*, was damaged by an underwater explosion on 17 April. However, Ruiz-Guinazu insisted that the ship had merely struck a mine, and had not been the victim of a U-Boat. Indeed, the Germans had every reason to avoid any appearance of a quarrel with Argentina. The great quality of Argentine neutrality was that it could not be other than damaging to the interests of the Western Allies. The United States could obviously not spare for a neutral country shipping and strategic materials which it needed most urgently for its own war effort. This meant that Argentina was forced to obtain from elsewhere resources which would otherwise have been available for purchase by the Allies. Argentine wheat poured into Chile in an almost tenfold increase from 1941 in return for greatly increased purchases of nitrates and coal which were important for the Allied war effort. Imports from Brazil almost trebled, including Brazilian rubber which was in critically short supply following the Japanese advances in the Pacific. On 22 April, Ruiz-Guinazu announced that Argentina would repair Allied ships only if their owners undertook to import within six months materials of equal value to that used in the repairs. Hull retorted angrily that material for this purpose had already been made available to the Argentines. His response was a new warning from Ruiz-Guinazu that Argentina would not be selling scrap-iron to the United States, as it needed all available supplies for its own war effort.

Ruiz-Guinazu's determination was strengthened by the arrival in Buenos Aires at this time of a Spanish trade and cultural mission, headed by Eduardo Aunos, ex-chief of Falange espionage in France and now ex-officio Inspector-General of the Falange Exterior in the Americas.[1] Roosevelt attempted to forestall the impending movement of Argentina completely into the Axis orbit by personal appeals on Argentine Independence Day to both Acting-President Castillo and President Ortiz who was now

[1] Allan Chase, *Falange,* G. P. Putnam's Sons, N.Y., 1943, p. 184

awaiting an examination by New York eye specialist, Ramon Castroviejo, to determine if his blindness could be ameliorated sufficiently to allow him to return to office. Roosevelt cabled Ortiz that he 'took pleasure in expressing my confidence that the spirit of resistance to aggression and devotion to democracy so nobly personified in your actions and your utterances will lead the people of your great country, as in the past, along those paths which alone can insure the continued preservation of those political and economic freedoms upon which our American civilisation is based'. To Castillo, he expressed his conviction, 'which I feel sure is shared by your Excellency, that because of their unity the peoples of the Republics of the Americas will preserve that freedom and liberty gained for them by their forefathers which is today challenged as never before in the history of their independence'. From a most unhappy Ortiz Roosevelt received the pathetically brave assurance that: 'The position of the people of my country, in the face of the suffering of those who have been subjugated or attacked, cannot be other than that marked out by the country's historic guiding rules and by the democratic feeling which has ever moulded its institutions . . . her reaction to any unjust aggression must be and always will be that of the most forthright repudiation and of complete solidarity.'[1] Ortiz no longer reigned in the Casa Rosada and knew that he never would again. No direct acknowledgement was received from Castillo, but Ruiz-Guinazu gave a reply of sorts when he publicly congratulated the rulers of Spain for their admirable wisdom in conserving peace and serenity, while Castillo reaffirmed his belief in a neutrality which ensured that 'in the middle of the catastrophe that affects all, we at least save the right of living at peace with all nations . . .'[2] He followed this by prohibiting newspapers from printing or commenting on any speech in Congress relating to international questions or to the state of siege itself or its application on the grounds that 'passionate discussion tends to divide the Argentine family', and that 'professional agitators are trying to spread ideals and principles contrary to national institutions'.[3]

---

[1] *La Presna,* 26 May 1942
[2] *La Presna,* 27 May 1942
[3] ibid., 28 May 1942

There were still limits to what could be done under a state of siege. Argentina had been a representative democracy for nearly eighty years. It had one of the proudest traditions of unfettered and informed news reporting in the world, and Castillo's new prohibition was made idiotic from the start by the remarkable proviso that the new order should itself not be published. On 2 June, Minister of the Interior Culaciatti, a man who could always be counted upon to make a bad policy seem worse, informed Congress that the prohibition was a lamentable error; that there was no intention of preventing the press from reporting anything said in Congress; and that the police must have made a mistake. On the same day, Castillo sought to recover some prestige by admitting that the tanker, *Victoria*, had been torpedoed, nearly seven weeks after he had pretended that it had been mined, and accordingly sent warning notes off to Hitler and Mussolini. The German reply was to extend unrestricted submarine warfare to the east coast of the United States, and to warn Argentina and Chile against entering this new blockade zone after 26 June. Castillo was as determined as Hipolito Yrigoyen ever had been to defend Argentine national dignity against any slights. He immediately ordered the Argentine Navy to be developed on a 'War Plan', although he diminished strongly the impact of this announcement by releasing the class of 1920, which had been kept with the colours since January, on the incredible grounds that the international crisis which had then required the strengthening of Argentina's army, had blown over. The Germans and Italians thereupon hastened to express their lively regret for the torpedoing of the *Victoria*, which they attributed to individual error, denied that they had any intention of offending the Argentine flag and offered compensation.

Castillo had gained a real diplomatic success. He needed one. All the factors which had made 1941 so ominous a year for Argentina still existed, but in intensified form. The United States was still demanding that Buenos Aires and Santiago should take action to cut communications with the Axis; Brazil was still trying to detach Paraguay from Argentina's sphere of influence, this time by an offer of 100,000 contos over six years to be spent on public works; and the nebulous Argentine-Uruguayan plans to fortify the River Plate had finally collapsed, with the offer from

Washington to Montevideo of $17,000,000 to build a huge air base for use by the United States. Chile was a positive embarrassment as a partner in neutrality. President Rios was in fact claiming that his country was of greater service to the democracies than some which had formally broken with the Axis. Even the success of the *Victoria* was wiped out the following day by the sinking of the *Rio Tercero* in broad daylight off the east coast of the United States, four days before the U-Boat blockade was supposed to start.

Castillo was not prepared to equivocate over this peculiarly untimely outrage. Once again Buenos Aires demanded from Berlin apologies, compensation, and a naval salute to the Argentine flag. An initial German reply was dismissed by Ruiz-Guinazu as giving inadequate satisfaction. Culaciatti intervened to cut telecommunications between Buenos Aires and the Axis capitals. This elicited a more conciliatory message from Berlin. On 15 July, Ruiz-Guinazu announced triumphantly that the seas of the world were safe for Argentine ships. Gaucho neutrality had exacted its price again. Castillo and Ruiz-Guinazu could at least draw comfort from the fact that the voices urging them to abandon this course were getting fewer and weaker. Ortiz had finally resigned on 24 June, assured by Castroviejo that there was no hope of his recovering his sight. Damonte Taborda, having already triumphantly survived an attempt by the Federal Interventor of Buenos Aires to dispose of him in a sabre duel,[1] offered his resignation to Congress after a stirring session in which cups of coffee were hurled across the floor of the Chamber. Congress voted against dispensing with his services by 92 to 12. Taborda repeated his offer when Ortiz died on 16 July. He accused Castillo and the military leaders of having appointed anti-Semites to his Committee of Inquiry and of having done everything possible to frustrate its work. Ruiz-Guinazu, in a furious reply, warned the delegates that Argentina was still in the European economic sphere; that the economic, military, and political expansion of the United States constituted a graver

---

[1] Taborda had never handled a sword in his life, while his opponent was an ex-Army officer. However, the vigour of the young Italian's attack more than compensated for his lack of experience.

danger than anything the Germans were doing; and that Washington was trying to lead the other American Republics by the nose. This, at least, had the effect of finally getting rid of Taborda. The Foreign Minister's outburst was not calculated to improve Argentina's external position, especially at a time when Santiago was openly boasting that the United States was helping to build up Chile's military establishment, while refusing arms to its Argentine partner in neutrality. Again the only relief came from Spain. Although Eduardo Aunos had been too busy inspecting 100,000 members of Nazi and Falange-type organizations in Argentina to make much headway with the trade negotiations which had been the ostensible object of his visit, he took time to arrange to have Franco award Castillo the Grand Collar of Isabella the Catholic, Spain's highest-ranking civilian decoration.

News of this great honour reached Castillo just as *La Presna* published an article by the American journalist, Waldo Frank, entitled *My Farewell to Argentina*, in which he claimed that, under Castillo, Argentina 'occupies a place of ambiguity, of cowardice or weakness, because it has not been able to gather together its public and spiritual forces to occupy a place of leadership . . . this nation is living through the greatest moral and spiritual crisis of modern times without morality'.[1] Castillo, whose own moral virtues had been so clearly recognized by Franco, immediately declared Frank *persona non grata* in Argentina. A more emphatic rejection of his views was registered by six members of nationalist organizations who beat Frank up in his hotel room, and who, after being arrested, were subsequently released on grounds of insufficient evidence. A far more significant event had taken place to emphasize Argentina's uncomfortable isolation. Vargas had decided long since that the traditional pro-United States policy of his country was the most rational course for him to follow in the circumstances, as well as being the one which offered the best prospects of challenging Argentine military predominance and preserving his own brand of indigenous Fascism intact and uncriticized. His hand was forced in any case by German intransigence. The wild hunt of U-Boats throughout the Atlantic was accompanied by increasingly belli-

[1] *La Presna,* 31 July 1942

gerent warnings from Berlin that manifestations of anti-German feeling in Brazil must be ended. On 17 August, three more Brazilian ships were sunk, making a total of seventeen lost to U-Boat action since 7 April. Rios helpfully proposed that a strong protest should be made to Berlin, and Guani declared Uruguay's complete accord with any more decisive action the Brazilians might take. It was not long in coming. On 22 August, Vargas formally declared war on the Axis powers, claiming that there was 'no way to deny that Germany and Italy practised acts of war against Brazil, creating a belligerent situation that we were forced to recognize in defence of our dignity and sovereignty, and that of America, and to repel with all our forces. . . .' His decision to declare war produced one surprising reaction : the Government of Portugal expressed its 'fraternal feelings with the noble Brazilian nation at this historic moment of their destiny'. Less surprising was the decision of Argentina to grant Brazil non-belligerent status on 24 August, followed by Uruguay, Colombia, Bolivia, Peru, and Paraguay. The Chileans characteristically extracted the greatest drama from the situation. At a meeting of the Inter-American Defence Conference, the Chilean chairman rose and embraced the Brazilian delegate, claiming that he could remain neither silent nor indifferent, and promising his 'loyal, sincere, effective, and practical collaboration'. Chile might be too cautious to fight, but it was always ready to cheer.

Castillo appreciated that something was required of him more than a cold assurance of non-belligerency. He accordingly told Vargas that he sent his best wishes for 'the definite triumph of principles that animate the juridical traditions' of the American Republics. He also announced in public that 'by defending her neutrality at all costs, Argentina assumes a noble and lofty attitude which should be praised instead of censured'. In a singular exercize in diplomacy on the cheap, he attempted to counter offers by Brazil and the United States of loans of $5,000,000 and $4,000,000 respectively to Paraguay, by cancelling a debt of $2,500,000 owing from Paraguay to Argentina since the War of the Triple Alliance, and since written off as irrecoverable. The erosion of Argentine influence continued. The United Kingdom agreed to hand over to Brazil six coast defence ships being built for the Royal Navy in Brazilian shipyards; Uruguay sent a mission to Brazil to confer on matters affecting the defence of the two countries against a still-awaited Axis attack; and the Export-Import Bank extended a further credit of $14,000,000 for the development of a railroad from Victoria to Minas Geraes. As a final display of no confidence in neutrality, crafty old Justo flew to Rio to take the stand with Vargas at a parade on Brazilian Independence Day and to offer his personal services in the defence of liberty against tyranny.

Once again, Spain provided the only breach in Argentina's isolation. Ruiz-Guinazu had been pressing Aunos to provide military equipment which could be obtained on the scale required only from Nazi Germany. This would merely continue the existing three-cornered pattern in which Spain had been shipping German manufactures to Argentina and transporting Argentine agricultural products and raw materials back to Germany. There were difficulties, however. Argentina was now demanding 'submarines, aircraft, tanks, anti-tank guns, and anti-aircraft artillery', at a time when the Axis was needing even more urgently every weapon that its factories could produce. A compromize was obviously necessary. Walter Funk, Nazi Minister of War Economics, arrived in Madrid to work out the details. On 8 September, Ruiz-Guinazu and Aunos signed a commercial and cultural treaty involving the exchange of goods and services valued at $46,000,000. Argentina was to increase shipments of meat and cereals to Spain. In turn, the Franco regime would provide iron and fruit, lease Argentina a tanker, and build a destroyer and three merchant ships to strengthen Argentina's sea-borne carrying capacity which was already swollen by the purchase of twelve blacklisted German vessels in defiance of United States wishes. In addition, Spain proposed to provide Argentina with a free port in the Mediterranean after the war. The political implications of these arrangements were made completely clear by Ruiz-Guinazu's declaration that ties between Spain and the New World must be strengthened, and that political emancipation did not extend to ideological freedom, delivered the day after Mussolini had affirmed that :

'The great unity of the Axis includes Nazis, Fascists and Spanish Falangists. There is no longer any distinction between Fascism, Nazism, and Falangismo.'

These provocations brought Sumner Welles' patience to an end. He was already infuriated by continued Chilean disregard of warnings that Allied ships were being sunk every day as a result of the activities of Axis spies in Chile, and by the fact that Foreign Minister Barros Jarpa was concealing the extent and significance of Axis espionage from Rios. In the first thoroughly hostile public statement made in the century by a United States diplomat about the governments of two Latin states, Welles attacked the policies of Argentina and Chile :

'I cannot believe that these two Republics will continue long to permit their brothers and neighbours of the Americas, engaged as they are in a life-and-death struggle to preserve the liberties and integrity of the New World, to be stabbed in the back by Axis emissaries, operating in the territory and under the free institutions of the Western Hemisphere . . . [and] their territory to be used by the officials and subversive agents of the Axis as a base for hostile acts against their neighbours.'

Barros Jarpa was in no position to make excuses. He merely stated that the dignity of Chile had been offended, and President Rios cancelled a scheduled visit to Washington, 'because of the unpleasant atmosphere that has been created'. Since it was not the intention of Washington to drive Chile into the arms of Argentina, Roosevelt immediately cabled back to Rios, telling him how much he was 'looking forward to exchanging views with you regarding the implementation of the desire of Chile . . . to co-operate with the United States and other Republics of the Americas in the defence of the Western Hemisphere', and hoping that the visit was merely postponed for a short time. Castillo, indeed, provided excuses, in the usual interminable language of Argentine diplomats under strain, to the effect that Welles's words 'constituted unconsidered affirmations made in imprecise general terms and contrary to the friendly attitude which this country jealously maintains towards the other American nations'. However, Damonte Taborda triumphantly claimed that Welles was merely repeating what he had often said himself in Congress, and Ruiz-Guinazu continued to stress the need for 'Spain and Argentina, which find themselves travelling the same road and have parallel interests . . . [to] be bound by still closer bonds, not with words but with deeds'.[1] Washington's response was to cancel the $110,000,000 Export-Import credit secured by Argentina in December 1940, while Mussolini congratulated the Chilean and Argentine Ambassadors in Rome on having safeguarded their independence alone in the Continent, and expressed his deep regret that America should be fighting Europe at all.

Mussolini soon had particular cause to regret America's participation in the war. In the last quarter of 1942, the fortunes of this most erratic of wars swung once again against the Axis. For almost ten months, only the huge British thousand-bomber raids and the American victory at Midway in June, had seriously marred a picture of otherwise apparently total Axis victory; but, on 23 October, the British went over to the offensive in Egypt in a manner which made it clear that the tide had turned for the last time in Africa. It was obviously time for Buenos Aires to count the odds again. On 4 November, Castillo instituted stricter control over Axis telecommunications, and Ruiz-Guinazu accepted from Ambassador Armour a memorandum on German activities in Argentina, although still professing himself disgusted with Sumner Welles. Castillo was, however, careful to suppress the findings of Damonte Taborda's long-defunct Committee, which had discovered among other things that:

'The Falange is a copy of the Nazi Party – a blueprint to such a point that it made a literal translation of all the principles that Fascism uses to plant the seeds of propaganda . . . The Spanish Falange aspires to set back the clock of history by two centuries, but it will not succeed. But insofar as it is alive, it is a factor of disorder that should be annihilated . . . 22,000 perfectly disciplined men are ready, plus 8,000 Germans from the Nazi Party, 14,000 members of the German Workers' Front, 3,000 Italian Fascists, 15,000 Falangists, and many other thousands affiliated with the Alianza Nacionalista Argentina – all ready to strike.'[2]

On 13 November, the new Argentine Ambassador in Spain, Palacio Costa, told his hosts that Spain and Argentina, being out

[1] *La Presna*, 13 October 1942.
[2] *Informe Confidencial de las Actividades Nazis en la Argentina*, B.A., 1942, p. 55

of the war, should 'at the opportune moment and inspired by
common Christian ideals co-operate to bring about a new world
order based on respect for human personality, family and love of
justice. We are trustees of moral values amidst the thunder of
arms.'[1] It behoved the trustees to show greater discretion than
they had in the past. Anglo-American forces had landed in French
North Africa on 8 November. Rios had immediately sent a
message congratulating Roosevelt, and promised him that 'for
our part we are continuing to increase the production of indis-
pensable materials and we are vigorously combatting all acts of
subversive propaganda and espionage'.[2] Argentina could scarcely
risk doing less. Ruiz-Guinazu accordingly followed Rios with a
cable of his own : 'The Argentine Government and people will
follow with a common interest the efforts of your great and
friendly nation to protect the security of the Americas, and they
repeat on this occasion their faith in the high ideals of neighbourly
continental relations.'[3]

The Argentine message had, at least, this element of substance:
it recognized that the Allied advances in Africa removed any
possibility of an Axis attack on the American hemisphere across
the Atlantic from Dakar. The American Republics could thus
breathe more easily, even though Argentina's leaders had always
doubted the possibility of such an attack. It also meant that there
was now no reason at all to conciliate Axis sensibilities. Culaciatti
accordingly announced on 18 November that strict measures
would be taken to prevent acts detrimental to the individual or
collective security of the American Republics, naming Germany,
Italy, and Japan specifically as countries against whose agents it
was necessary to take precautions, although he later named the
Communists as well. Rios, though, could always outbid Castillo's
Ministers. Five days after Culaciatti's *démarche*, as the Russians
completed the encirclement of von Paulus's forces at Stalingrad,
the Chilean President told the world that he was ready to break
relations with the Axis if the interests of his country and America
made it advisable, but that Chileans would have to defend their

---

[1] *La Presna,* 14 November 1942
[2] Bowers to Hull, *F.R.U.S.,* 8 November 1942
[3] Armour to Hull, ibid.

own country themselves 'as peoples and rulers, safeguarding to the point of exaggeration our national sovereignty and dignity [which] would never permit foreign forces . . . to occupy any part of our territory even with the excuse of protecting us in the presence of a menace from abroad'.[1]

Chile could rely on mere words. Argentina had to produce deeds. On 25 November, Culaciatti ordered the arrest of thirty-eight suspected German agents. On 3 December, he placed all radio and telecommunications between Argentina and foreign countries under the authority of the Director-General of Posts and Telegraphs, prohibited radio transmission in code except for diplomatic correspondence, and limited all foreign delegations to a maximum transmission of 100 words daily. This last provision operated only against the Axis legations, as those of the United Nations could use cables via Brazil and the United States. The German Naval and Air Attaché, Captain Dietrich Niebuhr, was then charged with espionage, and the German Government requested to recall him. The now-confident Allies were not so easily satisfied. On 31 December, the British Foreign Office formally deplored 'the policy of Argentina in remaining in diplomatic relations with the enemies of humanity', and reminded Ruiz-Guinazu that it had been at pains to leave the Argentine Government in no doubt as to its views. State Department at once professed its complete agreement with the terms of the British Note. Argentina was not to be let off the hook merely because it had chosen to acknowledge the fact that the Allies were starting to win at last. The situation at the beginning of 1943 was no better than at the beginning of 1942. The problem for Buenos Aires was still to preserve Argentine predominance in Latin America in the face of mounting pressure from Washington to fall in behind Brazil in a United States-dominated front against the Axis. It now seemed as if Gaucho predominance had been lost already. It was not a case of whether Argentina could hold out, but of whether there was anything to hold out for.

[1] *La Presna*, 24 November 1942

Chapter V

GUNS ACROSS THE
ATLANTIC

What Argentina could hold out for was precisely what Spain was holding out for. A Fascist victory now seemed improbable, but the victory of the United Nations need not mean the end of Fascism. Indeed, it was at least conceivable that the British and Americans might find it desirable to co-operate with the surviving Fascist powers after the war against their quondam Bolshevik ally. In the meantime, the United Nations did not need any more enemies. Spanish dictator Franco thus felt safe in sending to Hitler, on the first anniversary of Pearl Harbor of all occasions, a telegram expressing the hope that his arms 'might triumph in the glorious undertaking of freeing Europe from the Bolshevik terror'. In a defiant speech to leaders of the Falange, as well as to Allied and Axis diplomats in Madrid, Franco praised Mussolini as the founder of the 'social urge and national idea of the Fascist revolution'. He explained that German national socialism and other movements of this kind were not isolated phenomena, but were instead 'aspects of one and the same general movement and mass rebellion throughout the world . . . reactions against the hypocrisy and inefficiency of the old systems'. Franco further claimed that : 'When the war ends and demobilization begins, the moment will arrive to settle accounts and fulfil promises. Then whatever projects may exist now, the historical destiny of our era will be settled either according to the barbarous formula of Bolshevik totalitarianism, or according to the spiritual, patriotic formula Spain offers us, or according to any other formula of the Fascist nations. . . . Those are mistaken indeed who dream of the establishment of democratic liberal systems in Western Europe, bordering on Russian Communism.'[1]

It was a glorious destiny for Spanish-minded countries. Thus, Franco again reaffirmed the bewildering pretensions of Hispanidad. Even more impressive than the role that he had arrogated for the Hispanic world was the fact that he could express such views with impunity and even profit. It was not hard to explain. Five hundred thousand Spanish troops were poised in Spanish Morocco, on the flank of the Anglo-American forces advancing through French North Africa. Their intervention might have brought about the greatest of Allied military disasters. The United Nations therefore had the most practical reasons in the world for placating Franco. Even the news that he had called up the third military class in three months, to reinforce his Moroccan forces or the 100,000-strong Blue Legion fighting in Russia, drew only from United States Ambassador Carleton Hayes an attack on views that Fascism in Spain could not survive the victory of the United Nations and the assurance that the United States would continue to send substantial quantities of petroleum to Spain.

There was much in this to console the Argentinians, though their capacity to combine neutrality with intimidation did not really equal that of Spain's at the time. Their position was clearly about to be weakened still further by the defection of Chile from the neutral camp, despite warnings by ex-President Alessandri that to break relations with the Axis would render Chile a vassal of the United States. Castillo hastily began consultations with Rios, under cover of superfluous denials from Ruiz-Guinazu that any such consultations were taking place. Argentine diplomats and Axis agents worked assiduously to fan Chilean fears, which were always near the surface, that Peru might be planning to avenge its defeat in the War of the Pacific by launching a sneak attack against Chile, as it had previously done against hapless Ecuador. However, Rios's hand was forced by a vote of 30–10 in his Senate in favour of breaking relations. On 20 January, while Deputies began an impromptu parade down the Avenida Bernardo O'Higgins, Rios explained that Chile had complied with

[1] *New York Times,* 9 December 1942

its continental obligations by supplying essential war materials to the United Nations, but that now 'for the good of my country Chile must give ampler support to the friends of democracy . . . This rupture does not represent in any way a repudiation of the people of Italy, Germany, and Japan. We owe much of our economic life, our social organization, our military strength, our cultural growth and our racial formation to the people of those countries.' More importantly, he added that Chile would maintain the most cordial relations with other American republics, 'whatever the course of their politics'; Castillo remarked that Argentina's prudent neutrality would not be affected by the Chilean decision, but it was hard for it to remain unaffected by a further intervention from British Foreign Minister Anthony Eden, who said that he looked forward to the day when all Latin America would be united against the Axis and no longer in relations with the enemy; or by the news that the United States would be allocating $200,000,000 a year to buy strategic materials from Brazil. Understandable motives of prudence impelled Guani, now President-elect of Uruguay, to proclaim while on a visit to Washington that he would lose no opportunity to point out that though Uruguay's neighbour, Argentina, had not broken relations with the Axis, this had not created any ill will between the two Governments, and never would. Uruguayan independence of Argentine threats was strengthened by an offer from the United States of $20,000,000 for public works, which meant military bases on the Rio de la Plata. In the meantime, Brazil drew repressive Venezuela further away from the Argentine net by establishing a joint Chamber of Commerce to facilitate increased expansion of mutual trade.

Argentina's future had never looked less promising. It was evident that Castillo himself was immovably opposed to any action that might improve its prospects. On 18 February, War Minister Ramirez warned Castillo that his policy of neutrality was imperilling Argentina's position in the Americas since the other Republics were receiving increasing quantities of military equipment through Lend-Lease, while Argentina's own military establishment was no longer strong enough even to resist aggression. Castillo adamantly refused to alter his policy, and told Ramirez that if the Army were not strong enough it should be reinforced. Regional commanders were ordered to prepare by 1 March plans for raising a further 30,000 men to augment the normal call-up of 40,000. It was not men of which Argentina was seriously short, but modern equipment to arm them with. This was made the more evident by Rios's decision to send a mission to the United States to buy war equipment, following enthusiastic salutes in his public speeches to both the Red Army and the forces of the United States. At the same time, North American economic sanctions against Argentina were intensified. On 4 March, the Board of Economic Warfare recommended that no government credits should be extended to Argentina; that the effectiveness of the Proclaimed or Black List should be increased by examining proposed Argentine consignees of United Nations goods; and that further measures should be taken to cut off any transaction when it might be of direct or indirect benefit to the Axis. This was followed by a warning from Sumner Welles to all American Republics except Argentina, Chile, and Mexico that Argentina was not a member of the United Nations oil pool, and that American oil tankers were therefore being requested not to load oil products into any tanker under Argentine flag or charter, or to supply bunkers to any tanker or cargo vessel under Argentine flag or charter, without the previous approval of the State Department in each individual case.

Ruiz-Guinazu once again went through the increasingly ineffective responses open to him. Renewed offers of customs union were made to Chile regardless of any departures in that country's foreign policy. Guani was called to order by a decree banning the distribution in Argentina of any Uruguayan papers which dared to criticize the policy of neutrality. In a wonderfully obscure address, Ruiz-Guinazu tried to convey the idea that policy 'arises from Argentina's desire to avoid sterile moments in its constant effort to improve the moral and material conditions of all who make their home in Argentina'. He also promised 'effective collaboration with brother peoples who fight the battle of the ideals of peace'.[1]

This last sentiment was most untimely called in question by Raymond Lavalle, the former Argentine consular attaché in Tokyo, who announced in the United States that Argentina was

[1] *La Presna*, 16 April 1943

functioning as 'the eyes and ears of Japan in the Western Hemisphere'.[1] Lavalle's *démarche* was followed immediately by the report that Brazil had received its seventh submarine chaser from the United States, by a warning from Hull that 'this Government has no intention of depriving American shipbuilders or other producers of essential war material of fabricated steel equipment and diverting it to Argentina in a manner which will work a further hardship on other American interests without very definite assurance that the war effort can be served better by this course than by any other which is open', and by the dreaded visit of President Hinigo Morinigo of Paraguay to Rio. Ruiz-Guinazu frantically expended all his oratorical resources at a ceremony on the ninetieth anniversary of the Argentine Constitution, telling a mass patriotic rally that :

> 'In our midst, the totalitarian state, which absolutely subordinates the individual and the community to the idea of class, or nationality, of race in the normal and juridical order and in that of politics and economics, could never prosper. Essentially pagan and as a consequence incompatible with Christianity, it would lead to the omnipotence of the State in a blind and anxious destiny.'

He welcomed the opportunity to make it clear that the Argentine Government was not pro-Axis. On the contrary, he stated, its peaceful foreign policy was a practical and realistic one 'which should have as a basis universal economy [and] is the only one favourable to facilitate the elements of that resurrection of discipline today in operation in international law, freeing us from the error of subordinating political and juridical solidarity to the acceptance of utopian ideas impossible to apply in the activities of people. . . .' He warned in conclusion that :

> 'Every war has reserved to the victors an economic hegemony under the regime of which survive only those who can maintain their independence . . . Therefore the jealous care necessary in working with the nations whose parallel interests constitute a bond promising success . . . We shall have our place and shall

---

[1] *New York Times,* 20 April 1943

collaborate within the spirit of solidarity to the greatness of America.'[1]

His audience may well have had some difficulty in understanding what the Foreign Minister was talking about. Despite his jovial remark that this was his first chance to deny charges that he was a Nazi, his most enthusiastic popular response came from 10,000 nationalists who paraded down the Calle Santa Fe, chanting anti-United Nations slogans and distributing copies of the Fascist paper, *El Pampero*. What was really significant in Ruiz-Guinazu's speech was its clear debt to the ideas and rhetoric of General Franco, particularly in his assigning to the Communists a quality of totalitarianism which apparently the Fascist did not suffer from, at least to the same degree. Franco, indeed, showed his appreciation of Ruiz-Guinazu's words by hailing Argentina as 'Spain's favourite daughter', and by concluding a further trade agreement by which 100,000 tons of Argentine wheat were to be exchanged for iron products from Spain.

None of this markedly helped the position of the Castillo regime. On 6 May, the national convention of the Radicals voted by 84 to 37 in favour of co-operation with all other opposition parties, calling specifically for the rupture of relations with the Axis, active solidarity with all peoples fighting against Nazi-Fascist aggression, the suppression of electoral frauds and corrupt administration at home, and the nationalization of communications. Alarmed at this threat to conservative interests, War Minister Ramirez again approached Castillo, this time threatening to resign unless he got rid of some of the more obviously corrupt ministers, most particularly the spectacularly crooked and incompetent Culaciatti. Castillo had long since passed the stage at which he possessed any capacity for flexibility, even in self-defence. He blindly disregarded the most elementary dictate of prudence in Latin-American politics, which was never to put at defiance the armed forces of the state. Ramirez first threatened to resign; then he demanded Castillo's own resignation instead. When the Head of State refused, Colonel Arturo Rawson marched 10,000 men from the Campo de Mayo outside Buenos Aires to the Casa Rosada. Castillo threatened 'worthy punishment' for the leaders

[1] *La Presna*, 6 May 1943

of the rebellion, then fled for safety to the minesweeper, *Drummond*, after the First Field Regiment had failed to answer his call to help him fortify the Casa Rosada and defy the rebels. The age of Uriburu had returned.

It was, at first, far from clear what had returned with it. Rawson initially insisted that the Army had no intention at all of inaugurating a revolutionary regime. As he explained the matter to Buenos Aires and the world:

'The people of Argentina may feel confident that the movement initiated and carried through by the Army is purely Argentine and seeks only the welfare and security of our people, being entirely devoid of political inspiration. For that reason, the people must keep order and tranquillity, confident that the new authorities will know how to conduct the affairs of the nation ... The Army has been obliged to turn out, not in revolt, but to comply with constitutional precepts. The National Constitution concedes the Army the right to maintain law and order ... Communism threatens to encamp itself upon our soil, weakened by the lack of social welfare ... The Armed institutions have been neglected and the Armed Forces improvidently dealt with. The education of our children has been far removed from God's doctrines. ...'[1]

It certainly could scarcely have been called Castillo's fault if Communism were indeed encamped upon the soil of Argentina and God absent from its classrooms. The only possible sense in which his autocratic regime had fallen short of the pure ideals of Hispanidad lay in the fact that he had not formally renounced representative institutions. Even Rawson, however, had not done this. The Radicals accordingly felt justified in expressing the hope that the new leaders of the triumphant revolution would 'do the utmost possible to aid the moral and political health of the nation'. Few Deputies were displeased to see the egregious Culaciatti promptly placed under arrest when he and Castillo disembarked indignantly from the *Drummond*. This was only the

---

[1] *La Presna*, 6 June 1943

tip of the iceberg. Rawson himself gave every indication of believing that he had merely intervened in the traditional manner to replace a Chief Executive whose tenure of office was imperilling constitutional institutions and conservative interests. However, the movement of which he had been the respectable inaugurator really constituted the greatest challenge yet to traditional Argentine values. Even as Rawson laboriously explained the non-political nature of his coup, Army Chief of Staff, Juan Peron, circulated to his comrades of the *Grupo Unido Oficiales* a programme of action involving the industrialization of Argentina as a basis for domination of the southern continent, the introduction of a totalitarian regime in the country, and the establishment of an Argentine-dominated New Order incorporating the Andean Republics, Paraguay, and, ultimately, even Brazil. The achievement of this ambition would necessarily require the mobilization of all Argentine resources to the great goal of domination of the South. Industry would have to be developed to reduce dependency on the world outside, and also to provide the base for the resurgence of Argentine military power which would be necessary if the nation were to challenge successfully Brazil's bid for predominance; the cult of the *patria* would have to be fostered as never before; and all aspects of Argentine life would have to be organized as for a struggle for existence.

There was nothing really new about this. Argentine leaders had always seen the historical role of their nation as that of leader of the southern continent, in the same way as the United States was paramount in the north; they had always recognized Brazil as the one southern country which might effectively oppose their leadership; and they had always dreamed of a Gaucho Empire which would be recognized on both banks of the Pilcomayo and along the whole length of the Andes. Argentine objectives had not changed, but their problems had. Argentina's rivals had never been stronger, nor her own resources relatively weaker. There was also the very serious difficulty that Brazil could hardly be challenged at all without aid from the United States, and there was nothing less likely than that the North Americans would provide Argentina with the means of confronting so enthusiastic a partner of the United Nations. It was, indeed, far more likely that Washington would regard Argentina as virtually an ally of the Axis, and consequently increase the level of its assistance to the more co-operative Latin Republics.

The United Nations in general was prepared to hope for some effective conciliatory gesture from the new regime. Ambassador Armour assured Hull that one of the prime motives inspiring the revolution was to put the Armed Services in a position to obtain war materials, and the revolutionaries knew that to gain this, they must break off relations with the Axis.[1] Hull agreed that recognition of the new regime should be accorded as simultaneously as possible by the other American Republics, but he was not yet prepared to say when this should be done. The Uruguayan press pointed out the unfortunate fact that the only newspapers banned so far by the new regime had been Communist ones. Nor was there much comfort to be derived from the fact that all but two of the ministers appointed by Rawson were high-ranking officers of the Armed Services. Armour nonetheless reassured the other Latins that the United States had no intention of bargaining with the new regime over the question of recognition. He admitted that the choice of some of the new Ministers was unfortunate, but he was certain that Rawson would dominate the cabinet.[2]

This was an unfortunate prophecy. Rawson actually resigned the Presidency the following day after a furious all-night session at the Casa Rosada in which he expressed his regret that the triumph of the revolution had failed to unite all Argentines behind the ideal of greatness he had believed it would. The change seemed positively advantageous to the United Nations. The new President was the dry, bristling, little War Minister, Pedro Ramirez, who had first challenged Castillo over the condition of the Argentine armed forces. Ramirez undoubtedly seemed to know what Washington required of him. He immediately forbade the Nazi journal, *Pampero*, to be distributed through the mail; he prohibited the use of secret code in wireless transmissions to the world; he ended martial law, and informed the other Republics:

'The Argentine Republic reaffirms its traditional policy of friendship and loyal co-operation with the other nations of

---

[1] Armour to Hull, *F.R.U.S.*, 6 June 1943.
[2] Hull to Armour, ibid., 6 June 1943.

America in conformity with existing pacts. With regard to the rest of the world, its policy is, for the present, one of neutrality.'[1]

This, at least, held hope of better things to come. What these things might be was made plain by Ramirez's Foreign Minister, expansive, Italianate, Admiral Storni, who promised the world that, 'step by step, Argentina will arrive at the place where it should be in international affairs'. One could only presume from these words that it was not at present in the place where it should be. Storni's further assurance that Argentina's rapprochement with other American Republics would be accomplished 'by acts that will draw us even nearer to our American brothers' achieved the desired effect. Aranha and Vargas told the Brazilian Ambassador in Buenos Aires to enter into diplomatic relations with the new Government at once. Chile, Peru, Bolivia, and Uruguay hastened to follow the Brazilian lead. Armour warned Hull that the Argentine people would react favourably to Ramirez only if they could be sure that his regime was only temporary and that Ramirez would accordingly have to call elections soon. Washington was, however, losing interest in Armour's advice. In any case, the stampede to grant recognition was under way already. Hull duly announced that : 'this Government is entering into relations with the new Argentine Government in the hope and belief that Argentina will co-operate in the same spirit and measure as the other American Republics for the fulfilment of inter-American solidarity in all its aspects, and for the attainment of those general conditions of world order to which all free peoples aspire.'[2]

Hull was right, of course. Withholding recognition was certainly not going to induce any Argentine Government to act in a co-operative manner. Moreover, it seemed safe to assume that any regime must be more flexible and amenable than that of Castillo. The Brazilians had already devised a way to make it easy for Ramirez and Storni to co-operate in the manner desired. Aranha proposed ingeniously that Argentina should begin by breaking relations with Japan because that country had attacked another American Republic, and with Germany for having done the same with respect to Brazil. His advice seemed to make a strong

---

[1] *La Presna,* 8 June 1943
[2] Hull to Armour, *F.R.U.S.,* 9 June 1943

impression on the new men in Buenos Aires. Storni immediately reiterated that Argentina's policy would be based on the closest co-operation with the other American nations. Argentina was closely linked with Britain by ties of friendship, with Spain by common origin, and with France by intellect and culture. It was also, of course, linked with Italy by race and with Germany by arms deals, but Storni naturally did not comment on these associations.

Storni was saying nothing that could fail to give an impression of wholesale commitment to the cause of the United Nations. He made an excellent impression on Armour who was still desperately hoping for the best. Storni told him that he, personally, found dictatorship abhorrent; that he felt that Argentina should have declared war on the Axis long before; and that he had urged his cabinet colleagues to take up arms in the present struggle and not just to 'sit with crossed arms selling grain'. More practically, Storni was prepared to sign an agreement with the United States on the distribution of petroleum resources, and he had already taken measures to enforce the prohibition on the use of code in external wireless messages. In spite of these decisive actions, the policy of the new regime continued to be not so much ambiguous as thoroughly confused. Ramirez abruptly sacked a number of Supreme Court judges, including the vociferously anti-Nazi Miguel L. Jantus, on the grounds that it was necessary to 'restore to the judiciary powers that majesty and prestige necessary to the fulfilment of duty'. It was not clear, however, that this was best achieved by firing judges. He closed the British-owned Buenos Aires newspapers, *Standard* and *La Union*, for having published misinformation about a railway workers' strike, but allowed them to appear again twenty-four hours later subject to strict censorship.

The situation became progressively more confused. Ramirez gave a press conference on 15 June in which he promised that the military regime was 'come not to perpetuate itself but to clean and restore' Argentine political life. The Army had acted 'to find some solution to the sad plight of the people, particularly the working classes, who, weighed down by desperation caused by the impossibility of living, were the victims of the speculation of those lacking conscience'. This might well have served as a reference to

Culaciatti, who was, at the time, reflecting on his past career in the federal penitentiary.The pecuniary honesty, at least, of the new regime seemed confirmed by Ramirez's announcement that he and his ministers would continue to draw only their service pay and would donate their political salaries to good works. However, even the assurance of the new War Minister, General Edelmiro Farrell, that Argentina wanted to draw closer to the great republic of the United States in every way, did not erase the unfortunate impression made by warnings of suppression to the anti-Fascist Italian paper, *Italia Libre*, or by the appointment of Nazi sympathizer General Basilio B. Perine, a director of six German-owned firms, as Mayor of Buenos Aires.

Obfuscation was nothing new among Argentine politicians. Neither was a contrasting clarity of vision where business interests were involved. Storni promised that Argentina would gladly supply the oil needs of Uruguay, Paraguay, and Southern Brazil, thus releasing United Nations tankers to assist more directly in the war effort. The terms he required were 36,000 tons of drilling equipment for 360,000 cubic metres of petroleum products. The Brazilians protested furiously that there was no need for Argentina to break off relations with the Axis as long as it could extract from the United States terms more favourable than had been granted to any other American Republic. Hull immediately instructed Armour to tell Storni 'quite frankly that this Government had not from the moment the proposal was submitted . . . considered it a satisfactory one . . . Obviously this Government cannot enter into an agreement which would provide more favourable treatment to Argentina than to the other American Republics, which freely entered into the supply pool arrangement at its inception'.[1] It was not as easy as that. Armour was not merely displaying his usual ambassadorial caution when he pointed out to Hull that the United States could hardly show itself less conciliatory in dealing with the new regime than it had with that of Castillo. Nor would Armour's own capacity to negotiate be enhanced if proposals which he had himself accepted as a basis for discussion were abruptly ruled out as unacceptable by Washington. The United States had not left itself much room to manoeuvre.

[1] Hull to Armour, *F.R.U.S.*, 16 June 1943

Armour made the point even clearer in an urgent letter to Sumner Welles, in case Hull remained unconvinced:

'I should appreciate your giving your personal attention to the matter dealt with . . . I cannot overestimate the serious effect on our relations with the new Government and especially with Storni, should the Department insist on this . . . How can we expect this Government to co-operate with us on bigger things we look for if we are not willing to go along with them on a proposal which the Embassay was clearly given to understand we had virtually decided to conclude with the previous Government?'[1]

This was, undoubtedly, reasonable; but it overlooked the fact that, broadly speaking, no Argentine Government had ever shown itself willing to co-operate with Washington on anything. Storni was not the first Argentine Foreign Minister to have been lavish with promises for the sake of a bargain. He would be almost the first to make those promises good, if indeed he did. Hull had ample excuse for wishing to tie the Argentines down. He accordingly sent Armour a formidable list of positive steps which the new regime could take. These were to break off relations with the Axis, to cut telecommunications with Axis countries, to institute vigorous and effective control of subversive activities, to impose an efficient blockade plan on trade with the Axis, to control clandestine radio stations, to control press and radio propaganda, to supervize civil and commercial aviation, to control foreign funds, to co-operate on the Proclaimed List, to sever commercial and financial relations with the Axis, to co-operate with the United Nations on shipping, and to conclude the oil negotiations on an equitable basis.

Although there would be no need for the Argentines to go to war after this, there was no sign that they were going to comply. Ramirez suspended the Presidential elections scheduled for 5 September until 'such time as the objectives of the military revolution have been carried out'; suspended the *Standard* again for a day for daring to print an attack on Dr Goebbels; and prohibited meetings of all political parties or other organizations

[1] Armour to Welles, ibid., 18 June 1943

with any political aims. On the credit side, Storni earnestly told the press that the policy of the new regime was and would be 'friendship and co-operation with all nations of America. Every other nation of the world, without exception, which wants to establish future relations with us must bear this in mind . . . Within Pan-Americanism I declare that Brazilian-Argentine friendship is the cornerstone of our foreign policy'.

Talk was cheap in Buenos Aires, however. Hull waited a week, then told Armour again that Storni's proposals on petroleum were unfortunately unacceptable for the reasons already given. Armour tried to reassure him by referring to Storni's approaches to the Brazilians as an earnest of Argentine goodwill, and also to the suggestion, made by Under-Secretary of Foreign Affairs Gache, that Argentina might consider terminating its diplomatic relations with the Government of Vichy France. In practice, all this meant nothing. The Brazilians were counting so little on Argentine goodwill that they were deliberately making approaches of their own to Bolivia to counter Argentine promises about railroads and oil pipelines. Welles accordingly spelt the situation out to Armour in a lengthy reply :

'The change of Government in Argentina makes it desirable to review the objects of our policy with respect to that country . . . the outbreak of war in 1939 with Ortiz as President found the Argentine Government analysing the issues as clearly as . . . any other Government in the Hemisphere. With the untimely and unfortunate withdrawal of Ortiz from the Presidency on account of his illness, Argentine policy, under Castillo and Ruiz-Guinazu, took a new orientation. Its first manifestation was the reluctance to accept the arrangements suggested at the meeting of Foreign Ministers at Havana . . . The meeting at Rio de Janeiro brought out very clearly that the Argentine Government did not see in the Axis aggression the same threat to its own independence and freedom as the other American Republics did to theirs . . . Now a military coup d'etat has occurred. I judge from your reports that you believe this took place as a necessary step to the procurement of armament by the Argentine Army and Navy. So far as domestic issues are concerned the new Government seems no more inclined and probably less to observe constitutional forms and return to democratic political methods than its predecessor . . . In these circumstances the wise policy on our part would appear to be to wait and see what happens . . . It is my opinion that even though Argentina now completely breaks with the Axis this belated action would not be received with cheers on behalf of the other American Republics. They took a real risk during the darkest days of the war. Similar Argentine action now involves very little, if any, risk . . . Inter-American solidarity would receive a severe jolt if Argentina were at this late date to be welcomed into the fold like the prodigal son . . . There is no use in the Argentine Government's telling us what it intends to do; only positive action, under existing circumstances, means anything . . . Nor is there any use in Argentina's attempting a bargain to find out what rupture is worth to us . . . While Argentina cannot expect now to retrieve the past, such action would open to her a useful and constructive path of co-operation with the other American Republics in the future . . . I am afraid that the coming weeks are going to be rather trying ones for you because of my belief that the Government will be feeling you out on all sorts of half-way proposals . . . because of Espil's unwillingness to be forthright the major burden will have to rest upon your shoulders.'[1]

There were a few overstatements in all this. Ortiz may have analysed the international situation with great accuracy, but his Government had shown no more interest in co-operating with Washington than any other Government in Buenos Aires ever had done. Moreover, the other Republics had been more co-operative, not because they were more apprehensive about Axis aggression, but because they were far more vulnerable than Argentina was to United States pressure. The substance of his remarks was prudent and perceptive, however, and its implications were made very clear to Buenos Aires. Ramirez had already dispatched Colonel Carlos Wirth to Washington to inquire about the purchase of arms for the Argentine Services. He was told quite plainly that there could be no talk of Lend-Lease until Argentina broke off relations with the Axis.

[1] Welles to Armour, *F.R.U.S.*, 28 June 1943

Buenos Aires had an answer to that. Finance Minister, Jorge Santamaria, called on Armour to assure him that there definitely would be a break in relations with the Axis very shortly. Armour duly reported back to Hull, recommending again that 'we make a special effort to show our goodwill toward the new Government, and our appreciation of each new step which it takes to co-operate with us, such appreciation of course to take the form of our treating this country in the same manner as that adopted towards others which have co-operated with us'. His faith in the new regime was bolstered further by a surprise visit from Storni, who told him that he intended 'to go to the limit' in a speech which he was going to deliver at a state dinner on 4 July. The Foreign Minister was undoubtedly as good as his word, at least as far as words went. Storni told the assembled diplomats that Pan-Americanism was a geographical necessity; that Argentina would stand alongside the American nations in accordance with her pledges; and that any nation which endeavoured to hamper their solidarity and continental action was not with Argentina but against her. He also claimed that the people of the American Hemisphere were in the process of perfecting the greatest international union in history. Any act of aggression against any neighbour would lead to full and immediate mobilization of Argentina's entire strength. A united America would be invulnerable, even though the effectiveness of this mobilization would be influenced by considerations of distance, resources, and available transport.[1]

It was, of course, uncommonly improbable that any other American Republic was going to be subject to foreign aggression at this stage. Pantellaria had surrendered; the last great Panzer offensive had been halted in the Kursk salient; and the Anglo-Americans were poised for the assault on Sicily that would carry their attack from Africa to Europe. Argentine mobilization was not going to help the United Nations. All they needed was an Argentine breach with the Axis. The value of such a move was diminishing every day, as, consequently, was the price which the United Nations was prepared to pay. Still nothing was happening. Ramirez intensified press censorship by warning papers to 'avoid observations tending to hurt susceptibilities when dealing with

[1] *La Presna,* 5 July 1943

matters connected with the governmental organizations of foreign nations', which made it difficult to print any foreign news at all. He regretfully told Armour that the public and armed services in Argentina were not yet ready for a breach with the Axis; that he was hesitant to act unless he could be sure that his decision would not lead to civil war; and that he would need a month or five weeks to prepare the ground.

This was the familiar Argentine runaround. Ramirez certainly needed time to see if he could do a more favourable deal with the Axis. He had already approached Hans Harnisch, a German military intelligence agent, to discuss the possibility of Argentina's still being able to obtain arms from Germany so as to be able to resist pressure from those American Republics which were demanding a breach with the Axis.[1] This was a truly classical double play. On the one hand, Storni was asking the United Nations for arms so that Argentina could more effectively aid them against Axis aggression. On the other, Ramirez was asking the Axis for arms so that Argentina could hold out against U.N. pressure and create its own bloc of Axis-aligned neutrals. At the same time that he was putting into operation this supreme achievement of duplicity, Ramirez was promising at the annual dinner of the Argentine Armed Forces that he would 'maintain and strengthen the ties of friendship that bind us to all the nations of earth and particularly to those of the Americas'; and causing Armour seriously to question his sanity by the pious statement that the Argentine ideal of happiness was to have sufficient food and a good home so that children could pray for the *patria*.

Ramirez might have looked like a very simple soldier. He was in truth a singularly complicated one. He was surrounded by even more complicated soldiers. After listening to another thrilling account by Storni of how he had defied the Japanese Ambassador by threatening to declare war if Japan acted against any other American Republic, Armour sadly reported back to Hull that the policy of the Ramirez Government during its first month of office was confused and, at times, inconsistent. However, the Ambassador could still see signs of hope everywhere on the horizon. The intensified press censorship was due only to the

[1] Norman Mackenzie, *Argentina,* Gollancz, London, 1947, p. 49.

inexperience of the new ministers; anti-Nazi judges had been sacked merely to purge the judiciary of corruption; the closure of certain war relief committees, most of which had contributed to the Allied cause, was positively helping the United Nations; and it had to be admitted that the Argentine press, which still entirely supported the new regime for various reasons, wielded an influence which the press of Brazil had never enjoyed, even when it had been allowed more liberty than it was at present.[1]

It was difficult even for Armour to pretend much faith in the new regime after Storni had confessed to him that he was very discouraged by the general situation. It seemed that the Germans and Japanese were proceeding so cautiously that Argentina was not being given an opportunity to cause a breach in relations. As Storni now told the story, the Japanese Ambassador had been positively conciliatory, and it was Storni himself who had taken the offensive. Santamaria then added the argument that he had been told that the United States was no longer interested in Argentina's breaking off relations with the Axis, as this would come too late to be of any real use in the war. The dismissal of Mussolini by King Victor Emmanuel on 25 July did not apparently alter the position of the Ramirez regime. Storni merely said that Argentina would continue to wait.

It was, indeed, waiting for the opportunity to implement a major counter-attack against Brazilian attempts to gain a dominant position in the Continent. It had already become apparent that Aranha's offer to Bolivian President, Enrique Peneranda, of a port on the Atlantic at Santos and a railroad to link Santos with the frontier, was not going to bring about any swift change in Bolivia's orientation from the Pacific to the Atlantic. Bolivia's mineral deposits were only 500 miles from the Pacific. They were 1,500 miles from Santos : and two-thirds of the railroad to Santos was still to be built.[2] Bolivia was, in short, still in the market, and Ramirez had made a plan to bring that country completely into the Argentine camp. Edelmiro Farrell and Juan Peron co-ordinated military and political approaches with the exiled Bolivian head of the National Revolutionary Party, Paz

[1] Armour to Hull, *F.R.U.S.*, 6 July 1943
[2] *New York Times,* 8 July 1943

Estenssoro, in Buenos Aires, while awaiting the supplies of arms from Germany that would make a coup possible. Meanwhile, Santamaria told Armour that Argentina was perturbed about the presence of 200,000 Brazilian troops on its frontier.

This did not impress Hull, who expressed his concern that the Argentine Government seemed to be doing nothing except to find excuses for not breaking off relations. Armour suggested feebly that perhaps the Argentines thought they were making a contribution to the common cause by attacking Communism at home, as they regarded the United States and the United Kingdom as bulwarks against Communism despite their wartime alliance with Communist Russia. But Armour's position was completely destroyed by Storni himself, who told Armour that the Government had decided that it had missed the bus and could not break off relations now, as it would be cowardly and undignified to kick Italy when it was down, and Germany would be in the same position in a matter of months. Nor was this the only way in which such an act would be contrary to the Argentine code of honour. Chilean naval officers had suggested to him that Argentina would no longer be able to hold out against pressure from Brazil and, of all places, Paraguay. It was, therefore, necessary for Argentina to remain neutral in order to show that its Navy was not afraid of the new Brazilian equipment, but would fight even with knives if they had nothing better.

The Argentines had more than knives to fight with. They had two good modernized battleships against Brazil's two decrepit ironclads, three splendid new cruisers against Brazil's two relics, and fourteen destroyers, most of which were newer and more formidable than Brazil's fourteen destroyers and corvettes. The only category of fighting ship in which Brazil had a significant superiority was submarine chasers, but these would not be of value in a fleet action. It was not likely that Brazil would attack in any event, when the Brazilians were completing plans to send an Expeditionary Force to fight alongside the Anglo-Americans in Italy.

This was the end. Hull ordered the Office of Economic Warfare to halt all trade with Argentina by revoking all export licences issued for trade with that country before 1 May, and he recalled Armour to Washington for much-needed consultations. Argentine imports immediately fell by 39 per cent. Ramirez did not reply directly. Instead, he called a cabinet meeting to discuss more effective means of combatting Communism, which he described as 'the scourge which threatens to destroy society in its very fundamental bases'. Edelmiro Farrell boasted that Brazil with all its Lend-Lease material could not 'move a ship from one port to another without a United States okay'.[1] At least Brazil was getting the ships. Storni made a last bid for American understanding by writing directly to Hull:

'The situation of neutrality that the Argentine Republic has had to observe up to now, has not been understood ... Argentine ships are operating exclusively in the service of the allied nations . . . Argentina had passed decrees granting the status of non-belligerency exclusively to one of the belligerent parties . . . I cannot fail to point out the concern with which I view future possibilities if, because of the persistence in the present lack of comprehension, Argentina should continue to be denied the materials that it needs in order to increase its production and to arm itself . . . some time ago the Argentine Republic offered to increase shipments of fuels and heavy oils to American countries, for which purpose it sought from the United States the shipment of machinery necessary to increase its productive capacity. Unfortunately, thus far, this request has not been heeded . . . the Axis countries have nothing to hope for from our Government . . . but this evolution would be more rapid and effective for the American cause if President Roosevelt should make a gesture of genuine friendship toward our people; such a gesture might be the urgent provision of airplanes, spare parts, armaments and machinery to restore Argentina to the position of equilibrium to which it is entitled with respect to other South American countries.'

He concluded by remarking that it did not appear that the Argentine Government was acting 'under pressure or threats from foreign agents'.[2]

[1] *La Presna*, 5 August 1943
[2] Storni to Hull, *F.R.U.S.*, 5 August 1943

All this did was to prove that there were no limits to Argentine presumption. Storni was not trying to make a breach with the Axis possible. He was trying to avoid one with the United States. His request was simply that the Americans should arm a country which had not co-operated with them to protect it from the intentions of those which had. The absurdities of Storni's letter were highlighted by one that arrived in Washington on the same day from Counsellor Reed in Buenos Aires. This letter provided an interesting contrast to Ambassador Armour's former optimism. As Reed saw it, the present prospect for Argentine foreign policy was neutrality, and for internal policy, paternal dictatorship with a strong clerical influence, emanating largely from the redoubtable Father Wilkinson, chaplain at the Campo de Mayo. He considered, further, that recent developments had shown the Government to be a full military dictatorship characterized by 'administrative inexperience, bad judgement and confidence; the anti-Communist shibboleth, hypersensitive feelings regarding the honour and authority of the military; ill-conceived initiatives; religious spirit at times verging on the mystical; . . . antipathy to foreign capital already established in Argentina; isolationist neutrality; and what looks like an incipient attempt to create a Southern American bloc . . . This Government is heading for disaster. It is repeating and intensifying the Castillo mistakes.'[1]

Reed's analysis could not have been bettered as far as it went. The new regime, indeed, seemed to have no policy save a more extreme form of the one so unrewardingly pursued by Castillo. Ramirez fulminated about his determination to defend his aims with vigorous firmness; Storni said that Argentina would control immigration among refugees from Nazi oppression, welcoming young migrants willing to establish themselves in Argentina but banning those whose religion might make them undesirable, such as the Jews; and Espil seriously explained to Hull that the maintenance of relations with the Axis was a necessary consequence of Argentina's adherence to a policy of neutrality. The need for such stalling was already fading. Argentina was once again in a position to sell its way out of trouble. Chilean Foreign

[1] Reed to Hull, ibid., 7 August 1943

Minister Fernandez had been induced to visit Buenos Aires on his way to Washington. His visit was timed by the Argentine authorities to coincide with the triumphant announcement of General Diego Mason, Ramirez's Minister of Agriculture, that the United Kingdom had undertaken to buy Argentina's entire exportable surplus of meat for two years. There was now no danger of the American blockade seriously affecting Argentine prosperity. The other Latin Republics were not long in tumbling into Argentina's economic net. Fernandez signed a treaty on 24 August to establish a customs union between Chile and Argentina that would be open to all other American Republics that wished to join. Bolivia and Peru also hastened to conclude trade treaties with Buenos Aires.

Not all Argentina's plans were working so successfully. On 30 August, Hull dispatched a devastating reply to Storni's plea for equipment. He acknowledged that it was profoundly satisfactory to note that the people of Argentina felt themselves indissolubly linked with the other inhabitants 'of this continent of profoundly democratic origins', but he regretted that the Government and people of the United States had been forced to the conclusion that the sentiments of the Argentine people had not been implemented by action which was called for by the commitments freely entered into by their Government in common with the Governments of the other twenty American Republics. Warming to his subject, Hull told Storni, 'I must express my astonishment at your statement that for the Argentine Government to fulfil these obligations would afford grounds to believe that such action was taken under the pressure or threat of foreign agents . . . while the Argentine people were enjoying gasoline supplies equivalent to about 70 per cent of their normal civilian requirements, the peoples of Uruguay, Brazil, Paraguay, and Chile were receiving only approximately 40 per cent . . . Argentine assistance would have been of great value during this very difficult period . . . To furnish arms and munitions for the purpose indicated by Your Excellency would appear to this Government to be clearly inconsistent with the juridical and moral foundations upon which existing inter-American understanding and agreements are based . . . Since Argentina both by its words and actions has indicated clearly that the Argentine armed forces will not under present conditions be used in a manner designed to forward the cause of security of the New World . . . it would be impossible for the President of the United States to enter into an agreement to furnish arms and munitions to Argentina under the Lend-Lease Act.'[1]

This bombshell was considered by the Argentine Cabinet over the next week. Meanwhile, Italy surrendered, and the Chilean Government hailed this event as the best news in four years, while Vargas apprehensively promised the end of another Fascism by announcing that the democratic problems of Brazil would be solved by an appeal to all the social forces in that country. Hull's letter was then made public. Storni resigned, followed by Under-secretary Roberto Gache. In one sense, he could hardly have been blamed for the failure of his part in the conspiracy to obtain arms from either or both the belligerent parties; but his failure had been particularly resounding. Ramirez attempted to rally his discomfited officers by throwing a champagne lunch at the Casa Rosada for 1,000 serving officers from the rank of major upwards, at which he manfully placed the blame for everything that had gone wrong upon Storni's shoulders :

'. . . our sister nations may have the absolute certainty that our nation is firmly linked with their destinies and will know how to honour its historic past . . . the historic traditions of a nation cannot be diminished or pledged by the confidential statements of any official.'[2]

There was always the second string to the bow, anyway. Ramirez now instructed Storni's successor, Colonel Alberto Gilbert, to press on with the negotiations for an arms deal with Germany, while applauding the statement of the Spanish Ambassador in Buenos Aires, Don Jose Munoz Vargas, that Spain's neutrality had enabled that country to live in absolute normality amid a world at war.[3] Ramirez, indeed, went so far as to speak himself of 'the generosity and grandeur of the sentiments which determined Argentina's course', and promised to remain faithful to a policy of 'fraternal love' for all South American peoples, and peace and friendship

[1] Hull to Storni, *F.R.U.S.*, 30 August 1943
[2] *La Presna*, 13 September 1943
[3] ibid., 20 September 1943

with all other peoples of the world, at the same time that he continued the intimidatory build-up of Argentine military forces on the border of Paraguay. He then packed Rawson off to Rio as Ambassador, to get him out of the country, and closed down some 200 liberal newspapers for their failure to support his measures.

The Storni fiasco was not the only rebuff which Ramirez was forced to absorb in this supremely critical stage of Argentina's bid for continental supremacy. The economic base of his policy had been further strengthened by the decision of the British Government to buy Argentina's entire exportable surplus of eggs for the next two years. But this gratifying deal was followed by a quite unexpected note from the British Foreign Office denying that the egg deal had any political significance, because 'while His Majesty's Government naturally hopes for continuance of the long-established friendships and commercial intercourse between Great Britain and Argentina, they remain disappointed at the determination of successive Argentine Governments to maintain neutrality during the struggle which so potently threatens the principles for which your founders fought. It has, moreover, never been understood in Great Britain why Argentina, alone of the Western Republics, has failed to give effect to the recommendations of the Rio Conference . . . with the result that Axis nations are still free to conspire on Argentine soil against the interests and security of the United Nations . . . We trust that in the international sphere, the Argentine Government will, at an early date, range herself whole-heartedly on the side of the freedom-loving nations.'[1]

Argentina was by now accustomed to settle for cash in default of credit, but the British accusations could hardly be ignored, especially as they were immediately followed by mass strikes in Argentine cities in favour of alignment with the United Nations, and also by the recall to Rio of Brazilian Ambassador Rodriguez Alves, allegedly to visit a sick nephew, but in reality for consultations with Aranha. Alberto Gilbert duly lamented that 'it is still considered possible that security and interests of the United Nations may be conspired against from our territory. The most careful attention had always been given to any claims of enemy activities and all necessary measures had been taken to

[1] *New York Times,* 27 September 1943

investigate their veracity and to punish any act found susceptible to prejudice Anglo-Argentine relations . . . Not one known incident of this nature has occurred lately, and if, despite measures taken, such an incident should occur, punishment will be swift and inexorable.'[1] Ramirez solemnly toasted in Concordia 'the United American Republics forming a firm and solid bloc'.[2] Meanwhile, he took further precautions against unfavourable publicity by appointing to the Press Secretariat two of his most reliable Fascists, Leopoldo Lugones, an experienced torturer of political prisoners under Uriburu, and Martin Cobo, a vigorous censor of anti-Fascist films.

The pace of Argentina's economic counter-offensive was quickening. Ecuador followed Peru and Chile by signing a trade agreement with Buenos Aires. Even the Commodity Credit Corporation of the United States began surreptitiously buying feed grains in Argentina. Then the United States Ministry of Agriculture agreed to buy one million pounds of Argentine cheese, one and a half million pounds of poultry, and all Argentina's exportable surpluses of sunflower seed oil. Economic ties with Chile were strengthened by Fernandez's assurance that there was nothing that he desired more for Chile than a customs union, while Gilbert offered to direct Argentine capital investment into Chilean public works. Meanwhile, Ruiz-Guinazu flew to Spain as Ambassador to complete the arms deal that would place military predominance securely once more in the hands of Buenos Aires. One minor error of timing occurred. Ramirez somewhat impetuously yielded to clerical influence and closed all Jewish newspapers in Buenos Aires on 13 October. This drew from Roosevelt a sharp note that he 'could not forbear from expressing misgivings as the adoption in this hemisphere of action obviously anti-Semitic in nature and of a character so closely identified with the most repugnant features of the Nazi regime'.[3] There was obviously far too much at stake to be jeopardized by premature action of this kind. Ramirez promptly removed the ban. Two days later the arms deal was completed. Spain was, of course, to be the

---

[1] *La Presna,* 29 September 1943
[2] ibid., 2 October 1943
[3] *New York Times,* 16 October 1943

intermediary. Argentina would ship agricultural products to that country, as before. In return, Spain would provide everything needed for modern warfare to the best of its ability, and Germany would make up any deficiencies in Spain's capacity to meet Argentine requirements. Still firmer measures were taken in Argentina to guarantee secrecy. All wire and radio communications media were placed under the control of War Minister Edelmiro Farrell, on the grounds of their being essential for national defence, and foreign correspondents were required to submit all dispatches for approval by Farrell's officials. Meanwhile, Gilbert soothed the other Republics with assurances that the war 'has opened our eyes to the continental possibilities in South America . . . We want to be friends with everybody, and we'll break only with those powers which injure our dignity or offend our sovereignty'.[1] Then, the cat got out of the bag.

Ramirez had sent as his agent to Germany an Argentine national of German descent, Osman Hellmuth. Hellmuth was travelling in the guise of Argentine consul in Barcelona. He was, however, intercepted by the Allies at Trinidad. Ramirez desperately tried to evade responsibility after Hellmuth had been identified as a Nazi agent. He began, reasonably, by sacking Hellmuth. Then, he had the crew of the *Graf Spee*, who had been enjoying considerable liberty in Buenos Aires, rounded up and placed in military prison camps, on the grounds that they had been taking advantage of his leniency to make their escape. Foreign Minister Gilbert also attempted to repair Argentina's international image. He explained at Asuncion that the diplomatic position of Argentina was perfect and absolute neutrality. However, he was apparently not altogether satisfied with this definition himself, as he expressed the view the following day that there was no term in the vocabulary of politics which adequately defined the position of Argentina in world affairs.

This might well be the case; but diplomatic difficulties did not halt the spread of the Gaucho economic empire. Paraguay joined Ecuador and Peru in signing a trade agreement with Argentina, and joined Chile in accepting a commitment towards eventual customs union. Even mighty Brazil could not afford to stay out.

[1] *La Presna,* 2 November 1943

Trade talks between the two Latin giants began in Brazil on 1 December. The Argentines were no more reluctant than before to employ judicious intimidation. An early and satisfactory conclusion was ensured by freezing 29,000,000 pesos' worth of Brazilian credits on the eve of the talks.

The final detaching of Paraguay from Brazil and its effective incorporation into the Gaucho economic bloc proceeded apace. President Hinigo Morinigo was dazzled on his arrival in Buenos Aires from La Paz by the most lavish reception in Latin history, including a gigantic military parade down the Avenida Nuevo de Julio by 100,000 reservists. The two Presidents emotionally exchanged toasts. Ramirez swore that Argentina's ideology was crystal clear, and nothing should divert its course. Morinigo said that the Latins were one race and that Argentina was Paraguay's beloved brother. Meanwhile, Gilbert arranged the signing of a trade agreement that would link Paraguay inextricably with its giant overlord. Postal facilties between the countries would be improved; an airline opened, and a highway completed linking Asuncion and Buenos Aires; and Paraguay would be given the facilities of a free port in Buenos Aires by declaring certain docks and warehouses a Paraguayan zone. It was also agreed again that the ultimate objective of both countries was to complete a customs union.

There was still one more blow to be struck before this year of astounding Argentine recovery was ended. On 20 December, Paz Estenssoro and his military henchman, Guilberto Villaroel, made their bid for power in La Paz. The coup was equipped by Germany, trained by Argentina, and financed by Spain. It came at a time when Brazil was powerless to intervene, because its Expeditionary Force was about to sail for Italy, and when the other countries of the region had already linked their economies with that of Argentina. Estenssoro duly seized power, established a Fascist-type regime, and revoked the previous Government's declaration of war against Germany. Britain, Brazil, and the United States refused recognition of the new Government, and Sumner Welles furiously burst into print to denounce what he termed the 'Fascist blot on the Americas'. Even Welles had nothing to suggest in the way of positive action against what was happening in South America. He warned that: 'In the U.N.R.R.A., in which Argentina, as one of the great food-producing countries of the world, is vitally interested, the Argentine Republic, as a nation which has refused to sever its ties with the Axis Powers, has no place. For the same reason, she will have no voice in the shaping of the peace settlements . . . ' He was careful to point out, though, that 'unless the present Argentine dictatorship gives direct aid to the enemies of the New World, even the semblance of outside pressure should be avoided. Such a pressure would inevitably arouse a nationalistic reaction on the part of the Argentine people in favour of any Argentine Government . . . ' It was, also, all too likely to provide an opportunity for 'Colonel Peron, a young, forceful, fanatical Fascist, and bent upon becoming an Argentine dictator'. Welles's conclusion was effectively that all that could be done was for the United States to 'rightly regard as abhorrent the present Argentine Government and all that for which it stands'.[1] Buenos Aires could put up with unlimited insults. It was sufficient indication of the bankruptcy this time of United States policy that the Americans could consider only moral pressures against the southern maverick. There was, indeed, no reason except that of morality to apply any pressure at all. With the Allies established in Italy and the Russian winter offensive rolling on, an Argentine breach with the Axis could have no effect whatever on the outcome of the war. The significant fact was that Buenos Aires was triumphing yet again in its endless duel with Washington. Almost all the ground lost since Pearl Harbor had been recovered. Paraguay and Chile were on the way to becoming virtual economic satellites; Bolivia had become an ideological ally; Peru was linked by trade agreements; Brazil and Uruguay were under pressure. The Gaucho magic had worked again. The world could not do without Argentine agricultural products. As long as the Argentines could find the food, they did not need guns to make their will effective.

[1] *New York Times,* 29 December 1943

Chapter VI

THE MANDATE OF NOBLE
PRINCIPLES (1944-1945)

Economic strength and a total disregard for world opinion had
preserved Argentine independence once more. The second factor
had always been present. The first had been created by unflagging
cultivation of every commercial opportunity over the past two years.
Gilbert had been saying no more than the truth when he had told
foreign diplomats that the war had opened the eyes of Argentina's
leaders to the continental possibilities of South America. Argentine
trade during the war years had increased in value over five times
with Bolivia and Chile, four times with Uruguay, and three times
with Peru. Latin America as a whole accounted for 22·4 per cent
of Argentina's trade in 1943, compared with 8·3 per cent in 1938.
Even more important was the extent to which the Argentines had
been able to reduce their vulnerability to United States economic
pressure by expanding markets outside the hemisphere. Britain
took 35·6 per cent of Argentine trade in 1943, and the United
States only 24·3 per cent, at a time when comparative figures for
the whole of Latin America were 11·6 and 55 per cent. Trade with
Switzerland had increased by eight times, with Spain and Portugal
by sixteen times, and with South Africa by thirty-six times. The
result had been a vast improvement in Argentina's foreign
exchange position. Reserves had risen by only 24·5 per cent
between 1941 and 1942, compared with a Brazilian rise of 147
per cent. Between 1942 and 1943 the comparative figures were
47·7 per cent and 89 per cent. The financial gap between the two
Latin giants, which had narrowed dangerously between 1941 and

1942, was widening again. The United States blockade had failed. Another great Argentine boom was under way. Declining growth rates would inevitably force countries like Chile and Peru into ever-greater dependency on the only Latin country that could offer them ample markets and a source of investment capital. Moreover, growing exchange reserves meant that Argentina could afford to industrialize. Machine tools from Spain and Germany were already beginning to produce arms to render it independent of Lend-Lease. All that was needed for the final triumph of Gaucho diplomacy was the sense of timing and the indifference to morality which had never yet failed the leadership in Buenos Aires.

Surprisingly, these very qualities began to desert Ramirez and Gilbert now. The gamblers were demoralized by their own success. Ramirez had worked steadily to strengthen his dictatorship while discussions on the arms deal went on with the Germans in Madrid. He introduced a new press prohibition excluding all United States advertizing, in order ostensibly 'to ensure that the free expression of ideas shall not be affected by commercial interests'; he dissolved all activist political groups in Argentina, 'to bring about a truce in action of this kind while the country is under guidance'; and he declared that all goods necessary for national defence were liable to expropriation. All these totalitarian measures greatly heartened the European Fascists who saw sympathetic regimes being established across the Atlantic at the same time that their own power base in Europe was disintegrating. It did not alter the fact that Germany now needed all the arms it could produce for its own defence. The negotiations in Madrid broke down. Ruiz-Guinazu resigned, for the same reasons that Storni had left office. Ambassador Armour was amazed to be told by Gilbert that Argentina would break off relations with the Axis before the end of the week.

Ramirez could simply see no other course open to him. Two days after Gilbert had informed Armour of this new departure, he formally broke off relations, allegedly 'because of proofs provided by the Federal police regarding the existence of a vast espionage network to the detriment of countries linked to us by traditional ties and friendships . . . The seriousness and persistence of the acts ... make it necessary to redefine Argentine policy in the light of new circumstances.'[1] This was ironic coming from a dictator who had just been conspiring unsuccessfully with agents of that same vast espionage network to obtain arms with which to intimidate those countries linked to Argentina by traditional ties and friendships. Its effrontery almost convinced Franco that Ramirez might be serious. He hastened to reaffirm the neutrality of Spain, while diplomatic activity in Madrid reached a new peak of intensity. Excitement in other Latin capitals also redoubled when Ramirez closed Nazi newspapers, recalled Argentine ships to port, and warned the Axis against taking any reprisals. In Buenos Aires itself a fascinating ideological debate developed. Ambassador and ex-President Rawson congratulated Ramirez on the break, which he claimed fulfilled one of the fundamental principles of the military revolution, which was to 'return to the nation with all firmness its historic mission among the Americas'. Ramirez responded with impressive logic that the revolution had no purpose other than the recovery and strengthening of Argentina's sovereignty. It could never have had 'as one of its purposes, the rupture of relations with one of the belligerent parties, since it has always been the traditional policy of the country to maintain peace and harmony with all the people of the world'. Rawson thereupon resigned, repeating his claim that 'the revolution was made to restore Argentina to the community of her American sisters through the faithful fulfilment of her pacts and international treaties. Not to proclaim this now would be to detract from its historic importance ... Today, at the moment when I believed myself spiritually nearer to your Government, I find that I am even more distant than ever.'[2]

It was not only Rawson who was confused : So were Peron and his colleagues of the G.O.U. Fears began to spread that Ramirez might be considering making the break effective. His action had already given impetus to a groundswell towards war with the Axis among Argentina's Latin neighbours. Uruguay and Venezuela made pre-concerted declarations of war on 15 February. In the meantime, Ramirez ordered the arrest of the German and

---

[1] *La Presna,* 27 January 1944.
[2] *New York Times,* 30 January 1944.

Japanese Military Attachés in Buenos Aires, General Frederick Wolf and Rear Admiral Katsumi Yukeshito. This was too much for the officer corps. Gilbert was abruptly turned out of office after rumours began to spread that Argentina might be following Uruguay and Venezuela into war. He was replaced by the former Agriculture Minister, General Diego Mason. Ramirez tried to regain support by denying any intention of going to war, and by releasing Wolf and Yukeshito on the grounds that their freedom could no longer affect the investigation of Axis espionage. He then began to veer towards ideas of restoring something like representative democracy to Argentina. It was evidently time to replace him. On 25 February, Ramirez was arrested by Army officers while preparing a speech announcing his intentions of reintroducing liberal institutions into the country which had had a longer and deeper experience of them than any other south of the Rio Grande. The grounds for his removal were given at the time as ill-health brought on by the fatiguing labours of his office, although Ramirez himself explained later that he had really resigned 'because of a campaign of falsehoods which made my continuance as President incompatible with my dignity and honour'.[1]

Ramirez was succeeded by iron-willed General Edelmiro Farrell, who thereby helped to confirm the Argentine tradition that the Ministry of War was the next stop to the Casa Rosada. Farrell's first diplomatic act was to re-affirm Argentina's ties with Spain, which had been in a confused state ever since Ramirez had caught Franco off balance by breaking relations with the Axis. Any other diplomatic initiatives on the part of the new dictator would obviously have to wait until the world outside had made up its mind whether or not to recognize him. For there could be no question at all that Farrell's succession to power represented another and a mighty step by the Republic of the Pampas away from alignment with the United Nations. It had been possible to hope for better things from Rawson, simply because he was a change from Castillo, and because there seemed only one way to satisfy the demands of the Army which had brought him to office. It had also been possible to have hopes of Ramirez, if only

[1] *La Presna*, 11 March 1944

because he had been apparently able to command a situation which had been too much for the ingenuous Rawson. Nobody could have hopes of Farrell. That was made sufficiently obvious by the fact that he had come to power precisely to prevent Ramirez from following up the first initiatives made by any Argentine leader since Ortiz which were actually gratifying to Washington. To make things worse, his past history suggested that he combined the more formidable qualities of Yrigoyen and Justo. He was shrewder than Castillo, more efficient than Rawson, and tougher than Ramirez.

The United Nations met challenge with confrontation. Britain, Brazil, and the United States all withheld recognition from the Farrell regime, on the grounds that, like that of Villaroel and Estenssiro in Bolivia, it was simply a manifestation of the spread of Fascism in South America at the very moment of the defeat of that movement in Europe. Farrell replied imperturbably that he regretted any break in relations, but that Argentina would await the future with quiet confidence, convinced that truth would eventually triumph. He soon had reason for his confidence. President Rios of Chile reviewed the situation yet again, weighing Argentine economic power and rearmament against past Chilean promises to Rio and Washington; noted the imminent departure of the Brazilian Expeditionary Force for Italy; and opted, as he and his predecessors had always done, for alignment with the power his country seemed to have most reason to fear. He accordingly assured Farrell that Chile considered that the new regime was merely a continuation of that of Ramirez (which it most evidently was not) so that diplomatic relations between the two countries had never been interrupted. Farrell replied warmly that this gesture of recognition would never be forgotten. Bolivia and Paraguay then followed the Chilean example as expected, using the same formula of denying that there had been any interruption in their relations with Buenos Aires. Farrell then proceeded to link his country even more closely with Chile by re-opening the Andean Railroad which had been closed since 1934. Rios in return removed all restrictions on the sale of coal to Argentina from Chile's mines in the Magellanes, so that Argentina's new arms industries should not lack supplies of fuel which would otherwise have gone to the United Nations. Santiago, once so emphatically aligned with Rio, was now back with Buenos Aires more firmly than ever.

Rio itself was, of course, less willing to co-operate. There were, for a time, rumours in the Brazilian capital that the least aggressive of Latin powers might be preparing to fight for its vanishing dream of continental predominance. Young Brazilian officers lamented the fact that they had not made the most of their brief moment of technical superiority to sweep across the Rio de la Plata and settle Argentine pretensions, for a generation at least. It was even questioned whether the Brazilian Expeditionary Force should not be kept at home as a precaution against Gaucho aggression. This was only nostalgia. Brazil had never possessed the manpower necessary to conquer and subdue a country as vast as Argentina, and the great disadvantage of having one's arms supplied by the United States was that it meant that they could be used only in a North American cause. Lend-Lease hardware was for fighting Germans, not other Americans. The Argentines, by contrast, would be under no such restriction on the use of whatever weapons were now coming off the assembly lines in Buenos Aires and Cordoba. It was thus not surprising that even Aranha should have been uncertain how best to deal with the new regime. He began resolutely enough by arranging a deliberately discourteous reception for Gilbert's successor when he visited Rio, but the Argentine Fascists always had an uncanny knack of benefitting by someone else's timely death. Farrell was saved from embarrassment by the sudden demise of Brazilian Ambassador, Rodriguez Alves, just as Castillo had been aided by the deaths of Ortiz and Justo. He immediately declared three days of mourning throughout Argentina, and offered Aranha the use of Argentina's newest cruiser to carry the Ambassador's body back to Rio. Aranha could hardly refuse so magnificently Latin a gesture, any more than he could accept it without some show of courtesy and cordiality on his own part towards the new regime. Rio and Buenos Aires were talking again.

Farrell's diplomatic finesse made him a worthy successor of Saavedra Lamas or Justo. His domestic programme made him an equally worthy follower of Ramirez. The new regime was just as confused and erratic at home as the old one had been. In one area there was admittedly no confusion. Nationalization proceeded steadily. Argentina was certainly becoming more Argentine. The Primitiva Gas Company was expropriated, and all grain elevators declared public utilities. Civil liberties under the new regime expanded and receded in a truly fascinating manner. Farrell, for example, removed the ban on wireless reception by the Associated Press on 3 March, and proscribed broadcasts by the United Press on 18 March. He invited the Argentine press to print ideas on future foreign policy on 16 March, and prohibited on 27 April all press discussion of matters relating to freedom, political constitutions, or religion. He granted political opponents of his regime the right of broadcast on 3 April, and withdrew it on 14 April. However, two decrees that remained in force were those banning all May Day parades and all news broadcasts emanating from the United Nations.

All indications were that Farrell simply did not know what course to follow in domestic policy; but the lines of his defence policy were coming through quite unmistakably. The rumblings of Argentine rearmament grew louder every week. On 12 May, it was reported that Argentina was buying 1,000,000 pesos' worth of military equipment from Spain. A week later, the standing army was effectively doubled in size by a decree that students conscripted into the forces would be required to serve for twelve months, instead of for three as before. This was followed by the creation of a crack new Seventh Division, stationed, to the alarm of the Chileans, on the Andean border. Chilean concern was increased by the way in which the name of the nationalistic tyrant, Rosas, began to receive laudatory mention in speeches by Argentina's new leaders; by Colonel Juan Peron's declaration that war was an inevitable and beneficial social phenomenon, and that Argentina must organize a 'structure of total war'; and above all by the construction of enormous barracks on the Argentine side of the Patagonian border, where the new Seventh Division was being stationed.

There was no talk now of Argentines fighting for their honour with knives in their hands. On 4 June, Farrell began instead to refer vaguely to some new 35-ton tanks supposed to be coming 'in large numbers' from factories built in Argentina with Spanish and German equipment. He gave further details of this new development a fortnight later, stating that no less than eighty factories were producing the new tanks. Meanwhile, a new barter deal was completed with Spain, involving the exchange of 1,000,000 tons of wheat, 10,000 tons of cotton, and 500 tons of tobacco from Argentina, in return for 82,500 tons of iron and steel to be delivered by Spain before 4 December and a further 60,000 tons annually thereafter. On 26 June, a National Defence Council was created in Buenos Aires, and the world was informed that the aviation factory at Cordoba was now producing the first all-Argentine aircraft for Colonel Peron's new Air Force.

The continent was taking fright. Ecuador hastened to recognize the Farrell regime and to sign the inevitable trade agreement. Washington and London recalled their ambassadors for consultations. Farrell reassured his fellow-Latins that Argentina aspired only to national recovery, to which end it would turn all means, and had no aggressive intentions towards anybody. His comforting remarks were followed the next day by a display of Argentina's new military hardware which could only have been intended to give a distinctly contrary impression. For three hours, the striking power of the Argentine Republic passed in review before the junta of the military revolution. Most attention was attracted by the new tanks, interestingly named *Tigers*, or *Nahuels*, to use the Indian term. Fast, heavily armoured, and carrying as their main armament a 75-millimetre gun and four machine guns, they were fully comparable with their opposite numbers in the British or United States Armies. Ten of these formidable weapons passed the saluting base, followed by fifteen lighter tanks; and Farrell, affectionately resting his hand on a stationary *Nahuel*, remarked that there were plenty more where they came from. Ski troops formed another part of the parade, as a warning to Chile that the Andes were no longer a barrier. Overhead passed 284 aircraft, including seventy-eight Focke-Wulfs and eighteen of the local Cordoba products, six of which drew eighteen gliders carrying troops of the airborne regiment that Castillo had called into being after the German attack on Crete.

Nobody could be sure just how formidable a military capacity these units represented, of course, because nobody could be sure exactly what was coming out of Argentina's new factories to supplement them. The parade was by any count an astounding demonstration of the will and the resources of the new rulers of Argentina. They had bridged the gap. Denied Lend-Lease and Nazi aid alike, they had been able to stage a show of force more impressive than that seen elsewhere in the southern continent. The Brazilians, ever realistic, got the message at once. Aranha took it for granted that the race had been lost. He now appealed to Farrell to use Argentina's new-found strength for the security of the American Republics as a whole. There was to be no question of rivalry in arms between the two Latin giants. The Buenos Aires parade had done exactly what it had been supposed to do.

The armed forces of the great Latin American states had always been of primarily symbolic significance. Argentina, Brazil, and Chile had been too strong since the turn of the century to be challenged by any of the smaller states, singly or even in combination. They had, however, always been too weak to be able to make war effectively upon one another. Their military establishments accordingly existed essentially as indices of their respective material and diplomatic resources, to the extent that they did not merely show how successful the military in each country had been in extracting finance for its own ends from the Government. But Argentine power had always been in a rather different category from Chilean or Brazilian. It was not just that Argentina was always the strongest of the Latins. It was, rather, that Argentina alone gave the impression that it might really be tempted to deploy its strength against its neighbours. The Argentines were the most fanatically nationalistic of the Latin peoples. They were also the only ones with serious territorial ambitions, and were the only ones with the resources to implement these ambitions. All these considerations gave a threatening quality to the great Argentine rearmament which had been lacking in the case of Brazil. No one really thought that Edelmiro Farrell was thinking of war with Germany when he encouraged young Argentines to be ready to die for the *patria*. Argentina's neighbours might well ask themselves on whose territory the legions of the Pampas were supposed to do their dying.

They need not have worried. Argentina was not going to fight anyone. Argentine rearmament had three points of origin. It served notice to the world outside that no Brazilian-led combination of Latin states could coerce Buenos Aires; it both strengthened and gratified the armed forces on whose support the Farrell regime depended; and it responded to a quite genuine upsurge of nationalism, in the face of the most serious challenge yet made by Washington to Argentine hegemony in the southern continent. Argentina was literally in a state of siege. The North Americans were still withholding recognition. Hull responded to the great military parade in Buenos Aires by furiously denouncing what he chose to term Argentina's desertion of the Allied cause. Farrell, always a man to meet a challenge head-on, responded by recalling his ambassador from Washington. Meanwhile, his new Foreign Minister, General Orlando L. Peluffo, rejected Hull's accusations before an audience composed of representatives of those countries which had recognized the Farrell regime. He insisted that Argentina had indeed fulfilled all its international obligations; that it had not broken continental solidarity; that it was not supporting the Axis; and that the Argentine people and Government were firmly and amicably united.

Hull replied furiously that specious pleas by parties to the desertion of the Allied cause did not call for any comment. Peluffo admittedly was merely talking propaganda. Argentina had consistently failed to fulfil even those obligations which it pretended to recognize; it had devoted its energies since the time of Rosas to ensuring that no continental solidarity should be allowed to exist save under Argentine domination; and it had both traded and conspired with the Axis. Hull's own position, however, was little more tenable. The United States was itself a party to the disunity of the hemisphere by its decision to coerce a Government which was extremely unlikely to submit, and which four other Latin Governments had already recognized.

President Rios of Chile, indeed, expressed his deep regret at the split between Washington and Buenos Aires on the day after Hull's rejection of Peluffo's claims; but the split went wider even than the hemisphere itself. Authorities in London also found themselves embarrassed by Hull's intransigence. Argentina con-

tained the largest colony of British residents outside the Empire.
It was an increasingly important element in Britain's overseas
economic system, and British capital investment in Argentina was
still four times as valuable as that of the United States. Any
immoderate pressure by Washington on Buenos Aires could thus
seem to constitute an implicit challenge by the United States to
an enormously important sphere of British interest. Winston
Churchill thus clearly spoke more in sorrow than in anger when
he gave some support to Hull by admitting that Argentina had
allied itself with the evil as well as the losing side.[1] There were
influential voices nearer home which flatly rejected Hull's reason-
ing. Sumner Welles appeared in print again, this time actually
defending Argentina against the State Department. He criticized
the timing of Hull's hostile position on the grounds that Axis
activity in Argentina was now in fact less than it had been at any
time since the war began. He suggested, moreover, that only those
wholly unfamiliar with South American history and psychology
could imagine that Farrell represented a front for Hitler, or
indeed anything other than a crude variety of Spanish-American
dictatorship impelled by violent nationalism, itself heated to fever
pitch by fears of United States coercion. He proposed, accordingly, that the whole issue should be discussed by a consultative
meeting of American Foreign Ministers, which Argentina should
be invited to attend. The present policy of the State Department,
in his estimation, was destructive rather than constructive : it
would lead inevitably to the obliteration of the last trace of the
good-neighbour policy; and it could almost serve as a case-study
of how not to influence peoples and how to lose friends.[2]

This could only mean that the two men who had determined
more than any other United States policy towards Latin America
since 1932 now differed completely on the question of what to do
about Argentina. It was certainly not surprising that Hull's
patience should finally have evaporated. He had been dealing for
twelve years with people whose sole aim had been to mislead,
deceive, and frustrate him, and now that he was on the point of
getting out, he could afford to show them what he thought of

[1] *The Times*, 4 August 1944
[2] *New York Herald Tribune*, 8 August 1944

them. It was also more than evident that his views were shared by the man who was going to succeed him, Edward J. Stettinius, silver-haired, self-confident, and completely tactless. Stettinius considered it sufficient to reply to Welles by stating simply that 'we don't want Fascism in this hemisphere', and pointing to the failure of Venezuela and Colombia to recognize the Farrell regime as a proof of the unity of purpose animating the United Nations.[1] It was far more to the point to argue that these were, in fact, the only South American countries remote enough from Argentina to be able to affirm such a position. Their attitudes were really no more relevant than those of the Banana Belt. It was what was happening farther south that mattered. Every indication pointed to the accuracy of Sumner Welles's analysis. Coercion was only making the Argentines worse. Farrell had banned all seaborne trade with Uruguay when that country recalled its ambassador from Buenos Aires. The United States attempted to retaliate by ordering north-bound American shipping not to call at Argentine ports. Mexico then opened negotiations for massive purchases of Argentine corn. A half-hearted warning from Vargas that Brazil would not disarm when the war with the Axis was over drew, within a week, an announcement by War Minister Peron that all Argentine citizens between twelve and fifty years of age would be liable to military training for the defence of the *patria*, and that the Air Force would be established as a separate striking force with Luftwaffe officers, Major-General Steadman and Colonel-Instructor Walter Osterkamp, advising on its expansion. The Luftwaffe might be almost out of business in Europe, but there was work for it to do in South America. Vargas immediately responded by moving more of Brazil's few remaining home defence troops to the border of the Rio de la Plata. He mitigated the effect of this gesture, though, by appealing to Farrell and Mason to sell more beef to Brazil. Brazilian policy was never going to be provocative. Rio had long since resigned itself to having to live with Buenos Aires.

The mood of Washington seemed to be anything but one of resignation. The question of what action the North Americans might take next was seriously vexing Franco and his advisers.

[1] ibid., 11 August 1944

Hispanidad had been conceived as a fruitful basis for Spanish foreign policy at a time when an Axis victory seemed the most probable outcome of the world conflict. As the Russians closed in on Budapest, the Americans and French on Strasbourg, and the British on Antwerp, it became increasingly evident that the postwar role of Hispanic Fascism would have to be played in an environment less generally sympathetic than had initially been envisaged. Hispanidad now had to be expressed in terms more easily reconciled with the presumed ideals of the United Nations. Spain's own position had been made still more uncomfortable by Ramirez's quite unexpected breach with the Axis. Franco had thus two points to gain. He needed to bring about a reconciliation between Washington and Buenos Aires before North American concern over the spread of Fascism in the hemisphere endangered relations between Washington and Madrid. He also needed to find for Spain itself a foreign policy viable in the event of an Allied victory, no matter what happened to Argentina.

He started hopefully on 14 September by offering to mediate between the United States and Argentina. His proposal was rejected out of hand by Hull and Stettinius. A less direct approach had therefore to be attempted. Spanish Foreign Minister, Jose Felix Lequerica, began by explaining that the Hispanic world must remain united with the United States in the great task of elevating mankind. In an appeal to the whole American hemisphere he then claimed that the problems of peace would be the 'patrimony of all civilized peoples'. The Spanish and Portuguese-speaking countries constituted a world culture without whose participation world peace would be incomplete. The friendship and accord of the Latin countries was an imperative of Christian civilization. Hispanidad, besides being a factor in this American unity, was also 'the instrument of concord among the different countries of the Occidental Continent'. It was, in addition, 'a symbol of the very important value that Spain gives to the special relations she has always maintained towards the New World'.[1]

Franco had indeed given a significant indication of the importance with which he regarded relations with the Americas at the time, by appointing an office of Director-General for Spanish-

[1] *New York Times,* 3 December 1944

American Affairs in the Foreign Office, to take over the functions previously exercized by the appropriate organs of the Grand Council of Hispanidad and the Falange Exterior, both of which gave the impression of having outlived their immediate usefulness. Neither Washington nor Madrid was capable now of influencing the new mood in Buenos Aires. Intimidations and blandishments were alike ineffective against Farrell. Peluffo had hopefully proposed a Conference of the Pan-American Union to rationalize relations among the American Republics. When this was rejected by Washington, Farrell truculently announced that Argentina would have nothing more to do with the activities of the Union 'so long as Argentine rights continue to be disregarded and so long as the procedure of consultation continues to be allowed'. This further display of intransigence drew another condemnation of North American techniques from Sumner Welles : he went so far as to assert that the Argentine people would have returned to democracy long since but for the misguided attitude of the State Department : it was only Yankee intimidation that was keeping the Fascists of Buenos Aires in office.

In fact, this was all that Washington was succeeding in doing. Stettinius once more denounced Farrell's Government as a Fascist regime, but admitted that relations between the United States and Argentina had to be determined by the exigencies of the war effort of the United Nations. This meant in practice that no effective economic sanctions could be applied, and any other form of intervention was out of the question.[1] Although nothing seemed to be left but mud-slinging, Farrell was, in fact, already preparing to modify Argentine foreign policy. Argentina was not really doing as well as he would have wished in its present position of confrontation. National expenditure on arms was incredibly already six times what it had been in 1942, but there were still important shortages. Oil was decidedly in short supply. The United States had intervened again to frustrate an attempt to acquire rubber from Brazil in exchange for meat. Moreover, Welles's warnings about Argentina's postwar isolation had not been entirely ignored. Delegates of the other American Republics had assembled in Mexico City and agreed upon the terms of the

[1] *New York Herald Tribune,* 28 January 1945

Act of Chapultepec, by which congeries of totalitarianisms had expressed their devotion to the principles of democracy, freedom of speech, and the Atlantic Charter in general. It had been made discreetly clear that Argentina's accession to the United Nations depended upon its doing the same. The situation in Brazil had also taken a new turn. Vargas had sought to reconcile his own brand of Fascism with his commitments under the Act of Chapultepec by removing press censorship and promising free elections in Brazil. The result was a quite unexpected flood of criticism of the repressive aspects of his regime, and an offer by Air Force General, Eduardo Gomes, to run as democratic candidate against the little dictator.[1]

Farrell duly began to change course. On the same day that Gomes announced his candidature in Rio, Farrell told the Argentine people that their country had entered upon a phase of pre-electoral organization, and that he would be leading them back to a state of constitutional normality. Meanwhile, he introduced new and draconian penalties for all categories of crimes against security of the state, including specifically the dissemination of false information, meaning any statement of fact with which the regime chose to disagree. On 17 February, Farrell abruptly warned the German Government that unless they granted safe conduct to Argentine diplomats awaiting exchange in Goteburg, 'the Argentine Government will consider this an act of hostility and will reserve from this moment freedom of action to adopt whatever measures she may consider necessary in defence of her sovereignty and her citizens'.[2] The most blatant act of diplomatic hypocrisy ever committed by the most uninhibited of Foreign Offices was about to be consummated. Argentina was going to play and win the last trick.

It was only in a limited sense that Nazi Germany could be said to have a Government at all in February 1945. To the extent that it existed, that Government met Farrell's demand for safe conduct for his diplomats. Nothing that the Germans could have done would have made any difference. Five days later, Farrell repealed

---

[1] *New York Times,* 11 February 1945
[2] *La Presna,* 18 February 1945

the ban against Argentine ships entering the war zones.[1] On 7 March, as the Americans crossed the Rhine and the Russians advanced on Vienna, he adopted a resolution of solidarity with the other Republics already committed to the cause of the United Nations. The Brazilians might well have commented on the sheer effrontery of this new Buenos Aires *démarche*, but they were far too concerned with the future of Getulio Vargas. As the wave of public criticism mounted, Vargas hastily promised to hold elections within three months.[2] The Brazilian press suggested very reasonably that any such elections might well be only a farce. Vargas then gave assurances that he would not himself be a candidate, and explained that he had only established his Fascist regime in the first place to prevent the Fascists from doing so themselves. The most serious blow to his credibility came when Oswaldo Aranha announced that he would be supporting Gomes, not because he disliked Vargas, but merely because he disliked his regime. The political and constitutional situation of the country was then rendered totally obscure by the Brazilian Institute of Advocates, which ruled that any provisions Vargas made for new elections could not be legal, as he made them by virtue of his position under the terms of a merely nominal constitution, which itself conferred neither legality nor legitimate power. In the midst of all this confusion, the Argentine Republic went to war, in a manner of speaking.

The declaration of war itself was a masterpiece of the kind of eloquence which Argentine diplomats had made peculiarly their own. It contained nothing that was relevant and scarcely anything that was true. It began by affirming that 'the Argentine nation is and always has been an integral part of the union of American Republics . . . the Republic of Argentina has collaborated always with the states of the Americas in all activities tending to link the peoples of this hemisphere . . .' It was now responding to 'the imperative mandate of noble principles that has regulated always our international life . . . in view of the unanimous gesture of the sister nations that attended the Conference of Mexico City, the Government of the nation, animated by the most elevated ideals

[1] ibid., 23 February 1945
[2] *New York Times,* 29 February 1945

of hemisphere solidarity, and the directing norm of our international policy, cannot remain indifferent to the high spirit of American confraternity . . . the Government of the nation, consequent with its tradition of American solidarity, proposes once again to unify its policy in common with the other states of the Hemisphere to occupy the place that corresponds to it, and to the end of sharing the responsibilities that may devolve upon it.' In the words of Hipolito Yrigoyen, Argentina was to assume the position it deserved. It was aligning itself with the United Nations in order to acquire the means of imposing its will upon other members of the United Nations. It was going to reap a harvest to the preparation of which it had not intentionally made the slightest contribution. More precisely, it was going to secure all the benefits of adhering to principles every one of which it had flouted and conspired against during the past forty years. It could do so, as ever, with complete impunity. Edelmiro Farrell intensified press censorship, prepared his police to suppress any celebrations that might follow the taking of Berlin by Argentina's allies, and waited for his reward.

It came within the week. Stettinius was as well aware as Hull had ever been of the extent to which Buenos Aires was taking him for a ride. He could do no more about it than Hull had ever been able to. Argentina became numbered among the signatories of the Act of Chapultepec on 4 April. On the same day, Stettinius lifted all restrictions on trade between the United States and the Republic of the Pampas. The immediate response was a flood of sales and investment capital south from American companies which had been chafing for weeks against their exclusion by their own Government from one of the most attractive markets in the world. On 9 April, the United States and the other Republics formally recognized the regime of Edelmiro Farrell, while the dictator's police clubbed down citizens of Buenos Aires who had dared to celebrate the capture of Vienna by the Russians.

Farrell's position was not without its complications. What looked like becoming one of the worst of them was just arriving in Buenos Aires. President Harry S. Truman had appointed as Ambassador to Buenos Aires the massive Montanan, Spruille Braden. It might have seemed an inspired choice. Braden's impression of Argentine diplomats had been formed by his experience with Carlos Saavedra Lamas and Jose Maria Cantilo at the time of the Chaco War. He had achieved considerable success then in frustrating the efforts of the Great Peacemaker to keep the war going until he could be certain that nobody else would get any credit for stopping it. There was reason to believe that the same tactics might work again with similarly equivocal opponents. Farrell and Peron certainly did not appear to have a united nation behind them. The declaration of war had evoked no enthusiasm in Argentina. The public seemed to regard it as farcical and dishonourable, even though Farrell had tried to make it more acceptable by declaring war primarily against still-formidable Japan for having attacked another American Republic, and only incidentally against prostrate Germany, for being an ally of Japan's. The Armed Forces had no interest, as they knew that they would not be doing any fighting, and even War Minister Peron had been reluctant to make the symbolic break with a country from which he drew his political inspiration. Moreover, not even Farrell's censorship could conceal from the people of Argentina the fact that the Act of Chapultepec was supposed to guarantee them the blessings of democracy and that it was actually having that effect in Brazil.

On 18 April, students in Argentine universities began to stage massive demonstrations in protest against a further warning by Farrell that the police would use violence to suppress any public celebration of the imminent fall of Berlin. The celebrations took place when the Russians forced their way into the city on 24 April. Violence was accordingly used. Four hundred citizens were arrested, including the ever-present Colonel Arturo Rawson. Conflict between Buenos Aires and Washington took on a new intensity and a new style, but with the same old result.

Braden opened exchanges by calling on Farrell's new Foreign Minister, Cesar Ameghino, to remind him that the Act of Chapultepec required its signatories to make an effective break with the Axis and to extend democratic rights to their citizens. Ameghino assured him that he was having Axis companies in Argentina investigated and that the Argentine Government would unequivocally honour all its international obligations. Supported by an off-the-cuff statement by President Truman that he was 'not happy' about the situation in Argentina, Braden then visited War Minister Peron to present a similar reminder. It was an opportune meeting, as Edelmiro Farrell had just banned the pro-Allied women's organization, *Junta de Victoria*, and had seized 250,000 pesos' worth of medical supplies intended for the United Nations. Farrell himself repeated Ameghino's promise to fulfil the requirements of the Act of Chapultepec, but this assurance lost much of its effect when Minister of the Interior, Admiral Teisaire, warned *New York Times* correspondent, Arnoldo Cortesi, not to be surprised at anything that happened to him for his 'malicious efforts to create a difficult international situation for Argentina'.[1]

This threat hardly fulfilled the obligations of Chapultepec concerning the liberty of the press. Braden accordingly went again to see Farrell, Peron, and their Police Chief in Buenos Aires, Filimeno Velasco, to seek guarantees for the protection of American correspondents and the release of political prisoners. The regime promised to co-operate on both counts. In return, the United States agreed to let Argentina have almost its full pre-war equivalent supply of petroleum. This concession was partly extracted by Argentina's obvious willingness to hold a starving world to ransom, as it had done after the First World War. Buenos Aires had threatened to withhold grain supplies from Europe and actually to burn wheat as fuel unless the United States supplied sufficient petroleum. Heartened by this success, Farrell similarly threatened to withhold meat supplies unless a 25 per cent price increase were granted. Stettinius warned that though the United States had admitted Argentina to the ranks of the Allies, this did not mean 'a blanket endorsement of Argentine policies'.[2] He also pointed out that only 307 out of a minimum figure of 800 political prisoners had actually been released so far, despite Velasco's assurances to the contrary.

The internal situation in Argentina was now entering the last stage of a long metamorphosis. It was appropriate that the indebtedness of Buenos Aires to Berlin should be highlighted by

[1] *New York Times,* 8 June 1945.
[2] *New York Herald Tribune,* 21 June 1945

the belated arrival of the *Cabo de Hornes* with a final shipload of Nazi war equipment, six weeks after the last Nazi armies had themselves surrendered on the battlefield. For Nazi Germany had not just given Argentina arms. It had given it a blueprint for a new society. In the same way, the many new factories set up by Ramirez and Farrell had not just helped to reduce Argentina's economic vulnerability to United States pressure : they had also created a class basis for a genuine social revolution. Argentina had an industrial class at last. It could, therefore, sustain an authentic European-style Fascist revolution. On 16 June, the first rumblings of this revolution were heard when Juan Peron was assailed by 321 Argentine business organizations for attempting to introduce a new labour policy involving the fixing of price ceilings, pensions for workers, and schemes for sharing profits between business and management. Peron replied that capitalism was the real dictator in Argentina and robbed the workers of what was rightfully theirs. The class struggle had taken a new turn in Latin America.

This was, of course, the logical, if not the inevitable, outcome of everything that had happened since Roberto Ortiz handed power over to Ramon Castillo. Argentina's institutions of representative parliamentary democracy had been shattered beyond recovery by the authoritarian practices of the state of siege. The intervention of the armed forces and the development of industries to serve their needs had meant that power had fallen into the hands of a class of men socially far removed from the landed aristocrats and the millionaire servants of foreign enterprize who had managed affairs before 1942. This, in turn, meant that the traditional party of social progress had suddenly found itself without mass support or even a clear reason for existence. At the very moment that the Radicals were staging parades in Buenos Aires affirming their opposition to Farrell and demanding the release of all political prisoners, their hero, Damonte Taborda, having recovered in Rio from a sword thrust inflicted by a more skilful opponent in his second duel, was actively drumming up support in Washington for Peron as the true champion of the Argentine people.[1] Peron for his part warned the Radicals at home that he would take the risk of civil war if they attempted to

[1] *New York Times,* 4 July 1945

overthrow the regime. He claimed that he had the necessary force at his back in the form of 'our firm and united Army' and 'our valiant army of Labour'; and proudly accepted for himself the title of agitator of the Argentine masses.[1] He returned to this theme at an Armed Services dinner two days later, when Farrell promised that elections would be held before the end of the year, and at the same time warned the listening officers that 'days of struggle against demagogues and enemies of the country await us', and that the Army and Navy had assumed 'the responsibility of leading the country to the breath of authentic democracy'.[2]

The pace began to quicken. Peron organized a mass rally of Argentine industrial workers against what he called 'the capitalist oligarchy', in a deliberate bid for Communist support. On 20 July, the dream of Gaucho Empire of the G.O.U. took another giant step towards realization when the Bolivia of Villaroel and Estenssoro fell into Argentina's economic net, as Paraguay had done. Bolivia's external trade was tied, like that of Paraguay, to the Pacific by the provision of port facilities at the Argentine harbour of Rosario. These facilities were provided in an agreement on the construction of communications between Rosario and Bolivia's mines, and by the undertaking on the part of Villaroel to supply Argentina with oil products in return for a grant-in-aid of $15,000,000. The successful conclusion of these negotiations was followed by a vicious poster campaign in Buenos Aires against Braden, likening him to Al Capone, and attributing to him the responsibility for a disaster in the Chilean El Tiente mine in which Braden's grandfather had once owned shares but which he had subsequently sold. Ameghino was lavish with promises to stamp out the anti-Braden campaign, totally and mercilessly. These assurances were hardly to be taken seriously, however, since the originator of the campaign was known to be War Minister Peron himself, who was consequently denounced by United States Senators as constituting one half of 'a bush-league Axis', with Franco of Spain as his partner.

At this point, Braden received some genuine encouragement. The Army and Air Force were unquestionably strongly behind

[1] ibid., 5 July 1945
[2] *La Presna,* 8 July 1945

Peron. So probably was Argentina's new industrial proletariat and at least the lower ranks of management; but the aristocratic Navy was equally strongly out of sympathy. Some indication of the strength of anti-Peronista feeling was given on 6 August, when eleven admirals, surprisingly supported by thirty of the more favourably-connected generals, demanded that the Vice-President resign. Farrell's response was characteristically brisk and original. He lifted the state of siege initially imposed by Castillo three years before; took himself off on a state visit to Paraguay; and left the opposing forces to fight it out in his absence.

This was the signal for hell to break loose. Crowds which had turned out on the night of 14 August to celebrate the surrender of Japan, decided to improve the occasion by stoning the Casa Rosada as a demonstration of their dislike for Peron and the regime. They were savagely attacked in their turn by Peronistas armed with sticks and aided by sections of the Army and Velasco's city police. Two people were killed and at least eighty-seven wounded. Two more dead and another fifty wounded were counted after riots on the 17th, following orders by Peron that servicemen in Buenos Aires should carry arms for their own protection in the streets. The Vice-President was showing himself to be as good as his word in his willingness to provoke any degree of civil disorder in his dealings with his opponents. He was also maintaining his anti-Braden campaign in a manner which helped to ensure that relations between the two American powers were worse, now that they were allies, than they had ever been in their days of open estrangement. Nor did the gigantic Braden hesitate to take up the challenge. Appealing directly to Argentina's formerly-dominant landed aristocracy, he told the Rural Society, which Peron had already insulted by refusing to attend its meeting, that few peoples on earth were as well prepared as those of Argentina for the exercize of healthy democracy. In a further blast, he pronounced that it was no longer possible for a self-respecting world to accept a government that ruled through violence and humiliated man under dictatorship. His words were given support in Washington by the statement of Nelson Rocke-feller, Under-Secretary of State for Latin-American Affairs, that Argentina under its present regime could not be regarded as eligible for membership of the United Nations, and that it was time for the voice of the great Argentine people to be heard.[1]

It was quite certainly time for the United States and Argentina either to rationalize their relations, or to sever diplomatic ties once more. Braden could certainly not be left in Buenos Aires to represent North American interests with a Government he was devoting all his efforts to undermining. He was accordingly appointed to be Under-Secretary of Latin-American Affairs after Rockefeller's resignation. Braden himself claimed that the larger opportunities of the new post would make his efforts against Fascism even more effective.[2] The news of his impending departure from Buenos Aires certainly moved the Argentines to make some vigorous conciliatory gestures. Farrell, returning after the storm was over, replaced Ameghino with the Radical Juan Isaac Cooke, after Braden had delivered his most provocative speech yet accusing the regime by inference of displaying 'all the elements used by Fascism in its stupid strategems since the fall of Rome'.[3] Cooke hastened to assure Braden that he felt himself duty bound to inspire absolute solidarity with the United Nations and to consolidate American unity. He ordered the immediate removal of all posters insulting Braden (though this had no effect), and agreed with Braden that all Nazi influence must be extirpated from Argentina and constitutional representative democracy restored. As proof of his sincerity, he pointed out that 'all centres and organisms of sabotage have disappeared' in Argentina; that all Axis schools had been closed or were under Government control; and that measures had been taken against 136 Axis-controlled firms (in only two cases, however, did the measures seem to have any effect on the actual running of the firms concerned). In reality, the only significance of Cooke's appointment was to show that Farrell had no difficulty in finding leading Radicals who were not averse to being associated with the regime. Even more discouraging for Washington was the fact that the Radicals were, as a bloc, totally averse to being associated with the Conservatives in a common anti-Peronista front. The assorted forces of protest

[1] *New York Herald Tribune*, 25 August 1945
[2] ibid., 26 August 1945
[3] ibid., 30 August 1945

nonetheless managed to stage a massive 'liberty march' of 200,000 through the streets of Buenos Aires. This demonstration was saluted by the indefatigable Colonel Rawson as a 'symbol of the concept of human liberty'. It soon began to look like the reverse. Rawson was, of course, arrested again, and hauled before a military 'court of honour'; Farrell re-imposed the state of siege; and a sudden wave of arbitrary arrests netted some 2,000 suspected foes of the regime, including, of all people, those arch-nationalists Jose Maria Cantilo and Carlos Saavedra Lamas himself, who now found themselves, by this most incongruous quirk of history, being hailed as great statesmen and martyrs to liberty by the very same men in Washington who had cursed them for the past twenty years for being exactly the opposite.

It would certainly have been portentous if Fascism had developed in Argentina to the extent that Cantilo and Saavedra Lamas would have been ideologically out of step with the regime, as von Papen and von Seeckt might have found themselves out of step with the particular nationalism of the Nazi Revolution. A genuine power struggle between conflicting social ideologies was about to explode in Argentina. International pressure on Buenos Aires reached its most intense level as the British Ambassador, Sir David Kelly, warned Farrell of the unfortunate effect of the latest arrests on foreign public opinion; Under-Secretary of State, Dean Acheson, announced that the United States would refuse to be associated with Argentina in a multilateral military alliance for the defence of the hemisphere; and Getulio Vargas discourteously postponed a scheduled meeting with Edelmiro Farrell. Peron reacted to this by suddenly resigning his position as Vice-President and offering himself as a candidate in the promised Presidential elections, running on a platform of higher wages for the workers and profit-sharing. He was replaced as Minister of War by General Eduardo Avalos, a singularly hardfaced, bespectacled Fascist, whose only discernible ideological difference from Peron seemed to be a total freedom from Peron's concern for social justice, but whose activities in reality were determined by his desire to co-operate with the aristocratic Conservative Admiral of the Argentine High Seas Fleet, Verenengo Lima.

This partnership did not exactly seem to augur a new birth of freedom for Argentina. It was, in fact, as utterly confused a situation as even Buenos Aires had ever witnessed. For a week it seemed as if Farrell, Avalos, and Lima were ruling Argentina as a triumvirate; but what was really taking place was a final stand of Conservatives and Right-Wing Fascists against Peron. It failed totally through the usual incompetence of the conspirators, the inflexible will of Edelmiro Farrell, and Peron's foresight in granting wage rises to all Argentine workers before he resigned. It was not only by the irresistible appeal of more money that Peron had at length won the hearts of the Argentine masses. In an environment peculiarly receptive to personal magnetism and charisma, Peron appeared as the most compelling national leader of the century, with the possible exception of Yugoslavia's Tito. Extraordinarily handsome, brilliantly successful with women, and the best swordsman in the Argentine army, Peron was also a dramatically effective orator, a logical and disciplined ideologue, and the possessor of qualities of charm and courtesy which even North Americans who loathed him admitted to be unequalled in their experience of their fellow-men. He was the ideal demagogue. There was nothing more probable than that he would become ruler of Argentina.

Avalos and Vernengo Lima attempted to deal with this immensely formidable challenger with the conventional combination of bluster and weakness. The only safe way of dealing with Peron would be to have him shot. Instead, Avalos demanded that Farrell sack his old cabinet, arrest Peron, and appoint a civilian cabinet. Farrell refused to do any of these. Avalos therefore overruled the titular President by having Peron arrested on the minesweeper *Drummond*, already distinguished as the refuge sought by Ramon Castillo from Rawson's revolutionaries. Any possibility Avalos and Lima might have had of retaining the power they had seized was destroyed by the Argentine Supreme Court which claimed that, according to the constitution, executive power should devolve to it in a situation where the country seemed to be bereft of both President and Vice-President. Constitutional lawyers, like the United Nations, can always be counted upon to make a bad situation worse. Avalos and Lima thus found themselves deprived of legal backing, while the iron-willed Farrell defied the injunctions of the Court just as he had defied the demands of his co-rulers. The workers of Argentina, concerned for the welfare of their hero and alarmed for the fate of their pay rises and their share of future profits, demanded that Peron be released. Avalos somewhat unconvincingly denied that he had ever been arrested. Farrell finally put the conspirators out of their misery by announcing that all the Ministers appointed by Avalos and Lima had resigned and had been replaced by Peronistas. While 500,000 workers marched out of their factories to demonstrate for Peron, Lima headed wildly out into the Atlantic with those units of the High Seas Fleet still prepared to follow his flag, only to return ignominiously to port when Farrell threatened by radio to send the Air Force after him. The most inglorious coup in Argentine history was over. The most spectacular one was on its way.

Farrell cleared the way for Peron's election campaign by lifting the ban on political parties. His protégé then offered still more pay rises to railroad workers, moved ostentatiously from his luxury apartment in Buenos Aires to live in the workers' quarter, and formed his own political party, named, with obvious respect to the memory of Adolf Hitler, the National Labour Party. The Party programme was unquestionably commendable. It stood for freedom of suffrage, for order and progress, for equality without hatred, for work without slavery, and respect for the dignity of citizenship; for Argentine historical traditions; for the nationalization of energy, communications, and public works; and for the limitation of political power. It also stood for anti-Semitic pogroms unequalled in Latin-American history and for anti-Communism once the Communists had decided to align themselves with the anti-Peronista forces. This last factor finally won Peron the support of the Roman Catholic hierarchy in Argentina, which, although it did not order the faithful to vote for Peron, commanded them to vote against his opponents. The last opportunity for effective external intervention vanished when the Brazilian Army quietly removed Getulio Vargas from office and replaced him with Jose Lenharis on 2 November following an attempt by the little dictator to control the forthcoming elections through his own interventors. Once again, even honest elections in Latin America hardly seemed to further the cause of parliamentary democracy. The new President of Brazil, elected on 12 December with 60 per cent of the votes cast, was none other than

General Enrico Gaspar Dutra, Fascist and Integralista, who brought back into power with him his old friend, Fascist and Integralista, General Pedro Aurelio Goes Monteiro. The Latins were running true to form.

No one after this could have doubted that Peron would soon assume supreme office in Argentina. He had, in any event, his own ways of getting out the vote. On 21 December, he raised workers' wages in Argentina by a further 30 per cent, just in time for Christmas. The singularly unhappy combination of reactionaries, moderates, and Communists who opposed him could still, however, muster impressive support. Peron gained no more than 55 per cent of the votes cast in the Presidential elections in Argentina on 24 February 1946, the first held since Roberto M. Ortiz had come to office.

It was enough. Argentina was on the march, under its most dynamic leader since Rosas. Authority and predominance such as no Latin leaders had ever enjoyed fell without a struggle into the hands of Buenos Aires. Argentina had attained its destiny. For the few brief postwar years, Argentine nationalism reaped the harvest of Yrigoyen's dark intrigues, Lamas's ruthless ambition, Justo's jovial brutality, Castillo's intransigence, Ramirez's duplicity, and Edelmiro Farrell's relentless determination. Britain, Europe, and, through them, the United States were held to ransom by the Argentine power to withhold food supplies from a hungry continent. Argentina's exchange reserves, the highest of any nation in the world except the United States, financed grants of 750,000,000 pesos to Spain, and orders for sixteen more ships for Peron's merchant marine. The great financial and economic net of Buenos Aires swept over three-quarters of the continent. Paraguay was already secure. Ecuador was made virtually a dependency by an agreement of August 1946 in which Argentina accepted the little country's rubber, oil, and balsa in return for agricultural products. On 3 October, giant Brazil, which already sold more goods to Argentina than it did to any other country, contracted an agreement with the Gauchos on the sale of its exportable surpluses. Chile finally accepted a full and ultimately disastrous customs union arrangement on 13 December 1946. The two countries agreed to grant duty-free entry to non-competitive exports from each other, and Argentina at last gained its foothold on the Pacific, with free transit from Mendoza to Valparaiso. Shipping facilities were combined, preferential treatment accorded to export surpluses by the signatories, and a joint trading company formed with a capital of 300,000,000 pesos from each. In addition, Argentina extended Chile a loan of 300,000,000 pesos, and a further 100,000,000 on revolving credit. Seventeen days later, Uruguay accepted an Argentine investment of 450,000,000 pesos to develop hydro-electric power for mutual consumption. On 26 March 1947, Bolivia ratified a further customs union arrangement on the same lines as that undertaken by Chile, with duty-free entry for non-competitive exports, and free transit of goods through each other's territory. Argentina also extended its financial control over Bolivia with an investment of 100,000,000 pesos and the purchase of 650,000,000 pesos of Bolivian government bonds. Any lingering fear of a military challenge from Brazil was finally eliminated when Peron placed orders for a new aircraft-carrier, a cruiser, four destroyers, ten patrol boats, and three submarines to complete the modernization of the Argentine Navy. The Argentine triumph was complete. Buenos Aires had defied Washington and acquired hegemony over a continent. The great Gaucho Empire had been achieved at last. It was to endure for all of four years.

Conclusion

There are a number of extremely practical observations to be made about the events described in this book. One is that Anglo-Saxon diplomats face quite unusual linguistic difficulties in dealing with Latins. The post-1945 experience of the Cold War has of course tended to acquaint us all much more closely with the fact that people on one side of an ideological barrier will customarily use terms in a manner not only quite different from normal usage on the other side, but also sometimes quite incomprehensible to those who do not hold the same beliefs. There is nothing less relevant to real experience than the liberal myth that intelligent men of differing viewpoints can always discuss their differences fruitfully one with another. They more often cannot even understand one another.

The North Americans certainly found it uncommonly hard to understand the Latins. This did not necessarily mean that their own utterances were more honestly intended. Cordell Hull, Armour, and Sumner Welles frequently distorted or ignored inconvenient facts for the sake of evoking a desired response. Roosevelt almost always did. Even Woodrow Wilson was capable of staggering hypocrisies and partialities. But it could be affirmed as a general rule that statements from Washington relating to future policy usually bore quite a close relation to what the North Americans really intended to do. There was no such correlation between the promises and the real intentions of any Latin Government.

The North Americans thus faced exactly the same problems in dealing with the Latins that the other Powers faced in dealing with Hitler. It is simply the problem of playing a game with anyone who persistently pays no attention to the rules. Diplomacy admittedly is not a game, but a technique by which a nation seeks fortune and survival. The stakes for which the Latins were playing were particularly high. What was at issue was simply the ability of relatively weak nations to escape total cultural and material domination by an alien state which happened to be the richest and at times the most formidable in the world. On the other hand, total dishonesty is not normally a profitable style in diplomacy. International relations are more convenient to conduct when there is an element of mutual trust which arises out of the readiness of the parties concerned to observe the appropriate conventions. In practical terms, nations which play the diplomatic game can usually hope to receive more favourable treatment from their partners than those which appear to disregard the rules; but that did not apply in this case. The most staggering single feature of hemisphere relations in this period is the relative impunity with which the mavericks defied diplomatic conventions and threats of international coercion.

This is the most important lesson of the Latin experience. Argentina was able to challenge a superpower which was fifteen times richer than itself because there was little or no danger that the superpower could effectively exert its vastly superior strength. Military sanctions by the North Americans were ruled out because of the enormous British interest in Argentina, the sheer physical difficulty of conducting a campaign of such dimensions at such a distance, and because all administrations in Washington after Wilson's were committed to restoring an atmosphere of mutual trust and co-operation with the Latins. Financial sanctions were ineffective because of Argentina's capacity to earn foreign exchange. Economic sanctions were tried, but they failed for the same reason. Such measures are literally never effective against a community which produces materials that other nations want to buy and which has the purchasing power to buy what other nations want to sell. The diplomatic sanction of threatening to exclude Argentina from all postwar international settlements did, indeed, gain a certain token success, if that term can be applied to a gesture by the Farrell regime which cost Argentina nothing, gained it everything, and left relations between Buenos Aires and the United Nations worse in every way than they had been before.

The Argentine experience thus showed vividly the extent to which even a small nation can defy world opinion, including that of a superpower, if it is geographically difficult to get at, if it has the economic capacity to make it important to other nations as either a market or a source of supply, and if it can manage to remain sufficiently detached from foreign involvements to give a hostile superpower insufficient reason for going to war with it. Buenos Aires had lessons in the postwar decades for Paris, Belgrade, Bucharest, Pretoria, Salisbury, Lima, possibly Havana, and a host of other capitals where national self-determination was rated above the safety that might be derived from subservience to a protecting superpower. It also had lessons for those other capitals which dared either too much or not enough.

Latin diplomacy in this period needed no post-mortems. It simply achieved what it set out to do. The totality of its success, however, was, necessarily, the measure of the totality of Washington's failure. One has to consider whether a different approach by the United States might have achieved the goal of continental solidarity for which Hull, Welles, and Stettinius were aiming. Welles certainly thought that it might have done so. A more discreet presentation of United States policy might, indeed, have avoided the head-on confrontations and ensuing humiliations which the North Americans experienced increasingly after 1941. The fact remained that no amount of discretion on the part of Washington could have altered the fact that successive Argentine Governments saw the welfare and national destiny of their people as lying in their independence of the United States. The choice facing Washington was effectively one of conceding to Argentine intransigence gracefully, or of submitting under protest. Things might have been made easier if the regimes in Buenos Aires had not been what they were; but it is difficult to see what could have been done to alter them. More conciliatory treatment of Castillo might have averted the military coups of Rawson, Ramirez, and Farrell; but, in fact, Castillo was as unsatisfactory from Washington's point of view as any of his successors. Similarly, Braden's intemperance undoubtedly made Peron's rise to power much easier; but the only available alternatives to Peron seemed to be Farrell, Avalos, and Verenengo Lima, who again could scarcely be considered improvements in any sense. Moreover, all the conciliation in the world had been unable to keep Vargas in office in Brazil, or to prevent Paraguay, Uruguay, Bolivia, Chile, Ecuador, and Peru from lining up with Argentina in the great economic network of the Gaucho Empire.

The United States and the forces of democracy in Argentina undoubtedly had bad luck. It was unfortunate that Ortiz should have been stricken with diabetes as soon as he assumed the Presidency; that Justo should have died when he seemed to have a chance of displacing Castillo; and that Peron should have been as gifted with personal magnetism as he was. On the other hand, it is difficult to feel that any political movement which experienced so much bad luck could ever have been firmly grounded in the first place. The North Americans hoped to see Latin America develop as a community of democratic republics, as similar in constitution and practice to the United States as possible. What they still have is an unending series of experiments in personal rule. Their concern with Argentina was largely due to the fact that Argentina seemed to be the Latin country best equipped with the social forces favouring constitutional representative government. In fact even Argentina never looked like a parliamentary democracy on the Anglo-American pattern. It was not merely that its national heroes continued to be men like Bartolome Mitre and the tyrant Rosas, or that the only two Argentine Presidents who did not govern for some time as dictators were Alvear and Ortiz. What was really significant was that the moderate Alvear should have been rejected by the electorate in favour of the arbitrary and, indeed, insane Yrigoyen; and that Roberto M. Ortiz, the last best hope of Argentine democracy, should have been a millionaire servant of foreign interests who was engineered into power by the cunning Justo through an electoral fraud of breath-taking complexity. It can at least be said that Washington eventually learned from its bitter experience of 1920–1945. It has learned that the Latins do things their own way. It is still learning that other people do so too.

BIBLIOGRAPHY

OFFICIAL RECORDS

Argentina, Ministerio de Relaciones Exteriores y Culto, *Memorias*, 1917.

Ministerio de Relaciones Exteriores y Culto, *Boletin de Ligue de las Naciones*, 1920.

Ministerio de Relaciones Exteriores y Culto, *Memoria sobre la Ligue de las Naciones*, 1928.

Ministerio de Relaciones Exteriores y Culto, *Decretos sobre la Neutralidad de la Republica Argentina en el Estado de Guerra en Europa*, 1939.

Camera de Diputades, *Diarios*, 1933–1941.

Camera de Diputades, Commision Investigadora, *Informe Confidencial de las Actividades Nazis en la Republica Argentina*, 1941.

Camera de Senadores, *Diario*, 1933.

Brazil, Ministerio das Relacoes Exteriores, *Green Book*, 1920.

Ministerio das Relacoes Exteriores, *O Brasil e a II Guerra Mundial: Ruptura de Relacoes*, 1944.

Ministerio das Relacoes Exteriores, *O III Reich e o Brasil*, 1968.

Ecuador, *Informe que el Ministerio de Relaciones Exteriores presenta a la Nacion en 1917*.

Germany, *Documents on German Foreign Policy, Series D*, 1918–1945.

Diplomatische Korrespondenz, 1918–1939.

Great Britain, *Documents on British Foreign Policy*, 1918–1939.

Graf Spee 1939, The German Story, 1941.

Guatemala, *Boletin Oficial de la Secretario de Estado*, 1917.

Italy, *Italiani Documenti Diplomatici, Serie Seste a None*, 1918–1945.

United States, Department of State, *Foreign Relations of the United States, The American Republics*, 1917–1945.

Department of State, *Bulletin*, 1944.

Department of State, *Consultation Among the American Republics with respect to the Argentine Situation*, 1946.

League of Nations, *Records of the First Assembly*, 1920.

Doc. C.262, M.iii, 1934, VII.

Journal Officiel, 1934–1938.

U.S.S.R., *Soviet Relations with Latin America, 1918–1968* (Stephen Clissold ed.) O.U.P., 1970.

STATISTICS
International Monetary Fund, *International Financial Statistics.*
Jane's Fighting Ships, 1920–1946.
The Statesman's Yearbook, 1920–1946.
United Nations, *National and Per Capita Incomes, Seventy Countries,* 1949.
United States, Department of Foreign and Domestic Commerce, *International Transactions of the United States During the War.*

NEWSPAPERS
Berliner Zeitung
Correio da Manha
Deutsche Volkzeitung
Giornale d'Italia
New York Herald Tribune
New York Times
La Presna
Le Temps
The Times

MEMOIRS
Hull, Cordell, *Memoirs,* Hodder and Stoughton, London, 1948.
Labougle, F., *Mision en Berlin,* Editorial Guillermo Kraft, Buenos Aires, 1944.
Macedo Soares, J. C. de, *O Brasil e a Sociedade das Nacios,* Pedone, Paris, 1927.
Pickersgill, R., *The Mackenzie King Record,* University of Toronto Press, 1960.
Pinedo, F., *En Tiempos de la Republica,* Buenos Aires, 1946.
Yrigoyen, H., *Pueblo y Gobierno,* Buenos Aires, 1950.

BOOKS
Artucio, H. F., *The Nazi Octopus in South America,* Robert Hale, London, 1943.
Bello, J. M., *A History of Modern Brazil, 1887–1964,* Stanford University Press, 1966.
Chase, A., *Falange,* G. P. Putnam and Sons, New York, 1943.
De Barros, J., *A Politica Exterior do Brasil, 1930–1940,* Departmento de Impresna e Propaganda, Rio de Janeiro, 1941.
Dulles, John W. F., *Vargas of Brazil,* University of Texas Press, Austin, 1967.
Etcheparaborda and others, *Historia Argentina,* Plaza y Jares, Buenos Aires, 1968.
Ferns, H. S., *Argentina,* Benn, London, 1969.
Frye, Alton, *Nazi Germany and the American Hemisphere, 1933–1941,* Yale University Press, New Haven, 1967.

Galdames, Luis, *Histroia de Chile*, University of North Carolina Press, 1941.

Gunther, John, *Inside Latin America*, McGraw-Hill, New York, 1941.

Josephs, Ray, *Argentine Diary*, New York, 1944.

Langer, William L. and S. Everett Gleason, *The Undeclared War, 1940–1941*, New York, 1953.

Lascano, V., *Argentine Foreign Policy in Latin America*, Miami, 1946.

Mackenzie, N., *Argentina*, Gollancz, London, 1947.

Martin, P. A., *Latin America and the War*, John Hopkins, Baltimore, 1925.

Masur, Gerhard, *Nationalism in Latin America*, Macmillan, New York, 1966.

Mendonca, Renato, *Historia de la Politica Exterior del Brasil*, Mexico s.e., 1945.

Necochea, Hernan-Ramirez, *Los Estados Unidos y America Latina, 1930–1965*, Edition Palestra, Buenos Aires, 1966.

Perez-Guerrero, M., *Les Relations des Etats de l'Amerique Latine avec la Societe des Nations*, Pedone, Paris, 1936.

Peterson, H. F., *Argentina and the United States, 1810–1960*, University of New York, 1964.

Potash, Robert A., *The Army and Politics in Argentina, 1928–1945*, Stanford University Press, 1969.

Royal Institute of International Affairs, *Survey*, Oxford University Press, 1940.

Ruiz-Guinazu, E., *La Politica Argentina y el Futuro de America*, Liberia Humuel, Buenos Aires, 1944.

Ruiz-Moreno, I., *Historia de las Relaciones Exteriores Argentinas*, Editorial Perrot, Buenos Aires, 1961.

Seviri, L., *La Ligue de las Naciones, su origen y la obra realizada en la Republica Argentina*, Buenos Aires, 1928.

Skidmore, T. E., *Politics in Brazil, 1930–1964*, Oxford University Press, 1967.

Sodre, N. W., *Historia Militar do Brasil*, Rio, Civilizacao Brasiliera, 1966.

Souza, Antonio de, *O Brasil e a Terceira Guerra Mundial*, Biblioteca do Exercito, Rio, 1959.

Taylor, T., *The March of Conquest*, Edward Hulton, London, 1959.

Welles, Sumner, *Where Are We Heading?*, New York, 1946.

Wood, Bryce, *The United States and Latin American Wars, 1932–1942*, Cambridge University Press, New York, 1966.

INDEX

210